CHICKASAW BY BLOOD
ENROLLMENT CARDS
1898-1914

VOLUME V

TRANSCRIBED BY
JEFF BOWEN

NATIVE STUDY
Gallipolis, Ohio
USA

Originally published:
Baltimore, Maryland
2010

Reprinted by:

Native Study LLC
Gallipolis, OH
www.nativestudy.com

Library of Congress Control Number: 2020915583

ISBN: 978-1-64968-043-3

Made in the United States of America.

Other Books and Series by Jeff Bowen

1901-1907 Native American Census Seneca, Eastern Shawnee, Miami, Modoc, Ottawa, Peoria, Quapaw, and Wyandotte Indians (Under Seneca School, Indian Territory)

1932 Census of The Standing Rock Sioux Reservation with Births And Deaths 1924-1932

Census of The Blackfeet, Montana, 1897- 1901 Expanded Edition

Eastern Cherokee by Blood, 1906-1910, Volumes I thru XIII

Choctaw of Mississippi Indian Census 1929-1932 with Births and Deaths 1924-1931 Volume I

Choctaw of Mississippi Indian Census 1933, 1934 & 1937, Supplemental Rolls to 1934 & 1935 with Births and Deaths 1932-1938, and Marriages 1936-1938 Volume II

Eastern Cherokee Census Cherokee, North Carolina 1930-1939 Census 1930-1931 with Births And Deaths 1924-1931 Taken By Agent L. W. Page Volume I

Eastern Cherokee Census Cherokee, North Carolina 1930-1939 Census 1932-1933 with Births And Deaths 1930-1932 Taken By Agent R. L. Spalsbury Volume II

Eastern Cherokee Census Cherokee, North Carolina 1930-1939 Census 1934-1937 with Births and Deaths 1925-1938 and Marriages 1936 & 1938 Taken by Agents R. L. Spalsbury And Harold W. Foght Volume III

Seminole of Florida Indian Census, 1930-1940 with Birth and Death Records, 1930-1938

Texas Cherokees 1820-1839 A Document For Litigation 1921

Choctaw By Blood Enrollment Cards 1898-1914 Volumes I thru XVII

Starr Roll 1894 (Cherokee Payment Rolls) Districts: Canadian, Cooweescoowee, and Delaware Volume One

Starr Roll 1894 (Cherokee Payment Rolls) Districts: Flint, Going Snake, and Illinois Volume Two

Starr Roll 1894 (Cherokee Payment Rolls) Districts: Saline, Sequoyah, and Tahlequah; Including Orphan Roll Volume Three

Other Books and Series by Jeff Bowen

Cherokee Intruder Cases Dockets of Hearings 1901-1909 Volumes I & II

Indian Wills, 1911-1921 Records of the Bureau of Indian Affairs
Books One thru Seven;

 Native American Wills & Probate Records 1911-1921

Turtle Mountain Reservation Chippewa Indians 1932 Census with Births & Deaths,
1924-1932

Chickasaw By Blood Enrollment Cards 1898-1914 Volume I thru IV

Visit our website at **www.nativestudy.com** to learn more about these
and other books and series by Jeff Bowen

This whole series is dedicated to my
wife and best friend, Kathy.

ENROLLMENT CARDS FOR THE
FIVE CIVILIZED TRIBES
1898-1914

On 93 rolls of this microfilm publication are reproduced the enrollment cards that were prepared by the staff of the Commission to the Five Civilized Tribes between 1898 and 1914. These records are part of Records of the Bureau of Indian Affairs, Record Group (RG) 75, and are housed in the Archives Branch of the Federal Archives and Records Center, Fort Worth, Tex. An act of Congress approved March 3, 1893 (27 Stat. 645), authorized the establishment of the Commission to negotiate agreements with the Cherokee, Choctaw, Chickasaw, Creek, and Seminole tribes providing for the dissolution of the tribal governments and the allotment of land to each tribal member. Senator Henry L. Dawes of Massachusetts was appointed Chairman of this Commission on November 1, 1893, after which it has commonly been referred to as the Dawes Commission. The Commission was authorized by an act of Congress approved June 28, 1898 (30 Stat. 495), to prepare citizenship (tribal membership) rolls for each tribe. These final rolls were the basis for allotment. Under this act, subsequent acts, and resulting agreements negotiated with each tribe, the Commission received applications for membership covering more than 250,000 people and enrolled more than 101,000. The tribal membership rolls were closed on March 4, 1907, by an act of Congress approved on April 26, 1906 (34 Stat. 370), although an additional 312 persons were enrolled under an act approved August 1, 1914. The Commission enrolled individuals as "citizens" of a tribe under the following categories: Citizens By Blood, Citizens by Marriage, New Born Citizens By Blood (enrolled under an act of Congress approved March 3, 1905), Minor Citizens By Blood (enrolled under an act of Congress approved April 26, 1906), Freedmen (former black slaves of Indians, later freed and admitted to tribal citizenship), New Born Freedmen, and Minor Freedmen. Delaware Indians adopted by the Cherokee tribe were enrolled as a separate group within the Cherokee. Within each enrollment category, the Commission generally maintained three types of cards: "Straight" cards for persons whose applications were approved, "D" cards for persons whose applications were considered doubtful and subject to question, and "R" cards for persons whose applications were rejected. Persons listed on "D" cards were subsequently transferred to either "Straight" or "R" cards depending on the Commission's decisions. All decisions of the Commission were sent to the Secretary of the Interior for final approval.

An enrollment card, sometimes referred to by the Commission as a "census card," records the information provided by individual applications submitted by members of the same family group or household and includes notation of the actions taken. The information given for each applicant includes name, roll number (individual's number if enrolled), age, sex, degree of Indian blood, relationship to the head of the family group, parents' names, and references to enrollment on earlier rolls used by the Commission for verification of eligibility. The card often includes references to kin-related enrollment cards and notations about births, deaths, changes in marital status, and actions taken by the Commission and the Secretary of the Interior. Within each enrollment category, the cards are arranged numerically by a "field" or "census card" number, which is separate from the roll number. The index to the final rolls, which is reproduced on roll 1 of this publication, provides the roll number for each person while the final rolls themselves provide the census card numbers for each enrollee. No indexes have been located for the majority of the "D" and "R" cards. There are a few Mississippi Choctaw "Identified" and "Field Cards" as well as some Chickasaw "Cancelled" that refer to person never finally enrolled.

National Archives and Records Administration
American Indians Catalogue, p. 41

INTRODUCTION

The following Introduction describes the considerations employed in transcribing the Chickasaw enrollment cards that comprise the basis for this series. The Chickasaw by Blood enrollment cards, sometimes called "census cards" by the Dawes Commission, were pre-printed cards or loose sheets of paper labeled **Chickasaw Nation. Chickasaw Roll (Not Including Freedmen) with Residence County**. The heading **Post Office** appeared on the left side of each card, and **Card No., Field No.** on the right. The cards were further broken down into the categories *Dawes No., Name, Relationship to Person First Named, Age, Sex, Blood, Tribal Enrollment (Year, Town, Page), Name of Father, Year, Town, Name of Mother, Year, Town*, as well as *Tribal Enrollments of Parents*. For whatever reason, no card numbers were recorded in the corresponding field on any of the cards.

This and subsequent volumes have been transcribed from National Archives microfilm series M-1186: Roll 67, 1-662 and Roll 68, 663-1424. The page format of this transcription does not follow the microfilm exactly, owing to the space restrictions of the book format, but I have endeavored to include all categories of information supplied in the original. Also, the Dawes Roll No. has been relegated to the Notes area of each transcribed page. The notes section also contains information such as, Other name listings, Transfers to different cards, Birth dates, Death dates, listings on various payrolls with years, even sometimes a mention of a spouse in the doubtful category with card number, spouse possibly from another tribe, or a marriage license and certificate that was on file along with location. Sometimes the notes contain revealing information such as the following, "5/31/99. It is reported that Wm. Washington has this woman on his place and had parties to marry and they have never lived together—Investigate." Interestingly, this tidbit was found not under the representation of Wm. Washington but under that of Head of Household "Frank Osavior." Finally, the category "County" indicates the status of Non-Citizen, ethnicity, or Creek Roll, Cherokee Roll, Chocktaw Roll, etc.

Jeff Bowen
Gallipolis, OH
NativeStudy.com

Chickasaw Enrollment Cards 1898-1914
Chickasaw by Blood   Volume V

RESIDENCE: Pickens   COUNTY   CARD NO.

POST OFFICE: Oakland, Ind. Ter.   FIELD NO.

NAME	RELATION-SHIP TO PERSON FIRST NAMED	AGE	SEX	BLOOD	TRIBAL ENROLLMENT		
					YEAR	COUNTY	PAGE
1 Smith, John	NAMED	43	M	Full	1897	Pickens	12
2 " Ticy	Wife	43	F	"	1897	"	12
3 " Loman	Son	13	M	"	1897	"	12
4 " Ella	Dau	6	F	Full	1897	"	12
5 " Melton	Son	3	M	"	1897	"	12
6 " Ed	"	2	"	"			
7 Fulsom, Lela	Neice[sic]	20	F	"	1893	Pickens	80
8 Ned, Ellis	Bro in law	13	M	"	1893	"	160
9 Smith, Lelia	Dau	9mo	F	"			
10 " Luidsey	Dau	3	F	"			

TRIBAL ENROLLMENT OF PARENTS

	NAME OF FATHER	YEAR	COUNTY	NAME OF MOTHER	YEAR	COUNTY
1	Lo-wan-stub-by	Dead	Chickasaw roll	Si-ney	Dead	Chickasaw roll
2	London Net	"	" "	Becky Ned	"	" "
3	No. 1			No. 2		
4	No. 1			No. 2		
5	No. 1			No. 2		
6	No. 1			No. 2		
7	Dixon Fulsom	Dead	Pickens	Maggie Fulsom	Dead	Pickens
8	London Ned	"	Chickasaw roll	Becky Ned	"	Chickasaw roll
9	No. 1			No. 2		
10	No. 1			No. 2		

(NOTES)

No. 3 on Chickasaw roll as Lorson Smith
No. 7 "   "   " " Leila Folsom
No. 6 died October 9, 1899. Proof of death filed Aug. 13, 1901.
No. 7 on 1893 Chickasaw Pay roll No. 2 page 80
No. 8 " "   "   " " " " " 160
No. 9 Born Jan. 28, 1902; Enrolled Nov. 11, 1902.   (No. 9 Dawes' Roll No. 4126)
No. 10 Born July 2, 1899; Enrolled Nov. 21, 1902.   (No. 10 Dawes' Roll No. 4127)

P.O. Seems to be Russett I.T. 8/13/01   Sept. 27/98.

1

RESIDENCE: Tishomingo   COUNTY   CARD NO.

POST OFFICE: Vaughan, Ind. Ter.   FIELD NO.

NAME	RELATION-SHIP TO PERSON FIRST NAMED	AGE	SEX	BLOOD	TRIBAL ENROLLMENT		
					YEAR	COUNTY	PAGE
1 Polk, Lou	NAMED	23	M	I.W.			
2 " Nannie	Wife	18	F	1/4	1897	Tishomingo	29
3 " Jodie Ellify	Son	2mo	M	1/4			

TRIBAL ENROLLMENT OF PARENTS

NAME OF FATHER	YEAR	COUNTY	NAME OF MOTHER	YEAR	COUNTY
1 Taylor Polk		non citizen	Mary Polk		non citizen
2 John Kinney (I.W.)	1897	Tishomingo	Minnie Kinney	1897	Tishomingo
3 No. 1			No. 2		

(NOTES)

No. 2 on Chickasaw roll as Mamie Kinney   (No. 1 Dawes' Roll No. 34)

No. 3 Enrolled April 16, 1901.

11/6/02 P.O. Sulphur, I.T.   Sept. 27/98.

RESIDENCE: Tishomingo   COUNTY   CARD NO.

POST OFFICE: Buckhorn, Ind. Ter.   FIELD NO.

NAME	RELATION-SHIP TO PERSON FIRST NAMED	AGE	SEX	BLOOD	TRIBAL ENROLLMENT		
					YEAR	COUNTY	PAGE
1 Fletcher, David Peter	NAMED	26	M	1/8	1897	Tishomingo	P.R.#1 116
2 " Granville Merrill	Son	1	"	1/16			
3 " Maudie	Dau	3mo	F	1/16			
4 " Claudie	Son	3mo	M	1/16			

TRIBAL ENROLLMENT OF PARENTS

NAME OF FATHER	YEAR	COUNTY	NAME OF MOTHER	YEAR	COUNTY
1 Thos. Fletcher	1897	Pontotoc	Mary Fletcher	Dead	Non Citizen
2 No. 1			Dollie Fletcher		" "
3 No. 1		" "			" "
4 No. 1		" "			" "

(NOTES)

No. 2 affidavit of attending physician to be supplied. Received Oct. 11/98.

Evidence of death of No. 2 to be supplied by testimony of No. 1 Feby. 1, 1900.

Nos. 3 and 4 Enrolled May 24, 1900

No. 2 Died about Aug. 1, 1899; proof of death filed Aug. 19, 1902.

No. 1 Died Nov. 15, 1900; proof of death filed Aug. 19, 1902.   Sept. 27/98.

RESIDENCE: Pontotoc   **COUNTY**   **CARD NO.**

POST OFFICE: Waupaunuka, Ind. Ter.   **FIELD NO.**

	NAME	RELATION-SHIP TO PERSON FIRST NAMED	AGE	SEX	BLOOD	TRIBAL ENROLLMENT		
						YEAR	COUNTY	PAGE
1	Mosely, Palmer Simeon	NAMED	47	M	1/2	1897	Pontotoc	52
2	" Amanda J	Wife	30	F	Full	1897	"	52
3	" Flora	Dau	7	"	3/4	1897	"	52
4	" Nannie P.	"	6	"	3/4	1897	"	52
5	" Wilson H	Son	5	M	3/4	1897	"	52
6	" Palmer S., Jr.	"	2	"	3/4	1897	"	52
7	" Bessie	Neice[sic]	14	F	Full	1897	Panola	6
8	Simpson, Mattie	Ward	13	"	"	1897	Chick resodomg om Choctaw N. 3rd Dist.	74
9	Mosely, Garnett F.	Son	1	M	3/4			
10	" Varina Susie	Dau	3mo	F	3/4			

TRIBAL ENROLLMENT OF PARENTS

	NAME OF FATHER	YEAR	COUNTY	NAME OF MOTHER	YEAR	COUNTY
1	Simon Mosely	Dead	Choctaw roll	Belsie Mosely	Dead	Chickasaw roll
2	Harris Greenwood	"	Chickasaw roll	Sarah Greenwood	1897	Pontotoc
3	No. 1			No. 2		
4	No. 1			No. 2		
5	No. 1			No. 2		
6	No. 1			No. 2		
7	Harlin Mosely	Dead	Panola	Sophie Mosely	Dead	Panola
8	Joe Simpson	"	Pontotoc	Janie Simpson	Dead	Pontotoc
9	No. 1			No. 2		
10	No. 1			No. 2		

(NOTES)

No. 1 on Chickasaw roll as P.S. Mosley   *(No. 10 Dawes' Roll No. 4125)*
No. 4 "   "   "   " Nannie "
        First seven names on roll as Mosley
No. 9 enrolled Nov. 3/99
No. 10 Born Aug. 11, 1902, enrolled Nov. 6, 1902.

Sept. 27/98.

| RESIDENCE: Pickens COUNTY | | | | | CARD NO. | | |
| POST OFFICE: Newport, Ind. Ter. | | | | | FIELD NO. | | |

NAME	RELATION-SHIP TO PERSON FIRST NAMED	AGE	SEX	BLOOD	TRIBAL ENROLLMENT		
					YEAR	COUNTY	PAGE
1 Jones, Osceola	NAMED	30	M	I.W.	1897	Panola	83

TRIBAL ENROLLMENT OF PARENTS

NAME OF FATHER	YEAR	COUNTY	NAME OF MOTHER	YEAR	COUNTY
1 W.T. Jones	Dead	non-citizen	M.M. Jones		non citizen

(NOTES)

No. 1 on Chickasaw roll as Oceola Jones.   *(No. 1 Dawes' Roll No. 33)*

No. 1 was married to Martha Leacher a full blood Chickasaw woman in 1887 and lived with her till her death in 1888. Two children of Martha Leacher are Margaret Russell and Hix Leacher on Chickasaw card #858.

P.O. May 8/02. Ardmore, I.T.   Sept. 27/98.

| RESIDENCE: Pontotoc COUNTY | | | | | CARD NO. | | |
| POST OFFICE: Ada, Ind. Ter. | | | | | FIELD NO. | | |

NAME	RELATION-SHIP TO PERSON FIRST NAMED	AGE	SEX	BLOOD	TRIBAL ENROLLMENT		
					YEAR	COUNTY	PAGE
1 Letty, Mary	NAMED	27	F	Full	1897	Pickens	24
2 Lewis, Susan	Sister	18	"	"	1897	"	24
3 " Simon	Bro	10	M	"	1897	"	24
4 Letty, Carry	Dau	2	F	"			

TRIBAL ENROLLMENT OF PARENTS

	NAME OF FATHER	YEAR	COUNTY	NAME OF MOTHER	YEAR	COUNTY
1	Lewis	Dead	Chickasaw roll	Dicey Lewis	Dead	Chickasaw roll
2	"	"	" "	" "	"	" "
3	"	"	" "	" "	"	" "
4	John Letty		" "	No. 1		

(NOTES)

No. 3 also on Chickasaw roll, Pickens County, page 18

No. 4 enrolled Dec. 13/99.

Sept. 27/98.

RESIDENCE: Pickens   **COUNTY**   **CARD NO.**

POST OFFICE: Teller, Ind. Ter.   **FIELD NO.**

NAME	RELATION-SHIP TO PERSON FIRST NAMED	AGE	SEX	BLOOD	TRIBAL ENROLLMENT		
					YEAR	COUNTY	PAGE
1 Lewis, Levi	NAMED	29	M	Full	1897	Pickens	24
2 " Bettie	Dau	7mo	F	1/2			

TRIBAL ENROLLMENT OF PARENTS

	NAME OF FATHER	YEAR	COUNTY	NAME OF MOTHER	YEAR	COUNTY
1	Lewis	Dead	Chickasaw Roll	Dicey Lewis	Dead	Chickasaw Roll
2	No. 1			Effie Lewis		non citizen

(NOTES)

No. 1 was married to Effie Beavers a non-citizen Dec. 26, 1899.
    Evidence of marriage filed June 5, 1901.
No. 2 Enrolled Aug. 15, 1901.

Sept. 27/98.

RESIDENCE: Pickens   **COUNTY**   **CARD NO.**

POST OFFICE: Alex, Ind. Ter.   **FIELD NO.**

NAME	RELATION-SHIP TO PERSON FIRST NAMED	AGE	SEX	BLOOD	TRIBAL ENROLLMENT		
					YEAR	COUNTY	PAGE
1 Eldridge, Frances	NAMED	28	F	1/2	1897	Pickens	24
2 " Jim J.	Son	12	M	1/4	1897	"	24
3 " Emily	Dau	8	F	1/4	1897	"	24

TRIBAL ENROLLMENT OF PARENTS

	NAME OF FATHER	YEAR	COUNTY	NAME OF MOTHER	YEAR	COUNTY
1	Allen Latty		Cherokee citz	Emily Latty	1897	Tishomingo
2	Jim Eldridge		non citizen	No. 1		
3	" "		" "	No. 1		

(NOTES)

No. 1 on Chickasaw roll as Francis Eldridge
No. 3 "   "   "   " Amelia   "
No. 1 died May 10, 1900; proof of death filed October 24, 1902.

Sept. 27/98.

RESIDENCE: Tishomingo   COUNTY   CARD NO.
POST OFFICE: Baum, Ind. Ter.   FIELD NO.

NAME	RELATION- SHIP TO PERSON FIRST NAMED	AGE	SEX	BLOOD	TRIBAL ENROLLMENT		
					YEAR	COUNTY	PAGE
1 Brown, George	NAMED	25	M	Full	1893	Tishomingo	P.R.#1 53

TRIBAL ENROLLMENT OF PARENTS

NAME OF FATHER	YEAR	COUNTY	NAME OF MOTHER	YEAR	COUNTY
1 Aaron Brown	Dead	Chickasaw roll	Millie Hillhouse	Dead	Chickasaw Roll

(NOTES)

No. 1 died March 25, 1902; Proof of death filed July 8, 1902.   *(No. 1 Dawes' Roll No. 4124)*

The above notation as to death of No. 1 is an error and refers to George Brown on Chickasaw card #938.

See copy of letter from Geo. D. Rodgers filed Nov. 19, 1902.

Sept. 27/98.

RESIDENCE: Tishomingo   COUNTY   CARD NO.
POST OFFICE: Baum, Ind. Ter.   FIELD NO.

NAME	RELATION- SHIP TO PERSON FIRST NAMED	AGE	SEX	BLOOD	TRIBAL ENROLLMENT		
					YEAR	COUNTY	PAGE
1 Thomas, John	NAMED	50	M	1/2	1897	Tishomingo	30
2 " Jane	Wife	30	F	I.W.	1897	"	79
3 " Martha Belle	Dau	13	"	3/4	1897	"	30
4 " Rosabelle	"	8	"	3/4	1897	"	30
5 " Alta	"	3	"	1/4	1897	"	30
6 " John	Son	2	M	1/4			
7 " Gracie	Dau	5mo	F	1/4			

TRIBAL ENROLLMENT OF PARENTS

NAME OF FATHER	YEAR	COUNTY	NAME OF MOTHER	YEAR	COUNTY
1 *(Illegible)*Thomas	Dead	Non Citizen	Shtu-na-he	Dead	Chickasaw roll
2 Marion Brumley	"	" "	Add. Brumley		non citizen
3 No. 1			Sophie Hawkins Thomas	Dead	Chickasaw Roll
4 No. 1			" " "	"	" "
5 No. 1			No. 2		
6 No. 1			No. 2		
7 No. 1			No. 2		

(NOTES)

Affidavits of parties present at marriage to be supplied.   *(No. 2 Dawes' Roll No. 321)*

No. 3 on Chickasaw roll as Martha Thomas

No. 4 "   "   "   "   Rosa   "

6

No. 5 "   "   " "   Etta "
No. 3 is now the wife of J.H. Stanfield, non-citizen. Evidence of marriage filed Oct. 31, 1902.

Sept. 27/98.

RESIDENCE: Choctaw Nation (1st Dist.)	COUNTY			CARD NO.			
POST OFFICE: San Bois, Ind. Ter.				FIELD NO.			
NAME	RELATIONSHIP TO PERSON FIRST NAMED	AGE	SEX	BLOOD	TRIBAL ENROLLMENT		
					YEAR	COUNTY	PAGE
1 Scott, George W.	NAMED	26	M	1/8			

TRIBAL ENROLLMENT OF PARENTS

	NAME OF FATHER	YEAR	COUNTY	NAME OF MOTHER	YEAR	COUNTY
1	G.W. Scott	Dead	non citizen	Eliza Scott	Dead	Chickasaw Roll

(NOTES)

On Choctaw Census Record No. 2, Page 417, San Bois County, transferred to Chickasaw roll by Dawes Com.
On Choctaw Roll, 1896, Sans Bois County, No. 11095.
Wife and child on Choctaw Card No. 2837.

Sept. 27/98.

CANCELLED Stamped across card

RESIDENCE: Tishomingo COUNTY				CARD NO.			
POST OFFICE: Mill Creek, Ind. Ter.				FIELD NO.			
NAME	RELATIONSHIP TO PERSON FIRST NAMED	AGE	SEX	BLOOD	TRIBAL ENROLLMENT		
					YEAR	COUNTY	PAGE
1 Harris, Tipton Shirley	NAMED	29	M	1/2	1897	Tishomingo	27
2 " Bertie	Wife	29	F	I.W.	1897	"	79
3 " Delos	Son	8	M	1/4	1897	"	27
4 " Fred	"	7	"	1/4	1897	"	27
5 " Irene	Dau	5	F	1/4	1897	"	27
6 " Jennie	"	3	"	1/4	1897	"	27

TRIBAL ENROLLMENT OF PARENTS

	NAME OF FATHER	YEAR	COUNTY	NAME OF MOTHER	YEAR	COUNTY
1	Cyrus Harris	Dead	Chickasaw Roll	Hettie Harris	1897	Tishomingo
2	Wm Healey	"	Non Citizen	Susan Healey	Dead	Non Citizen
3	No. 1			No. 2		
4	No. 1			No. 2		
5	No. 1			No. 2		
6	No. 1			No. 2		

(NOTES)

No. 1 on Chickasaw roll as Tip Harris
No. 5 "   "   " " Iram "
No. 2 Died April 14, 1900; Proof of death filed Nov. 10, 1902.

RESIDENCE: Tishomingo   **COUNTY**   **CARD NO.**
POST OFFICE: Nebo, Ind. Ter.   **FIELD NO.**

	NAME	RELATION- SHIP TO PERSON FIRST NAMED	AGE	SEX	BLOOD	TRIBAL ENROLLMENT		
						YEAR	COUNTY	PAGE
1	Hawkins, Scott	NAMED	55	M	Full	1897	"	28
2	" ~~Minnie~~	~~Dau~~	~~20~~	~~F~~	~~"~~	~~1897~~	~~"~~	~~28~~
3	" Ruby	Dau	6	F	1/2	1897	"	28
4	" Jessie	"	2	"	1/2	1897	"	28
5	" Fannie Doria	"	6mos	"	1/2			
6	" Abbie Dee	Dau	3mo	F	1/2			
7	" Eliza Jane	Wife	35	"	I.W.			

TRIBAL ENROLLMENT OF PARENTS

	NAME OF FATHER	YEAR	COUNTY	NAME OF MOTHER	YEAR	COUNTY
1	La-pon-e-tub-by	Dead	Chickasaw roll	Ah-le-nus-se	Dead	Chickasaw roll
2	~~No. 1~~			~~Becky Hawkins~~	"	" "
3	No. 1			Eliza Wade Hawkins		White woman
4	No. 1			" " "		" "
5	No. 1			" " "		" "
6	No. 1			" " "		" "
7	Franklin Anders	dead	non-citz	Rebecca Anders	dead	non citz

(NOTES)

No. 1 husband of Eliza Wade Hawkins Chickasaw Card No. D.82
No. 3 on Chickasaw roll as Rubin
No. 6 Enrolled January 31, 1901.
     Evidence of birth of No. 5 received and filed March 15, 1902.
No. 7 transferred from Chickasaw card No. D-82. Nov. 28-1906
     See decision of Nov. 12-1906.

P.O. Sulphur IT   Sept. 27/98.

8

Chickasaw Enrollment Cards 1898-1914
Chickasaw by Blood   Volume V

RESIDENCE: Pontotoc   **COUNTY**

POST OFFICE: Minco, Ind. Ter.

CARD NO.

FIELD NO.

NAME	RELATION-SHIP TO PERSON FIRST NAMED	AGE	SEX	BLOOD	TRIBAL ENROLLMENT		
					YEAR	COUNTY	PAGE
1 Herman, Vicy	NAMED	78	F	Full	1897	Pontotoc	65

TRIBAL ENROLLMENT OF PARENTS

	NAME OF FATHER	YEAR	COUNTY	NAME OF MOTHER	YEAR	COUNTY
1		Dead	Chickasaw Roll		Dead	Chickasaw Roll

(NOTES)

Also known as Granny
On Chickasaw roll as Gramvicy Herman.
No. 1 Also on Chickasaw roll, 1897, Page 97, as Vicie Sampson.

Sept. 27/98.

RESIDENCE: Pontotoc   **COUNTY**

POST OFFICE: Minco, Ind. Ter.

CARD NO.

FIELD NO.

NAME	RELATION-SHIP TO PERSON FIRST NAMED	AGE	SEX	BLOOD	TRIBAL ENROLLMENT		
					YEAR	COUNTY	PAGE
1 Saffron, Lizzie E.	NAMED	20	F	Full	1897	Pontotoc	57

TRIBAL ENROLLMENT OF PARENTS

	NAME OF FATHER	YEAR	COUNTY	NAME OF MOTHER	YEAR	COUNTY
1	Ben Saffron	Dead	Chickasaw roll	Hannah Saffron	Dead	Chickasaw roll

(NOTES)

Sept. 27/98

RESIDENCE: Pontotoc   **COUNTY**

POST OFFICE: Minco, Ind. Ter.

CARD NO.

FIELD NO.

NAME	RELATION-SHIP TO PERSON FIRST NAMED	AGE	SEX	BLOOD	TRIBAL ENROLLMENT		
					YEAR	COUNTY	PAGE
1 Jefferson, Morris	NAMED	22	M	1/8	1897	Chick residing in Choctaw N. 3rd Dist.	74
2 " Hilda E.	Dau	2 1/2mo	F	1/16			

TRIBAL ENROLLMENT OF PARENTS

	NAME OF FATHER	YEAR	COUNTY	NAME OF MOTHER	YEAR	COUNTY
1	Canos Jefferson	Dead	Choctaw roll	Elsie Jefferson	Dead	Chickasaw Roll
2	No. 1			Sarah Jefferson		non citizen

9

(NOTES)

No. 1 is now the husband of Sarah Jefferson a non citizen, evidence of marriage filed March 10, 1902.

No. 2 Born Dec. 30, 1901; enrolled March 10, 1902.

Sept. 27/98

RESIDENCE: Pontotoc COUNTY					CARD NO.		
POST OFFICE: Minco, Ind. Ter.					FIELD NO.		
NAME	RELATION-SHIP TO PERSON FIRST NAMED	AGE	SEX	BLOOD	TRIBAL ENROLLMENT		
					YEAR	COUNTY	PAGE
1 Bond, James H.	NAMED	57	M	I.W.	1897	Pontotoc	81
2 " Adelaide	Wife	57	F	1/4	1897	"	65
3 " Reford	Son	22	M	1/8	1897	"	65
4 " Edward	"	13	"	1/8	1897	"	65

	TRIBAL ENROLLMENT OF PARENTS						
	NAME OF FATHER	YEAR	COUNTY	NAME OF MOTHER	YEAR	COUNTY	
1	John Bond	Dead	non Citizen	Jemima Bond	Dead	non Citizen	
2	Charles Johnson	"	" "	Rebecca Courtney Johnson	"	Chickasaw roll	
3	No. 1			No. 2			
4	No. 1			No. 2			

(NOTES)

No. 1 on Chickasaw roll as J.H. Bond.   *(No. 1 Dawes' Roll No. 320)*

No. 2 "   "   " " Adalda Bond.

No. 3 lives at Chickasha, I.T.   Sept. 27/98

RESIDENCE: Tishomingo COUNTY					CARD NO.		
POST OFFICE: Berwyn, Ind. Ter.					FIELD NO.		
NAME	RELATION-SHIP TO PERSON FIRST NAMED	AGE	SEX	BLOOD	TRIBAL ENROLLMENT		
					YEAR	COUNTY	PAGE
1 Gilliam, Mary Elizabeth	NAMED	17	F	1/4	1897	Tishomingo	30
2 " Olivette Herndon	Sister	15	"	1/4	1897	"	30
3 " James Sanders	Bro	14	M	1/4	1897	"	30
4 " John Overstreet	"	14	"	1/4	1897	"	30
5 " Sallie Louisa	Sister	14	F	1/4	1897	"	30
6 " Lula Maude	"	9	"	1/4	1897	"	30
7 " Howard Preston	Bro	7	M	1/4	1897	"	30
8 " John O.	Father	49	M	I.W.	1897	Pickens	79

Chickasaw Enrollment Cards 1898-1914
Chickasaw by Blood   Volume V

			TRIBAL ENROLLMENT OF PARENTS				
	NAME OF FATHER	YEAR	COUNTY	NAME OF MOTHER	YEAR	COUNTY
1	John O. Gilliam		White man	Susan B. Gilliam	Dead	Tishomingo
2	" " "		" "	" " "	"	"
3	" " "		" "	" " "	"	"
4	" " "		" "	" " "	"	"
5	" " "		" "	" " "	"	"
6	" " "		" "	" " "	"	"
7	" " "		" "	" " "	"	"
8	James S. Gilliam		Non Citizen	Martha Ann Gilliam	"	Non Citizen

(NOTES)

No. 1 on Chickasaw roll as Lizzie Gilliam
No. 2 "   "   "   " Jennie "
No. 3 "   "   "   " Earlie "
No. 4 "   "   "   " Johnie "
No. 5 "   "   "   " Sallie "
No. 6 "   "   "   " Manda "
No. 7 "   "   "   " Howard "
No. 8 on Chickasaw roll as William J.O. Gilliam
No. 8 transferred from Chickasaw Card #D.130. See decision of August 17, 1904 Sept. 1, 1904.
   John O. Gilliam, father of Nos 1-7 inclusive on Chickasaw D.130.

Sept. 27/98

RESIDENCE: Choctaw Nation (3ʳᵈ Dist.)	~~COUNTY~~		CARD NO.	

RESIDENCE: Choctaw Nation (3rd Dist.)   ~~COUNTY~~   CARD NO.
POST OFFICE: Coalgate, Ind. Ter.   FIELD NO.

NAME	RELATION-SHIP TO PERSON FIRST NAMED	AGE	SEX	BLOOD	TRIBAL ENROLLMENT		
					YEAR	COUNTY	PAGE
1 James, Daniel		17	M	3/4			

			TRIBAL ENROLLMENT OF PARENTS				
	NAME OF FATHER	YEAR	COUNTY	NAME OF MOTHER	YEAR	COUNTY
1	Silas James		Atoka County Choctaw Roll	Malinda James	Dead	Chick residing in Choctaw N. 3ʳᵈ Dist.

(NOTES)

   On Choctaw Census Record No. 2 Page 306, transferred to Chickasaw roll by Dawes Com.
   On Choctaw Roll, 1896, Atoka County, No. 7311.
No. 1 is son of Silas James on Choctaw card #297
No. 1 Died Aug. 12, 1901; proof of death filed May 6, 1902.

Sept. 27/98

CANCELLED Stamped across card

Chickasaw Enrollment Cards 1898-1914
Chickasaw by Blood   Volume V

RESIDENCE: Choctaw Nation	COUNTY				CARD NO.			
POST OFFICE: San Bois, Ind. Ter.					FIELD NO.			

NAME	RELATION-SHIP TO PERSON FIRST NAMED	AGE	SEX	BLOOD	TRIBAL ENROLLMENT		
					YEAR	COUNTY	PAGE
1 Riddle, John	NAMED	27	M	1/2			

TRIBAL ENROLLMENT OF PARENTS

	NAME OF FATHER	YEAR	COUNTY	NAME OF MOTHER	YEAR	COUNTY
1	Mose Riddle	Dead	Choctaw roll	Easter Riddle	Dead	Chickasaw roll

(NOTES)

On Choctaw Census Record No. 2, Page 407, San Bois Co., transferred to Chickasaw roll by Dawes Com.
On Choctaw Roll, 1896, Sans Bois County, No. 10669.

Sept. 27/98

CANCELLED Stamped across card

RESIDENCE: Pickens COUNTY					CARD NO.			
POST OFFICE: Ardmore, Ind. Ter.					FIELD NO.			

	NAME	RELATION-SHIP TO PERSON FIRST NAMED	AGE	SEX	BLOOD	TRIBAL ENROLLMENT		
						YEAR	COUNTY	PAGE
1	Wallace, Nannie	NAMED	37	F	Full	1897	Pickens	16
2	" Esther B	Dau	13	"	1/2	1897	"	16
3	" Elizabeth Vashti	"	12	"	1/2	1897	"	16
4	" Albert Ned	Son	8	M	1/2	1897	"	16
5	" Samuel Lee	"	6	"	1/2	1897	"	16
6	" Leo Edmond B.	"	5	"	1/2	1897	"	16
7	" George Blanchee	"	3	"	1/2	1897	"	16
8	" William G.	Hus	41	M	I.W.	1897	"	83

TRIBAL ENROLLMENT OF PARENTS

	NAME OF FATHER	YEAR	COUNTY	NAME OF MOTHER	YEAR	COUNTY
1	Duncan Ned	Dead	Chickasaw roll	Ar-no-le-ho-yo	Dead	Chickawaw roll
2	W.G. Wallace (I.W.)	1897	Pickens	No. 1		
3	" " "	1897	"	No. 1		
4	" " "	1897	"	No. 1		
5	" " "	1897	"	No. 1		
6	" " "	1897	"	No. 1		
7	" " "	1897	"	No. 1		
8	Harvey Wallace		non citizen	Elizabeth Wallace		non citizen

(NOTES)

No. 1 wife of W.G. Wallace, Chickasaw Card No. D.80.

No. 2 on Chickasaw roll as Ester B. Wallace

No. 3 "   "   "   " Elizabeth   "

No. 4 "   "   "   " Avert   "

No. 5 "   "   "   " Sam   "

No. 6 "   "   "   " Edmon   "

No. 7 "   "   "   " George   "

Nos. 1 to 7 inclusive admitted by Dawes Commission in 1896 as Chickasaws by blood
Chickasaw case #98; no appeal

No. 8 transferred from Chickasaw card #D.80 April 7, 1904.   *(No. 8 Dawes' Roll No. 319)*
See decision of March 15, 1904.

Sept. 27/98

RESIDENCE: Choctaw Nation   ~~COUNTY~~   **CARD NO.**

POST OFFICE: Kiowa, Ind. Ter.   **FIELD NO.**

	NAME	RELATION-SHIP TO PERSON FIRST NAMED	AGE	SEX	BLOOD	TRIBAL ENROLLMENT		
						YEAR	COUNTY	PAGE
1	Thompson, Wilson	FIRST NAMED	12	M	1/8	1897	Chick residing in Choctaw N. 1st Dist.	71
2	" Angeline	Sister	10	F	1/8	1897	" " " "	71
3	Bollinger, Minnie M.	Mother	36	F	I.W.			

TRIBAL ENROLLMENT OF PARENTS

	NAME OF FATHER	YEAR	COUNTY	NAME OF MOTHER	YEAR	COUNTY
1	Cobb Thompson	Dead	Chick residing in Choctaw N. 1st Dist.	Minnie Bolinger		non citizen
2	" "	"	" " " "	" "		" "
3	Wilson B. Manners		Non citizen	Cyntha A. Manners		" "

(NOTES)

Grandchildren of Martha Thompson, Chickasaw roll, Card No. 667   *(No. 3 Dawes' Roll No. 545)*

No. 3 formerly wife of Richard C. Thompson a recognized Chickasaw by blood who died in the year 1870.

No. 3 married to Addison Bollinger a U.S. Citizen Oct. 7, 1894.

No. 3 originally listed for enrollment on Chickasaw card #D.230 Mar. 22/99
transferred to this card Nov. 26, 1904. See decision of Nov. 10, 1904.

Sept. 27/98.

Chickasaw Enrollment Cards 1898-1914
Chickasaw by Blood Volume V

RESIDENCE: Choctaw Nation ~~COUNTY~~   CARD NO.
POST OFFICE: Kiowa, Ind. Ter.   FIELD NO.

	NAME	RELATION-SHIP TO PERSON	AGE	SEX	BLOOD	TRIBAL ENROLLMENT		
						YEAR	COUNTY	PAGE
1	Thompson, Martha	FIRST NAMED	52	F	1/2	1897	Chick residing in Choctaw N. 1st Dist.	71
2	" Robert	Son	17	M	1/4	1897	" " " "	71
3	" Alexander	"	10	M	1/4	1897	" " " "	71

TRIBAL ENROLLMENT OF PARENTS

	NAME OF FATHER	YEAR	COUNTY	NAME OF MOTHER	YEAR	COUNTY
1	Theodore Watkins	Dead	non citizen	Tennessee Colbert	Dead	Chickasaw roll
2	Alexander Thompson	"	" "	No. 1		
3	" "	"	" "	No. 1		

(NOTES)
No. 2 is the husband of Nettie Thompson on Choctaw card #4467.
No. 3 on Chickasaw roll as Alex Thompson.

Sept. 27/98.

RESIDENCE: Pickens COUNTY   CARD NO.
POST OFFICE: Brownsville, Ind. Ter.   FIELD NO.

	NAME	RELATION-SHIP TO PERSON FIRST	AGE	SEX	BLOOD	TRIBAL ENROLLMENT		
						YEAR	COUNTY	PAGE
1	Colbert, Amos Henry	NAMED	35	M	Full	1897	Pickens	23
2	" Icy	Wife	30	F	"	1897	"	23
3	" Alice	Dau	11	"	"	1897	"	23
4	" Humphreys	Son	3	M	"	1897	"	23
5	" Edna	Dau	7wks	F	"	DIED PRIOR TO SEPTEMBER 25 1902		

TRIBAL ENROLLMENT OF PARENTS

	NAME OF FATHER	YEAR	COUNTY	NAME OF MOTHER	YEAR	COUNTY
1	Abijah Colbert	Dead	Chickasaw Roll	Rhody Colbert	Dead	Chickasaw roll
2	James Hamilton	"	Pickens	Sallie Hamilton	1897	Pickens
3	No. 1			Adeline Colbert	Dead	"
4	No. 1			No. 2		
5	No. 1			No. 2		

(NOTES)
No. 1 on Chickasaw roll as A.H. Colbert
No. 4 "   "   "   " Humfres "
No. 1 Died Sept. 19, 1901; Proof of death filed Nov. 7, 1902
No. 5 enrolled Dec. 17/98.

14

No. 5 Died Nov. 1901; Proof of death filed Nov. 7, 1902.

Sept. 27/98.

		RELATION-SHIP TO PERSON FIRST NAMED	AGE	SEX	BLOOD	TRIBAL ENROLLMENT		
NAME						YEAR	COUNTY	PAGE
	RESIDENCE: Pontotoc **COUNTY**					**CARD NO.**		
	POST OFFICE: Wiley, Ind. Ter.					**FIELD NO.**		
1	Holden, Amos		37	M	Full	1897	Pontotoc	56
2	" Sukey	Wife	29	F	"	1897	"	56
3	" James	Son	9	M	"	1897	"	56
4	" Annie	Dau	6	F	"	1897	"	56
5	" Armon	Son	2	M	"	1897	"	56
6	" Richmond	Nephew	6	"	"	1897	"	56
7	Colbert, Lydia	Dau	17	F	"	1897	"	58
8	" Martha	Dau of No. 7	7mo	F	"			
9	Holden, Emily	Dau	2mo	F	"			

TRIBAL ENROLLMENT OF PARENTS

	NAME OF FATHER	YEAR	COUNTY	NAME OF MOTHER	YEAR	COUNTY
1	Ah-no-le-tub-by Holden	Dead	Chickasaw Roll	Se-mi-o-ke	Dead	Chickasaw Roll
2	Jimson-e-shock-ey	"	" "	Rachael	"	" "
3	No. 1			No. 2		
4	No. 1			No. 2		
5	No. 1			No. 2		
6	Edmund Holden	1897	Pontotoc	Jennie Holden	Dead	Pontotoc
7	No. 1			Betsey Holden	"	"
8	Sim Colbert	1897	Panola	No. 7		
9	No. 1			No. 2		

(NOTES)

No. 2 on Chickasaw roll as Suckey Holden
No. 3 "   "   " " Jane   "
No. 7 "   "   " " Lydia Wolfe
No. 7 is now the wife of Sim Colbert on Chickasaw Card #1094. Evidence of death of his first wife requested,
    and certified copy of the marriage certificate between No. 7 and Sim Colbert filed Oct. 3, 1901.
No. 8 Enrolled Oct. 3, 1901
No. 6 Died Jan. 1899; Proof of death filed Nov. 8, 1902.
No. 9 Born Feby. 16, 1901; enrolled April 30, 1902.

P.O. Filmore, IT 1/23/03   Sept. 27/98.

RESIDENCE: Pickens   COUNTY   CARD NO.
POST OFFICE: Kingston, Ind. Ter.   FIELD NO.

NAME	RELATION-SHIP TO PERSON FIRST NAMED	AGE	SEX	BLOOD	TRIBAL ENROLLMENT		
					YEAR	COUNTY	PAGE
1 Townsley, Pheby	NAMED	20	F	Full	1897	Pickens	22
2 " Rosie	Dau	2	"	1/2	1897	"	22
3 " Maggie	"	2mo	"	1/2			

TRIBAL ENROLLMENT OF PARENTS

NAME OF FATHER	YEAR	COUNTY	NAME OF MOTHER	YEAR	COUNTY
1 Jim Hamilton	Dead	Pickens	Sallie Hamilton	1897	Pickens
2 Jim Townsley		Non Citizen	No. 1		
3 " "		" "	No. 1		

(NOTES)

No. 2 on Chickasaw roll as Mosey
No. 3 enrolled Dec. 13/99.

Sept. 27/98.

RESIDENCE: Pickens   COUNTY   CARD NO.
POST OFFICE: Kingston, Ind. Ter.   FIELD NO.

NAME	RELATION-SHIP TO PERSON FIRST NAMED	AGE	SEX	BLOOD	TRIBAL ENROLLMENT		
					YEAR	COUNTY	PAGE
1 Hamilton, Sallie	NAMED	50	F	Full	1897	Pickens	22

TRIBAL ENROLLMENT OF PARENTS

NAME OF FATHER	YEAR	COUNTY	NAME OF MOTHER	YEAR	COUNTY
1 Sha-pe-ok-ke	Dead	Chickasaw Roll	Stem-ma-ko-ke	Dead	Chickasaw roll

(NOTES)

Sept. 27/98.

RESIDENCE: Choctaw Nat'n Kiamitia   COUNTY   CARD NO.
POST OFFICE: Antlers, I.T.   FIELD NO.

NAME	RELATION-SHIP TO PERSON FIRST NAMED	AGE	SEX	BLOOD	TRIBAL ENROLLMENT		
					YEAR	COUNTY	PAGE
1 Locke, Elisha I.	NAMED	40	M	I.W.			
2 " Jane	Wife	36	F	1/2			
3 " Elisha	Son	5	M	1/4			
4 " Mary	Dau	3	F	1/4			
5 " Bertie	"	6mo	"	1/4			

16

6	Hampton, Susan	S.Dau	11	"	1/4				
7	Locke, Jesse	Son	7wks	M	1/4				

TRIBAL ENROLLMENT OF PARENTS

	NAME OF FATHER	YEAR	COUNTY	NAME OF MOTHER	YEAR	COUNTY
1	Frank Locke	Dead	Non Citz	Mary Locke	Dead	Non Citz.
2	Barney Davenport	"	Choctaw Roll	Saliney Yakambe	"	Chick Roll
3	No. 1			No. 2		
4	No. 1			No. 2		
5	No. 1			No. 2		
6	Julius Hampton	1896	Choctaw Roll	No. 2		
7	No. 1			No. 2		

(NOTES)

No. 2 on 1893 Pay Roll, Choctaw Nat'n. Page 10, No. 113. Cedar Co, as Jane Davenport
No. 6 on 1893 Pay Roll, Choctaw Nat'n, Page 10, No. 114, Cedar Co.
    Transferred to Chickasaw Roll by Dawes Commission
No. 5 Affidavit of birth to be supplied. Rec'd May 18/99.
No. 7 Born November 16, 1901; Enrolled Jan. 3, 1902

5/12/99

CANCELLED Stamped across card

RESIDENCE: Choctaw Nation, Kiamitia **COUNTY**	**CARD NO.**
POST OFFICE: Antlers, I.T.	**FIELD NO.**

	NAME	RELATION-SHIP TO PERSON FIRST NAMED	AGE	SEX	BLOOD	TRIBAL ENROLLMENT		
						YEAR	COUNTY	PAGE
1	Frazier, Joanna		17	F	1/4			
2	" Clara	Dau	4mo	F	1/2			

TRIBAL ENROLLMENT OF PARENTS

	NAME OF FATHER	YEAR	COUNTY	NAME OF MOTHER	YEAR	COUNTY
1	Allington Ward	1896	Choctaw Roll	Phoebe Ward	1896	Chickasaw
2	Harris Frazier	1896	Choctaw Roll	No. 1		

(NOTES)

On 1896 Choctaw Roll as Joanna Ward. Page 360, No. 13745, Kiamitia County.
    Transferred to Chickasaw Roll by Dawes Commission
Husband on Choctaw Card No. 1675
No. 2 Enrolled Feby. 26, 1900.

5/12/99

CANCELLED Stamped across card

Chickasaw Enrollment Cards 1898-1914
Chickasaw by Blood   Volume V

RESIDENCE: Choctaw Nation, Jacks Fork COUNTY   CARD NO.
POST OFFICE: Antlers, I.T.   FIELD NO.

	NAME	RELATION-SHIP TO PERSON	AGE	SEX	BLOOD	TRIBAL ENROLLMENT		
						YEAR	COUNTY	PAGE
1	Nash, Lizzie	FIRST NAMED	24	F	1/4	1897	Chickasaw residing in Choc. Nation 2nd Dist.	72
2	" Esther	Dau	2	"	1/8			
3	" Ruth	"	3mo	"	1/8			
4	" Mary	Dau	1mo	F	1/8			
5	" Henry C.	Husb	42	M	I.W.	1896	Chickasaw residing in Choctaw Nation	82

TRIBAL ENROLLMENT OF PARENTS

	NAME OF FATHER	YEAR	COUNTY	NAME OF MOTHER	YEAR	COUNTY
1	Thomas Griggs	1897	Choctaw Roll	Mary Griggs	Dead	Chick Roll
2	Henry C. Nash	1897	Non Citz	No. 1		
3	" " "	"	" "	No. 1		
4	" " "	"	" "	No. 1		
5	F.H. Nash	1896	Non citizen	Frances Nash	1896	non citz.

(NOTES)
No. 1 is also on 1893 Pay Roll, Choctaw Nation, Page 31, No. 258, Kiamitia County as Lizzie Griggs
    also on 1896 Choctaw Roll Page 250, No. 9881 as Lizzie Noah, Jacks Fork.
No. 5 Husband of No. 1 and father of No. 2 on Choctaw Cartd No. 1693 was admitted by
    Dawes Commission as an Intermarried Choctaw
No. 3 Enrolled Dec. 14/99
No. 4 Born Aug. 15, 1902; enrolled Sept. 24, 1902.
No. 5 transferred from Choctaw card #1693
    See decision of March 9, 1904.

5/15/99.

RESIDENCE: Choctawe Nat'n. Jacks Fork COUNTY   CARD NO.
POST OFFICE: Antlers, I.T.   FIELD NO.

	NAME	RELATION-SHIP TO PERSON	AGE	SEX	BLOOD	TRIBAL ENROLLMENT		
						YEAR	COUNTY	PAGE
1	Locke, Sina J.	FIRST NAMED	24	F	1/2			
2	" Mattie P.	Dau	5	"	1/4			
3	" Victor B.	Son	7mo	M	1/4			

TRIBAL ENROLLMENT OF PARENTS

	NAME OF FATHER	YEAR	COUNTY	NAME OF MOTHER	YEAR	COUNTY
1	Jim Miller	Dead	Choctaw Roll	Mahaley Miller	Dead	Chick Rolls

18

2	James L. Locke	1896	"	"	No. 1		
3	" " "	"	"	"	No. 1		

(NOTES)

No. 1 on 1896 Choctaw Roll, Page 208, No. 8365, Jacks Fork Co., as S. Locke.
No. 2 " 1896 " " " 208 " 8366 " " " " M.P. Locke
    Transferred to Chickasaw Roll by Dawes Commission
    Husband of No. 1, James L. Lock, on Choctaw Card No. 1750.

5/19/99

CANCELLED Stamped across card

RESIDENCE: Choctaw Nation, Cedar   COUNTY   CARD NO.

POST OFFICE: Kosoma, I.T.   FIELD NO.

NAME	RELATION-SHIP TO PERSON FIRST NAMED	AGE	SEX	BLOOD	TRIBAL ENROLLMENT		
					YEAR	COUNTY	PAGE
1 Sherred, Emma	NAMED	28	F	1/2			
2 " McKennon	Son	2wks	M	1/4			
3 Miller, Rena P.	Dau	8	F	1/4			
4 " Myrtle	"	6	"	1/4			
5 Sherred, Shub	Son	3mo	M	1/4			

TRIBAL ENROLLMENT OF PARENTS

	NAME OF FATHER	YEAR	COUNTY	NAME OF MOTHER	YEAR	COUNTY
1	James Miller	Dead	Choctaw Roll	Mahale Miller	Dead	Chick Roll
2	Josephus Sherred	1896	" "	No. 1		
3	Mike Erwin	Dead	Non Citz.	No. 1		
4	Henry John	1896	Choctaw Roll	No. 1		
5	Josephus Sherred	1896	Choctaw Roll	No. 1		

(NOTES)

No. 1 on 1896 Choctaw Roll Page 293 No. 11358, Cedar County
No. 3 " 1896 " " " 214 " 8598 " " as Rena Miller
No. 4 " 1896 " " " 214 " 8599 " "
    Transferred to Chickasaw Roll by Dawes Commission
    Josephus Sherred on Choctaw Card No. 1790
No. 5 Enrolled April 16, 1901

5/16/99

CANCELLED Stamped across card

Chickasaw Enrollment Cards 1898-1914
Chickasaw by Blood   Volume V

RESIDENCE: Jacks Fork   COUNTY   CARD NO.

POST OFFICE: Kosoma, I.T.   FIELD NO.

NAME	RELATION-SHIP TO PERSON FIRST NAMED	AGE	SEX	BLOOD	TRIBAL ENROLLMENT		
					YEAR	COUNTY	PAGE
1 Cooper, Sina	NAMED	28	F	1/2			
2 Wilson, Jeff	Ward	3	M	1/4			

TRIBAL ENROLLMENT OF PARENTS

NAME OF FATHER	YEAR	COUNTY	NAME OF MOTHER	YEAR	COUNTY
1 Kamotabe	Dead	Jacks Fork	Silis Kamotabe	Dead	Jacks Fork
2 Craven Wilson	1896	?ashoba	Clistie Kamotabe	"	" "

(NOTES)

No. 1 on Choctaw Roll, Page 71, No. 3008, Jacks Fork County
    Transferred to Chickasaw Roll by Dawes Commission
    Columbus Cooper, husband of No. 1 on Choctaw Roll No. 1813
No. 1 on 1896 roll as Sam Cooper

5-16-99

CANCELLED Stamped across card

RESIDENCE: Choctaw Nation, Kiamitia   COUNTY   CARD NO.

POST OFFICE: Grant, I.T.   FIELD NO.

NAME	RELATION-SHIP TO PERSON FIRST NAMED	AGE	SEX	BLOOD	TRIBAL ENROLLMENT		
					YEAR	COUNTY	PAGE
1 Parshall, Lula	NAMED	18	F	1/8	1897	Pontotoc	96

TRIBAL ENROLLMENT OF PARENTS

NAME OF FATHER	YEAR	COUNTY	NAME OF MOTHER	YEAR	COUNTY
1 L.B. Parshall	Dead	Non Citz.	Virginia Parshall	Dead	Chick Roll

(NOTES)

On 1896 Choctaw Roll as Lula Paishall, Page 266, No. 10458, Kiamitia Co.
Transferred to Chickasaw Roll by Dawes Com.

5/19/99

RESIDENCE: Choctaw Nat'n Jacks Fork   COUNTY   CARD NO.

POST OFFICE: Hartshorne, I.T.   FIELD NO.

NAME	RELATION-SHIP TO PERSON FIRST NAMED	AGE	SEX	BLOOD	TRIBAL ENROLLMENT		
					YEAR	COUNTY	PAGE
1 Ward, Charles	NAMED	21	M	1/2			

TRIBAL ENROLLMENT OF PARENTS						
NAME OF FATHER	YEAR	COUNTY	NAME OF MOTHER	YEAR	COUNTY	
1 Williston Ward	Dead	Choc Roll	Patsy Ward	Dead	Chick Roll	

(NOTES)

On 1896 Choctaw Roll, Page 369, No. 14087
Transferred to Chickasaw Roll by Dawes Com.

5/22/99

CANCELLED Stamped across card

RESIDENCE: Choctaw Nation Jacks Fork   **COUNTY**   **CARD NO.**
POST OFFICE: Tushkahomma, I.T.   **FIELD NO.**

NAME	RELATION-SHIP TO PERSON FIRST NAMED	AGE	SEX	BLOOD	TRIBAL ENROLLMENT		
					YEAR	COUNTY	PAGE
1 McGee, George	NAMED	23	M	Full	1896	Choc. Dist. 3rd	73

TRIBAL ENROLLMENT OF PARENTS						
NAME OF FATHER	YEAR	COUNTY	NAME OF MOTHER	YEAR	COUNTY	
1 Folsom McGee	1896	Jacks Fork	Susan McGee	Dead	Jacks Fork	

(NOTES)

Enrolled on Page 73, 3rd Dist. of Chickasaw Rolls in Choctaw Nation.
Wife on Choctaw rolls, No. 1921.

RESIDENCE: Choctaw N. Sans Bois   **COUNTY**   **CARD NO.**
POST OFFICE: Sans Bois, I.T.   **FIELD NO.**

NAME	RELATION-SHIP TO PERSON FIRST NAMED	AGE	SEX	BLOOD	TRIBAL ENROLLMENT		
					YEAR	COUNTY	PAGE
1 Frazier, Jane	NAMED	42	F	Full			
2 " Edmund	Son	20	M	3/4			

TRIBAL ENROLLMENT OF PARENTS						
NAME OF FATHER	YEAR	COUNTY	NAME OF MOTHER	YEAR	COUNTY	
1 Garland William	Dead	Chickasaw Roll	Eliza William	Dead	Chickasaw Roll	
2 Campbell (illegible)	"	Gaines	No. 1			

(NOTES)

No. 1 on 1896 Choctaw Roll, Page 93, No. 3831
No. 2 " 1896   "   "   " 93 " 3827

5-22-99

CANCELLED Stamped across card

RESIDENCE: Choctaw Nation, Jacks Fork   COUNTY   CARD NO.

POST OFFICE: Tushkahomma, I.T.   FIELD NO.

NAME	RELATIONSHIP TO PERSON FIRST NAMED	AGE	SEX	BLOOD	TRIBAL ENROLLMENT		
					YEAR	COUNTY	PAGE
1 Benton, Sallie	NAMED	23	F	1/2			
2 " Willie	Son	8	M	1/4			
3 " Everidge	"	5	"	1/4			
4 " Margaret	Dau	2	F	1/4			
5 " Adeline	S.Dau	14	"	1/4			
6 " George	Son	3mo	M	1/4			

TRIBAL ENROLLMENT OF PARENTS

	NAME OF FATHER	YEAR	COUNTY	NAME OF MOTHER	YEAR	COUNTY
1	Allington Anderson	Dead	Choctaw Roll	Louisa Impson	1896	Chick Roll
2	George Benton	"	" "	No. 1		
3	" "	"	" "	No. 1		
4	" "	"	" "	No. 1		
5	" "	"	" "	Sissy Benton	Dead	Chick Roll
6	" "	"	" "	No. 1		

(NOTES)

No. 1 on 1896 Choctaw Roll, Page 48, No. 1978, Jacks Fork County

No. 2 " 1896 " " " 48 " 1980 " " "

No. 3 " 1896 " " " 48 " 1981 " " "

All transferred to Chickasaw Roll by Dawes Commission

No. 5 on 1896 Choctaw Roll Page 48, No. 1979, Jack Fork Co.

Transferred to Chickasaw roll by Dawes Commission.

No. 6 Enrolled Nov. 4/99.

5/22/99
No. 5 - 5/24/99

CANCELLED Stamped across card

RESIDENCE: Choctaw Nation, Jacks Fork   COUNTY   CARD NO.

POST OFFICE: Stringtown, I.T.   FIELD NO.

NAME	RELATIONSHIP TO PERSON FIRST NAMED	AGE	SEX	BLOOD	TRIBAL ENROLLMENT		
					YEAR	COUNTY	PAGE
1 Williams, Amanda	NAMED	2	F	1/4			

TRIBAL ENROLLMENT OF PARENTS

	NAME OF FATHER	YEAR	COUNTY	NAME OF MOTHER	YEAR	COUNTY
1	Joe B. Williams	1896	Choctaw Roll	Carrie Williams	Dead	Chick Roll

(NOTES)

Father on Choctaw Card No. 1956.

5/22/98.

CANCELLED Stamped across card
and transferred to Choctaw card #1956 with father

RESIDENCE: Choctaw Nation, Jacks Fork	COUNTY				CARD NO.			
POST OFFICE: Tushkahomma, I.T.					FIELD NO.			
NAME	RELATION-SHIP TO PERSON FIRST NAMED	AGE	SEX	BLOOD	TRIBAL ENROLLMENT			
					YEAR	COUNTY	PAGE	
1 Hihcha, Lottie		49	F	Full	1897	Chickasaw residing in Choctaw N. 3rd Dist.	73	

TRIBAL ENROLLMENT OF PARENTS

	NAME OF FATHER	YEAR	COUNTY	NAME OF MOTHER	YEAR	COUNTY
1	Emakatabe	Dead	Chick Roll	Ishtemaha	Dead	Chick Roll

(NOTES)

No. 1 on 1897 roll as "Lottie".
No. 1 is mother of Osborne Anderson, Chickasaw Card #1655
No. 1 is now wife of Thomas Tuffer, on Choctaw Card #1975
  Evidence of marriage filed *(remainder illegible)*

5/23/99

RESIDENCE: Choctaw Nation, Jacks Fork	COUNTY				CARD NO.			
POST OFFICE: Tushkahomma, I.T.					FIELD NO.			
NAME	RELATION-SHIP TO PERSON FIRST NAMED	AGE	SEX	BLOOD	TRIBAL ENROLLMENT			
					YEAR	COUNTY	PAGE	
1 Moore, Gertie		12	F	1/2				

TRIBAL ENROLLMENT OF PARENTS

	NAME OF FATHER	YEAR	COUNTY	NAME OF MOTHER	YEAR	COUNTY
1	Isaac Gibson	Dead	Choctaw Roll	Nancy Moore	Dead	Chick Fork.

(NOTES)

On 1896 Choctaw Roll as Gurdie Moore, Page 223, No. 8892
Transferred to Chickasaw Roll by Dawes Com.

5/23/99

CANCELLED Stamped across card

RESIDENCE:	Choctaw Nat'n, Jacks Fork	COUNTY				CARD NO.		
POST OFFICE:	Tushkahomma, I.T.					FIELD NO.		

NAME	RELATION- SHIP TO PERSON FIRST	AGE	SEX	BLOOD	TRIBAL ENROLLMENT		
					YEAR	COUNTY	PAGE
1 Moore, Gilbert	NAMED	65	M	1/2			

	TRIBAL ENROLLMENT OF PARENTS						
NAME OF FATHER	YEAR	COUNTY	NAME OF MOTHER	YEAR	COUNTY		
1 Gilbert Moore	Dead	Chick Roll	Hettie Underwood	Dead	Chick Roll		

(NOTES)
On 1893 Choctaw Pay Roll, Page 59, No. 528, Jacks Fork Co.
transferred to Chickasaw Roll by Dawes Commission
Wife on Card D.236.

5/24/99.

CANCELLED Stamped across card

RESIDENCE:	Choctaw Nat'n, Gaines	COUNTY				CARD NO.		
POST OFFICE:	Hartshorne, I.T.					FIELD NO.		

NAME	RELATION- SHIP TO PERSON FIRST	AGE	SEX	BLOOD	TRIBAL ENROLLMENT		
					YEAR	COUNTY	PAGE
1 Thomas, Jimmie	NAMED	7	M	1/2			

	TRIBAL ENROLLMENT OF PARENTS						
NAME OF FATHER	YEAR	COUNTY	NAME OF MOTHER	YEAR	COUNTY		
1 Dave Thomas	1896	Choctaw Roll	Becky Thomas	Dead	Chick Roll		

(NOTES)
On 1896 Choctaw roll Page 310, No. 11991, Gaines County
Transferred to Chickasaw Roll by Dawes Commission.
No. 1 is the son of Dave Thomas on Choctaw card #2008.

5/24/99

CANCELLED Stamped across card

RESIDENCE:	Choctaw Nation	COUNTY				CARD NO.		
POST OFFICE:	Talihina, I.T.					FIELD NO.		

NAME	RELATION- SHIP TO PERSON FIRST	AGE	SEX	BLOOD	TRIBAL ENROLLMENT		
					YEAR	COUNTY	PAGE
1 Hitcher, Harrison	NAMED	40	M	Full			

Chickasaw Enrollment Cards 1898-1914
Chickasaw by Blood   Volume V

TRIBAL ENROLLMENT OF PARENTS

	NAME OF FATHER	YEAR	COUNTY	NAME OF MOTHER	YEAR	COUNTY
1	Hih-cha	Dead	Chick Roll	Siney Hih-cha	Dead	Chick Roll

(NOTES)

On 1896 Choctaw Roll, Page 131, No. 5400
transferred to Chickasaw Roll by Dawes Commission.
Wife and children on Choctaw Card No. 2128.

5/30/99.

CANCELLED Stamped across card

RESIDENCE: Choctaw Nation   COUNTY   CARD NO.
POST OFFICE: Lenox, I.T.   FIELD NO.

	NAME	RELATION-SHIP TO PERSON FIRST NAMED	AGE	SEX	BLOOD	TRIBAL ENROLLMENT		
						YEAR	COUNTY	PAGE
1	Potts, Bessie	NAMED	45	F	Full			
2	Pitchlynn, Williamson	Son	13	M	1/2			
3	" Louisa	Dau	9	F	1/2			
4	" Livingston	Son	7	M	1/2			

TRIBAL ENROLLMENT OF PARENTS

	NAME OF FATHER	YEAR	COUNTY	NAME OF MOTHER	YEAR	COUNTY
1	Hih-cha	Dead	Chick Roll	Siney Hih-cha	Dead	Chick. Citz.
2	Tom Pitchlynn	"	Choctaw Roll	No. 1		
3	" "	"	" "	No. 1		
4	" "	"	" "	No. 1		

(NOTES)

No. 1 On 1896 Choctaw Roll, Page 262, No. 10303, Wade Co.
No. 2 " 1896 " " " 262 10304 " "
No. 3 " 1896 " " " 262 10305 " "
No. 4 " 1896 " " " 262 10306 " "

All transferred to Chickasay[sic] Roll by Dawes Commission
Husband of No. 1 on Choctaw Card No. 2129.

5/30/99.

CANCELLED Stamped across card

Chickasaw Enrollment Cards 1898-1914
Chickasaw by Blood   Volume V

RESIDENCE:	Choctaw Nation	~~COUNTY~~				CARD NO.			
POST OFFICE:	Talihina, I.T.					FIELD NO.			

	NAME	RELATION-SHIP TO PERSON FIRST	AGE	SEX	BLOOD	TRIBAL ENROLLMENT		
						YEAR	COUNTY	PAGE
1	King, Robert	NAMED	37	M	1/2			
2	" Emma	Wife	24	F	I.W.			
3	" Osie	Dau	7	"	1/4			
4	" Willis	Son	5	M	1/4			
5	" Gilbert	"	2	"	1/4			
6	" Oscar	"	3mo	"	1/4			

TRIBAL ENROLLMENT OF PARENTS

	NAME OF FATHER	YEAR	COUNTY	NAME OF MOTHER	YEAR	COUNTY
1	William King	Dead	Choctaw Roll	Wiona King	Dead	Chick Roll
2	Ransom Paris	"	Non Citz.	Ann Lolley	1896	Non Citz.
3	No. 1			No. 2		
4	No. 1			No. 2		
5	No. 1			No. 2		
6	No. 1			No. 2		

(NOTES)
As to marriage of Nos. 1 and 2 see testimony of G.W. Dukes.
No. 6 Affidavit of birth to be supplied: Received May 30, 1899.
No. 1 On 1896 Choctaw Roll, Page 186 No. 7510 Wade Co.
No. 3 " 1896   "   "   " 186 No. 7512   "   "
No. 4 " 1896   "   "   " 186 No. 7513   "   "
All transferred to Chickasaw Roll by Dawes Commission.
No. 2 On 1896 Choctaw Roll, Page 392 No. 14721, Wade Co. as Amanda King.
No. 6 Born Oct. 16, 1901; Enrolled Jan. 24, 1902.

5/30/99.

CANCELLED Stamped across card

RESIDENCE:	Choctaw Nation, Wade	COUNTY				CARD NO.			
POST OFFICE:	Lenox, I.T.					FIELD NO.			

	NAME	RELATION-SHIP TO PERSON FIRST	AGE	SEX	BLOOD	TRIBAL ENROLLMENT		
						YEAR	COUNTY	PAGE
1	Hitcher, Jackson	NAMED	31	M	Full			

TRIBAL ENROLLMENT OF PARENTS

	NAME OF FATHER	YEAR	COUNTY	NAME OF MOTHER	YEAR	COUNTY
1	Hitcher	Dead	Chick Roll	Siney Hitcher	Dead	Chick Roll

(NOTES)

On 1896 Choctaw Roll, Page 132, No. 5404, Wade County
Transferred to Chickasaw Roll by Dawes Commission.

6/1/99.

CANCELLED Stamped across card

RESIDENCE: Choctaw Nation	~~COUNTY~~				CARD NO.		
POST OFFICE: Howe, I.T.					FIELD NO.		
NAME	RELATION-SHIP TO PERSON FIRST NAMED	AGE	SEX	BLOOD	TRIBAL ENROLLMENT		
					YEAR	COUNTY	PAGE
1 Church, Celie		19	F	1/4			
2 Wyatt, Maud Lee	Dau	3w	F	1/8			

TRIBAL ENROLLMENT OF PARENTS

	NAME OF FATHER	YEAR	COUNTY	NAME OF MOTHER	YEAR	COUNTY
1	Chas Church		Non Citz.	Newklie Church	1896	Chick Roll
2	E.L. Wyatt		Non Citz.	No. 1		

(NOTES)

On 1896 Choctaw Roll, Page 54, No. 2240, Sugar Loaf County
No. 2 Enrolled January 15, 1901.
Evidence of marriage of No. 1 and E.L. Wyatt to be supplied. Received and filed Jany. 31, 1901.

6/5/99.

CANCELLED Stamped across card

RESIDENCE: Chickasaw Nation	~~COUNTY~~				CARD NO.		
POST OFFICE: Pocola, I.T.					FIELD NO.		
NAME	RELATION-SHIP TO PERSON FIRST NAMED	AGE	SEX	BLOOD	TRIBAL ENROLLMENT		
					YEAR	COUNTY	PAGE
1 Brown, Henry		23	M	I.W.			
2 " Eliza	Wife	24	F	1/2			

TRIBAL ENROLLMENT OF PARENTS

	NAME OF FATHER	YEAR	COUNTY	NAME OF MOTHER	YEAR	COUNTY
1	George Brown	Dead	Non Citz.	Rose Brown	Dead	Non Citz.
2	Moses Riddle	Dead	Choc. Roll	Easter Riddle	"	Chick Roll

(NOTES)

No. 2 1896 Choctaw Roll, Page 16, No. 588, transferred to Chickasaw Roll by Dawes Commission.

6/6/99.

CANCELLED Stamped across card

Chickasaw Enrollment Cards 1898-1914
Chickasaw by Blood   Volume V

RESIDENCE: Choctaw Nation ~~COUNTY~~				CARD NO.			
POST OFFICE: Howe, I.T.				FIELD NO.			

NAME	RELATION-SHIP TO PERSON FIRST NAMED	AGE	SEX	BLOOD	TRIBAL ENROLLMENT		
					YEAR	COUNTY	PAGE
1 Hitcher, Henry	NAMED	26	M	Full			

TRIBAL ENROLLMENT OF PARENTS

NAME OF FATHER	YEAR	COUNTY	NAME OF MOTHER	YEAR	COUNTY
1 Hitcher	Dead	Chick Roll	Siney Hitcher	Dead	Chick Roll

(NOTES)

On 1896 Choctaw Roll, Page 128, No. 5262, Sugar Loaf County.

No. 1 the husband of Dicey Hitcher on Choctaqw Card #2384.

6/7/99.

CANCELLED Stamped across card

RESIDENCE: Choctaw Nation ~~COUNTY~~				CARD NO.			
POST OFFICE: Tamaha, I.T.				FIELD NO.			

NAME	RELATION-SHIP TO PERSON FIRST NAMED	AGE	SEX	BLOOD	TRIBAL ENROLLMENT		
					YEAR	COUNTY	PAGE
1 Deshan, Albert	NAMED	20	M	1/2	1893	Choc. Dist.	
2 " Dovie	Dau	1/2	F	1/4			
3 " Iva A	Wife	13	F	I.W.			

TRIBAL ENROLLMENT OF PARENTS

NAME OF FATHER	YEAR	COUNTY	NAME OF MOTHER	YEAR	COUNTY
1 Billy Deshan	Dead	Non Citz.	Sarah Deshan	Dead	Chickasaw
2 No. 1			Ivy Rilla Deshan		
3 George Barns	dead	non citz.	Sarah Barn	1896	non citz.

(NOTES)

Found on "Ishatubbee Roll". Is well known by Peter Maytubby.

Wife on Card No. D.239

Evidence of marriage attached to Chickasaw D.239.

No. 2 Enrolled May 24, 1900.

No. 3 transferred from Chickasaw card #D.239, April 1, 1903.

See decision of March *(remainder illegible)*

6/14/99.

	NAME	RELATION-SHIP TO PERSON FIRST NAMED	AGE	SEX	BLOOD	TRIBAL ENROLLMENT		
						YEAR	COUNTY	PAGE
1	McCann, Austin	NAMED	41	M	1/2			
2	" Alice	Wife	22	F	I.W.			
3	" Julia	Dau	1	"	1/4			

RESIDENCE: Choctaw Nation   ~~COUNTY~~   *CARD NO.*
POST OFFICE: Starr, I.T.   *FIELD NO.*

TRIBAL ENROLLMENT OF PARENTS

	NAME OF FATHER	YEAR	COUNTY	NAME OF MOTHER	YEAR	COUNTY
1	Alex. McCann	Dead	Choctaw	Ho-ya-ho-ke	Dead	Chickasaw
2	Hampton	"	Non Citz	Emiline Mantis	1896	Non Citz.
3	No. 1			No. 2		

(NOTES)

No. 1 on 1896 Choctaw Roll, Page 226, No. 9026
    transferred to Chickasaw Roll by Dawes Com.
No. 3 Affidavit of birth to be supplied; Rec'd 7/1/99,

6/15/99.

CANCELLED Stamped across card

RESIDENCE: Choctaw Nation   ~~COUNTY~~   *CARD NO.*
POST OFFICE: Red Oak, I.T.   *FIELD NO.*

	NAME	RELATION-SHIP TO PERSON FIRST NAMED	AGE	SEX	BLOOD	TRIBAL ENROLLMENT		
						YEAR	COUNTY	PAGE
1	McCurtain, Sampson W.	NAMED	39	M	1/2			
2	Jessie, Buster	Neph.	14	"	1/2			

TRIBAL ENROLLMENT OF PARENTS

	NAME OF FATHER	YEAR	COUNTY	NAME OF MOTHER	YEAR	COUNTY
1	Wm McCurtain	Dead	Choctaw	Sa-ni-cho	Dead	Chickasaw
2	Joshua Jessie	"	"	Melissa Jessie		"

(NOTES)

No. 1 on 1896 Choctaw Roll, Page 230, No. 9165, Gaines County
No. 2 " 1896   "   "   " 159, " 6502 Sugar Loaf County
    Transferred to Chickasaw Roll by Dawes Commission.
    Wife of No. 1 on Choctaw Card No. 2852.

6/19/99

CANCELLED Stamped across card

RESIDENCE: Sans Bois *COUNTY*   **CARD NO.**

POST OFFICE: Sans Bois, I.T.   **FIELD NO.**

	NAME	RELATION-SHIP TO PERSON FIRST NAMED	AGE	SEX	BLOOD	TRIBAL ENROLLMENT		
						YEAR	COUNTY	PAGE
1	Garland, Harriet	NAMED	30	F	Full			
2	" Louisa	Dau	8	F	1/2			
3	" Louena	Dau	5	F	1/2			
4	" Henry	Son	3	M	1/2			
5	Kianotubbe, Mitchell	Son	13	M	1/2			

TRIBAL ENROLLMENT OF PARENTS

	NAME OF FATHER	YEAR	COUNTY	NAME OF MOTHER	YEAR	COUNTY
1	Charius Wright	Dead	Gaines	Sha-ho-yih-cha	Dead	Gaines
2	Joel Garland	1896	Sans Bois	No. 1		
3	" "	"	" "	No. 1		
4	" "	"	" "	No. 1		
5	Kianotubbe	Dead	Gaines	No. 1		

(NOTES)

No. 1 on Choctaw 1896 Roll, P. 112 No. 4602
No. 2 "   "   1896 "   " 112 No. 4603
No. 3 "   "   1896 "   " 112 No. 4604
No. 4 "   "   1896 "   " 112 No. 4605
No. 5 "   "   1896 "   " 112 No. 7446

   All transferred to Chickasaw roll by Dawes Commission.
No. 1 Husband on Choctaw card No. 2854.

6/15/99.

CANCELLED Stamped across card

RESIDENCE: Choctaw Nation   ~~COUNTY~~   **CARD NO.**

POST OFFICE: Sans Bois, I.T.   **FIELD NO.**

	NAME	RELATION-SHIP TO PERSON FIRST NAMED	AGE	SEX	BLOOD	TRIBAL ENROLLMENT		
						YEAR	COUNTY	PAGE
1	Cooper, Jeff D.	NAMED	22	M	1/2			

TRIBAL ENROLLMENT OF PARENTS

	NAME OF FATHER	YEAR	COUNTY	NAME OF MOTHER	YEAR	COUNTY
1	Thompson Cooper	Dead	Choctaw	Kittie Cooper	Dead	Chickasaw

(NOTES)

On 1896 Choctaw Roll, Sans Bois County, Page 51, No. 2091
Transferred to Chickasaw Roll by Dawes Commission.

6/19/99.

CANCELLED Stamped across card

RESIDENCE: Choctaw Nat'n. ~~COUNTY~~					CARD NO.			
POST OFFICE: Red Oak, I.T.					FIELD NO.			

NAME	RELATION-SHIP TO PERSON FIRST NAMED	AGE	SEX	BLOOD	TRIBAL ENROLLMENT		
					YEAR	COUNTY	PAGE
1 Jefferson, Jane		66	F	1/2			

TRIBAL ENROLLMENT OF PARENTS

NAME OF FATHER	YEAR	COUNTY	NAME OF MOTHER	YEAR	COUNTY
1 Wm McCurtain	Dead	Choctaw	Polly McCurtain	Dead	Chickasaw

(NOTES)

On 1896 Choctaw Roll, Page 157, No. 6410, Sans Bois Co.
Transferred to Chickasaw Roll by Dawes Commission.

CANCELLED Stamped across card

RESIDENCE: Sugar Loaf COUNTY					CARD NO.			
POST OFFICE: Faushaw, I.T.					FIELD NO.			

NAME	RELATION-SHIP TO PERSON FIRST NAMED	AGE	SEX	BLOOD	TRIBAL ENROLLMENT		
					YEAR	COUNTY	PAGE
1 McCurtain, Joshua		39	M	1/2			
2 Adams, Jincy	Niece	22	F	1/2			

TRIBAL ENROLLMENT OF PARENTS

NAME OF FATHER	YEAR	COUNTY	NAME OF MOTHER	YEAR	COUNTY
1 Wm McCurtain	Dead	Sugar Loaf	Saw-i-cha McCurtain	Dead	Sugar Loaf
2 William Adams	"	" "	Fannie Adams	"	" "

(NOTES)

No. 1 on Choctaw Rolls 1896, Page 228, No. 9118.
    Transferred to Chickasaw Roll by Dawes Commission
    Children on Choctaw Card No. 2887.
No. 2 on Choctaw roll 1896, Pagae 2, No. 58
    Transferred to Chickasaw roll by Dawes Commission
    On 1896 Choctaw Roll as Winnie Adams.

6/19/99.

CANCELLED Stamped across card

RESIDENCE: Choctaw Nation COUNTY					CARD NO.			
POST OFFICE:					FIELD NO.			

NAME	RELATION-SHIP TO PERSON FIRST NAMED	AGE	SEX	BLOOD	TRIBAL ENROLLMENT		
					YEAR	COUNTY	PAGE
1 Noel, Robert		20	M	1/4			

Chickasaw Enrollment Cards 1898-1914
Chickasaw by Blood   Volume V

| 2 | " Edmund | | Bro | 11 | M | 1/4 | | | |

TRIBAL ENROLLMENT OF PARENTS

	NAME OF FATHER	YEAR	COUNTY	NAME OF MOTHER	YEAR	COUNTY
1	Peter Noel	Dead	Sans Bois	Corinda Noel	Dead	Sans Bois
2	" "	"	" "	" "	"	" "

(NOTES)

No. 1 On 1896 Choctaw Roll, page 241, No. 9545
No. 2 " 1896 Choctaw Roll   " 241 No. 9547
    Both transferred to Chickasaw roll by Dawes Commission
    Brother Moses and wife on Chick card No. 1467
No. 1 is now the husband of Mary Cole.

6/19/99.

CANCELLED Stamped across card

RESIDENCE: Choctaw Nation   **COUNTY**   **CARD NO.**
POST OFFICE: Red Oak, I.T.   **FIELD NO.**

NAME	RELATION-SHIP TO PERSON FIRST NAMED	AGE	SEX	BLOOD	TRIBAL ENROLLMENT		
					YEAR	COUNTY	PAGE
1 Luke, David	NAMED	52	M	1/2			

TRIBAL ENROLLMENT OF PARENTS

	NAME OF FATHER	YEAR	COUNTY	NAME OF MOTHER	YEAR	COUNTY
1	Anderson Luke	Dead	Sans Bois	On-ti-ma-ye	Dead	Sans Bois

(NOTES)

On 1896 roll as Dave Luke, Page 191- No. 7694, transferred to Chick Roll by Dawes Com
    Wife on Choctaw Card No. 2890.

CANCELLED Stamped across card

RESIDENCE: Choctaw Nation   ~~COUNTY~~   **CARD NO.**
POST OFFICE: Red Oak, I.T.   **FIELD NO.**

NAME	RELATION-SHIP TO PERSON FIRST NAMED	AGE	SEX	BLOOD	TRIBAL ENROLLMENT		
					YEAR	COUNTY	PAGE
1 Jefferson, Wallace	NAMED	37	M	1/2			

TRIBAL ENROLLMENT OF PARENTS

	NAME OF FATHER	YEAR	COUNTY	NAME OF MOTHER	YEAR	COUNTY
1	Soben Jefferson	Dead	Choctaw	Jinnie Jefferson	1896	Chickasaw

(NOTES)

On 1896 Choctaw Roll, Sans Bois Co, Page 157, No. 6406
Transferred to Chickasaw Roll by Dawes Commission
Wife and children on Choctaw Card No. 2904.

Chickasaw Enrollment Cards 1898-1914
Chickasaw by Blood   Volume V

6/20/99.

CANCELLED Stamped across card

RESIDENCE: Choctaw Nation	COUNTY				CARD NO.		
POST OFFICE: Red Oak, I.T.					FIELD NO.		

NAME	RELATION-SHIP TO PERSON FIRST NAMED	AGE	SEX	BLOOD	TRIBAL ENROLLMENT		
					YEAR	COUNTY	PAGE
1 Pope, Gilbert		21	M	1/2			

TRIBAL ENROLLMENT OF PARENTS

	NAME OF FATHER	YEAR	COUNTY	NAME OF MOTHER	YEAR	COUNTY
1	Sampson Pope	Dead	Gaines	Liney Pope	Dead	Gaines

(NOTES)
On 1896 Choctaw Roll, Page 256, No. 10106
Transferred to Chickasaw roll by Dawes Commission
Wife and daughter on Choctaw Card No. 2933.

6/20/99

CANCELLED Stamped across card

RESIDENCE: Choctaw Nation	~~COUNTY~~				CARD NO.		
POST OFFICE: Red Oak, I.T.					FIELD NO.		

NAME	RELATION-SHIP TO PERSON FIRST NAMED	AGE	SEX	BLOOD	TRIBAL ENROLLMENT		
					YEAR	COUNTY	PAGE
1 Hancock, Jincey		30	F	1/2			
2 " Amanda	Dau	9	"	1/4			
3 " Aaron	Son	4	M	1/4			
4 " Rhoda	Dau	3	F	1/4			
5 " Bazada	"	1 1/2	"	1/4			
6 " Corah	"	8mo	F	1/4			

TRIBAL ENROLLMENT OF PARENTS

	NAME OF FATHER	YEAR	COUNTY	NAME OF MOTHER	YEAR	COUNTY
1	Soben Jefferson	Dead	Choctaw	Jinnie Jefferson	1896	Chickasaw
2	Simon Hancock	"	"	No. 1		
3	Willis Hancock	1896	"	No. 1		
4	" "	"	"	No. 1		
5	" "	"	"	No. 1		
6	" "	"	"	No. 1		

(NOTES)
No. 2 on 1896 Choctaw Roll as Maud Hancock.

33

No. 1 on 1896 Choctaw Roll, Sans Bois Co., Page 125, No. 5148
No. 2 " 1896   "   "   "   "   "   "   " 125 " 5150 as Maud Hancock
No. 3 " 1896   "   "   "   "   "   "   " 125 " 5149
No. 4 " 1896   "   "   "   "   "   "   " 125 " 5151
    All transferred to Chickasaw Roll by Dawes Com.
    Husband of No. 1, Willis Hancock, on Choctaw Card 2905.
No. 6 Born Jan. 17, 1901; Enrolled Nov. 8, 1901.

6/20/99.

CANCELLED Stamped across card

RESIDENCE: Choctaw Nation	~~COUNTY~~				CARD NO.			
POST OFFICE: Red Oak, I.T.					FIELD NO.			
NAME	RELATION-SHIP TO PERSON FIRST NAMED	AGE	SEX	BLOOD	TRIBAL ENROLLMENT			
					YEAR	COUNTY	PAGE	
1 Hancock, Isaac		58	M	1/2				

	NAME OF FATHER	YEAR	COUNTY	NAME OF MOTHER	YEAR	COUNTY
	TRIBAL ENROLLMENT OF PARENTS					
1	Yarlis Hancock	Dead	Choctaw	Un-te-al-ye	Dead	Chickasaw

(NOTES)

On 1896 Choctaw Roll, Sans Bois Co., No. 5146
transferred to Chickasaw Roll by Dawes Com.

6/19/99

CANCELLED Stamped across card

RESIDENCE: Choctaw Nation	COUNTY				CARD NO.			
POST OFFICE: Red Oak, I.T.					FIELD NO.			
NAME	RELATION-SHIP TO PERSON FIRST NAMED	AGE	SEX	BLOOD	TRIBAL ENROLLMENT			
					YEAR	COUNTY	PAGE	
1 James, John		9	M	1/2				

	NAME OF FATHER	YEAR	COUNTY	NAME OF MOTHER	YEAR	COUNTY
	TRIBAL ENROLLMENT OF PARENTS					
1	Joseph James	1896	Sans Bois	Patsy James	Dead	Sans Bois

(NOTES)

On 1896 Choctaw Roll, Page *(illegible)*, No. 6419
Transferred to Chickasaw Roll by Dawes Com
Father and brothers on Choctaw Card No. 2937

6/20/99.

CANCELLED Stamped across card

RESIDENCE:	Choctaw Nation	~~COUNTY~~			CARD NO.			
POST OFFICE:	Iron Bridge, I.T.				FIELD NO.			

	NAME	RELATION-SHIP TO PERSON FIRST NAMED	AGE	SEX	BLOOD	TRIBAL ENROLLMENT		
						YEAR	COUNTY	PAGE
1	Billy, Susan	NAMED	18	F	1/2			
2	Jackson, Jonas	Son	1	M	1/4			
3	Billy, James	Bro	14	"	1/2			

TRIBAL ENROLLMENT OF PARENTS

	NAME OF FATHER	YEAR	COUNTY	NAME OF MOTHER	YEAR	COUNTY
1	Dixon Billy	1896	Choctaw Roll	Sally Billy	Dead	Chickasaw
2	Ben Jackson	1896	" "	No. 1		
3	Dixon Billy	1896	" "	Sally Billy	Dead	Chickasaw

(NOTES)

No. 1 on 1896 Choctaw Roll, Sans Bois Co., Page 17, No. 643
No. 3 " 1896 " " " " " " 17 " 644
All transferred to Chickasaw Roll by Dawes Com.

6/20/99

CANCELLED Stamped across card

RESIDENCE:	Choctaw Nation	~~COUNTY~~			CARD NO.			
POST OFFICE:	Le Flore, I.T.				FIELD NO.			

	NAME	RELATION-SHIP TO PERSON FIRST NAMED	AGE	SEX	BLOOD	TRIBAL ENROLLMENT		
						YEAR	COUNTY	PAGE
1	Le Flore, Joseph	NAMED	53	M	1/2			

TRIBAL ENROLLMENT OF PARENTS

	NAME OF FATHER	YEAR	COUNTY	NAME OF MOTHER	YEAR	COUNTY
1	Wallace Le Flore	Dead	Wade	Pollea Le Flore	Dead	Chick Roll

(NOTES)

On 1896 Choctaw Roll, Sugar Loaf Co, Page 193, No. 7786
Transferred to Chickasaw Roll by Dawes Commission
Wife and children on Choctaw Card No. 2908.

6/20/99

CANCELLED Stamped across card

RESIDENCE: Choctaw Nation	COUNTY				CARD NO.			
POST OFFICE: Red Oak, I.T.					FIELD NO.			

	NAME	RELATION-SHIP TO PERSON FIRST NAMED	AGE	SEX	BLOOD	TRIBAL ENROLLMENT		
						YEAR	COUNTY	PAGE
1	Colbert, Malissa	NAMED	40	F	1/2			
2	" Sukey	Dau	6	F	1/4			
3	" Annie	"	5	F	1/4			
4	" Agnes	"	3	F	1/4			
5	" Joe	Son	8mo	M	1/4			
6	" Gill	Son	1	M	1/4			

TRIBAL ENROLLMENT OF PARENTS

	NAME OF FATHER	YEAR	COUNTY	NAME OF MOTHER	YEAR	COUNTY
1	William McCurtain	Dead	Sugar Loaf	Sa-wi-cha	Dead	Sugar Loaf
2	Nat Colbert	1896	" "	No. 1		
3	" "	"	" "	No. 1		
4	" "	"	" "	No. 1		
5	" "	"	" "	No. 1		
6	" "	"	" "	No. 1		

(NOTES)

No. 1 On 1896 Choc Roll, Page 54, No. 2235 Sugar Loaf Co., as Milissie
No. 2 " 1896   "   "   " 54 " 2237 "   " " " Sukie
No. 3 " 1896   "   "   " 54 " 2238 "   " "
No. 4 " 1896   "   "   " 54 " 2239 "   " "
    All transferred to Chickasaw roll by Dawes Com
    Husband on Choctaw card No. 2943
No. 6 Born Aug. 24, 1901; enrolled Sept. 9, 1902.

6/20/99.

CANCELLED Stamped across card

RESIDENCE: Choctaw Nation	~~COUNTY~~				CARD NO.			
POST OFFICE: Red Oak, I.T.					FIELD NO.			

	NAME	RELATION-SHIP TO PERSON FIRST NAMED	AGE	SEX	BLOOD	TRIBAL ENROLLMENT		
						YEAR	COUNTY	PAGE
1	Jesse, Eastman	NAMED	22	M	1/2			

TRIBAL ENROLLMENT OF PARENTS

	NAME OF FATHER	YEAR	COUNTY	NAME OF MOTHER	YEAR	COUNTY
1	John Jesse	Dead	Choctaw Roll	Malissa Jesse		Chick Roll

Chickasaw Enrollment Cards 1898-1914
Chickasaw by Blood   Volume V

On 1893 Pay Roll, Page 56, No. 533, Sugar Loaf County, Choctaw Nation, as Esmond Jesse
Transferred to Chickasaw Roll by Dawes Commission
Also on 1896 Choctaw Roll, Sugar Loaf Co, Page 161, No. 6562.

6/20/99.

CANCELLED Stamped across card

	NAME	RELATION-SHIP TO PERSON FIRST NAMED	AGE	SEX	BLOOD	TRIBAL ENROLLMENT		
						YEAR	COUNTY	PAGE
1	Witt, Marion	NAMED	33	M	I.W.			
2	" Peggy	Wife	33	F	1/2			
3	" Mary A.	Dau	2	"	1/4			
4	" John	Son	1mo	M	1/4			
5	Darden, William	S.Son	7	"	1/4			
6	" Minnie	S.Dau	6	F	1/4			
7	" Charley	S.Son	3	M	1/4			
8	Witt, Fanie	Dau	3mo	F	1/4			

RESIDENCE: Choctaw Nation ~~COUNTY~~ CARD NO.
POST OFFICE: Red Oak, I.T. FIELD NO.

TRIBAL ENROLLMENT OF PARENTS

	NAME OF FATHER	YEAR	COUNTY	NAME OF MOTHER	YEAR	COUNTY
1	Jesse Witt		non citz	Polly A. Witt	Dead	non citz
2	Wm McCurtain	Dead	Choctaw	Swega McCurtain	"	Chick Roll
3	No. 1			No. 2		
4	No. 1			No. 2		
5	James Darden	Dead	Non Citz	No. 2		
6	" "	"	" "	No. 2		
7	" "	"	" "	No. 2		
8	No. 1			No. 2		

No. 2 on 1896 Choctaw Roll, Sugar Loaf Co., Page 337, No. 12856, as Pikie Witt
No. 5 " 1896   "   "   "   " "   " 78 " 3248
No. 6 " 1896   "   "   "   " "   " 78 " 3250
No. 7 " 1896   "   "   "   " "   " 78 " 3249
No. 3-4 Affidavits of birth to be supplied; Rec'd July 27/99
No. 8 Enrolled Sept. 4, 1901.

6/21/99.

CANCELLED Stamped across card

Chickasaw Enrollment Cards 1898-1914
Chickasaw by Blood   Volume V

RESIDENCE: Choctaw Nation   COUNTY   CARD NO.
POST OFFICE: Sans Bois, I.T.   FIELD NO.

NAME	RELATION-SHIP TO PERSON FIRST NAMED	AGE	SEX	BLOOD	TRIBAL ENROLLMENT		
					YEAR	COUNTY	PAGE
1 Noel, Moses	NAMED	18	M	1/4			
2 " Ida	Wife	17	F	I.W.			

TRIBAL ENROLLMENT OF PARENTS

NAME OF FATHER	YEAR	COUNTY	NAME OF MOTHER	YEAR	COUNTY
1 Peter Noel	Dead	Sans Bois	Lucinda Noel	Dead	San Bois
2 John Deason	1896	Non Citz	Alice Deason	1896	Non Citz.

(NOTES)

No. 1 On 1896 Choctaw Roll, Page 241, No. 9546
        Transferred by Dawes Commission to Chickasaw roll
        Brothers on Cick. Card No. 1455.

No. 1 6/19/99
No. 2 6/22/99

CANCELLED Stamped across card

RESIDENCE: Choctaw Nation   COUNTY   CARD NO.
POST OFFICE: Red Oak, I.T.   FIELD NO.

NAME	RELATION-SHIP TO PERSON FIRST NAMED	AGE	SEX	BLOOD	TRIBAL ENROLLMENT		
					YEAR	COUNTY	PAGE
1 Jefferson, Nicholas	NAMED	56	M	1/2			

TRIBAL ENROLLMENT OF PARENTS

NAME OF FATHER	YEAR	COUNTY	NAME OF MOTHER	YEAR	COUNTY
1 En-lo-mon-Tubbee	Dead	Choctaw Roll	Ho-te-a-key	Dead	Chick Roll

(NOTES)

On 1896 Choctaw Roll, Sans Bois Co., Page 157, No. 6411
Transferred to Chickasaw Roll by Dawes Com.

6/20/99.

CANCELLED Stamped across card

Chickasaw Enrollment Cards 1898-1914
Chickasaw by Blood   Volume V

RESIDENCE: Choctaw Nation   ~~COUNTY~~   CARD NO.
POST OFFICE: Red Oak, I.T.   FIELD NO.

NAME	RELATION-SHIP TO PERSON FIRST NAMED	AGE	SEX	BLOOD	TRIBAL ENROLLMENT		
					YEAR	COUNTY	PAGE
1 Harlen, Sila	NAMED	30	F	Full			
2 " Edmund	Son	5	M	1/2			
3 " Daniel	"	2	"	1/2			

TRIBAL ENROLLMENT OF PARENTS

	NAME OF FATHER	YEAR	COUNTY	NAME OF MOTHER	YEAR	COUNTY
1	Willie Thompson	1896	Chickasaw	Charlotte Thompson	Dead	Chickasaw
2	Logan Harlen	1896	Choctaw	No. 1		
3	" "	"	"	No. 1		

(NOTES)

No. 1 on 1896 Choctaw Roll, Gaines Co., Page 129, No. 5320, as Sally Harlen
No. 2 " 1896   "   "   "   "   " 129 " 5321
   All transferred to Chickasaw Roll by Dawes Com
   Husband on Card No. 2923, Choctaw.

                                                        6/20/99.

   CANCELLED Stamped across card

RESIDENCE: Choctaw Nation   ~~COUNTY~~   CARD NO.
POST OFFICE: Red Oak, I.T.   FIELD NO.

NAME	RELATION-SHIP TO PERSON FIRST NAMED	AGE	SEX	BLOOD	TRIBAL ENROLLMENT		
					YEAR	COUNTY	PAGE
1 James, Watkins	NAMED	16	M	Full			

TRIBAL ENROLLMENT OF PARENTS

	NAME OF FATHER	YEAR	COUNTY	NAME OF MOTHER	YEAR	COUNTY
1	Jacob James	Dead	Chick Roll	Lady James	Dead	Chick Roll

(NOTES)

On 1896 roll, Choctaw Sans Bois Co., Page 157, No. 6415
Transferred to Chickasaw Roll by Dawes Commission.

                                                        6/20/99.

   CANCELLED Stamped across card

RESIDENCE: Choctaw Nation ~~COUNTY~~					CARD NO.			
POST OFFICE: Lodi, I.T.					FIELD NO.			

NAME	RELATION-SHIP TO PERSON FIRST NAMED	AGE	SEX	BLOOD	TRIBAL ENROLLMENT		
					YEAR	COUNTY	PAGE
1 Jefferson, Thomas	NAMED	64	M	1/2			

TRIBAL ENROLLMENT OF PARENTS							
NAME OF FATHER	YEAR	COUNTY	NAME OF MOTHER	YEAR	COUNTY
1 (Name Illegible)	Dead	Choctaw Roll	Ha-te-ak?	Dead	Chick Roll

(NOTES)

On 1896 Choctaw Roll, Skullyville Co, Page 158, No. 6429.
Transferred to Chickasaw Roll by Dawes Commission.

6/12/99

CANCELLED Stamped across card

RESIDENCE: Choctaw Nation COUNTY					CARD NO.			
POST OFFICE: Le Flore, I.T.					FIELD NO.			

NAME	RELATION-SHIP TO PERSON FIRST NAMED	AGE	SEX	BLOOD	TRIBAL ENROLLMENT		
					YEAR	COUNTY	PAGE
1 Atohko, Simon	NAMED	26	M	1/2			
2 " Sarphin	Bro	24	"	"			

TRIBAL ENROLLMENT OF PARENTS							
NAME OF FATHER	YEAR	COUNTY	NAME OF MOTHER	YEAR	COUNTY
1 Simeon Atohko	Dead	Choctaw	Sophie Atohko	Dead	Chickasaw
2 " "	"	"	" "	"	"

(NOTES)

No. 1 on 1896 Choctaw Roll, Sugar Loaf Co., Page 2, No. 72 as Simms Atohko
No. 2 " 1896   "   "   "   " " " 2 " 74

6/22/99.

CANCELLED Stamped across card

RESIDENCE: Choctaw Nation ~~COUNTY~~					CARD NO.			
POST OFFICE: Ola, I.T.					FIELD NO.			

NAME		RELATION-SHIP TO PERSON FIRST NAMED	AGE	SEX	BLOOD	TRIBAL ENROLLMENT		
						YEAR	COUNTY	PAGE
1 Brown, Belle	Void	NAMED	20	F	1/2			
2 " Wesley Ann	Void	Dau	4mo	"	1/4			
3 " Lula May	Void	Dau	3mo	F	1/4			

Chickasaw Enrollment Cards 1898-1914
Chickasaw by Blood   Volume V

	TRIBAL ENROLLMENT OF PARENTS					
NAME OF FATHER	YEAR	COUNTY	NAME OF MOTHER	YEAR	COUNTY
1 Thos. Mitchell	Dead	Choctaw	Selphie Mitchell	Dead	Chickasaw
2 Milton Brown		"	No. 1		
3 " "		"	No. 1		

(NOTES)

Husband on Choctaw Card No. 3103
No. 2 Affidavit of birth to be supplied; Rec'd. Aug. 9/99
No. 3 born Oct. 4, 1901; Enrolled Jany. 14, 1902.

Aug. 1/99

CANCELLED Stamped across card

RESIDENCE: Choctaw Nation   ~~COUNTY~~   CARD NO.

POST OFFICE: Damon, I.T.   FIELD NO.

NAME	RELATION-SHIP TO PERSON FIRST NAMED	AGE	SEX	BLOOD	TRIBAL ENROLLMENT		
					YEAR	COUNTY	PAGE
1 Reed, George	NAMED	8	M	1/2			

	TRIBAL ENROLLMENT OF PARENTS					
NAME OF FATHER	YEAR	COUNTY	NAME OF MOTHER	YEAR	COUNTY
1 Josiah Reed		Choctaw	Mollie Reed	Dead	Chickasaw

(NOTES)

On 1896 Choctaw Roll, Page 275. No. 10751, Gaines County.
Transferred to Chickasaw Roll by Dawes Commission.
Father on Choctaw Carc No. 3148.

Aug. 2/99.

CANCELLED Stamped across card

RESIDENCE: Gaines   COUNTY   CARD NO.

POST OFFICE: Hartshorne, I.T.   FIELD NO.

NAME	RELATION-SHIP TO PERSON FIRST NAMED	AGE	SEX	BLOOD	TRIBAL ENROLLMENT		
					YEAR	COUNTY	PAGE
1 Haklotubbe, Adeline	NAMED	21	F	Full	1896		
2 " Garrett	Son	7mo	M	1/2			

	TRIBAL ENROLLMENT OF PARENTS					
NAME OF FATHER	YEAR	COUNTY	NAME OF MOTHER	YEAR	COUNTY
1 Joseph Haklotubbe	Dead	Gaines	Losina Haklotubbe	Dead	Gaines
2 Illegitimate child			No. 1		

(NOTES)

On 1896 Choctaw Roll, Page 22, No. 840, Gaines County.
Transferred to Chickasaw Roll by Daes Commission.
On roll as Adeline Baldwin
No. 2 Enrolled May, 25, 1900.

CANCELLED Stamped across card

RESIDENCE: Pontotoc COUNTY					CARD NO.			
POST OFFICE: McGee. I.T.					FIELD NO.			
NAME	RELATION-SHIP TO PERSON FIRST NAMED	AGE	SEX	BLOOD	TRIBAL ENROLLMENT			
					YEAR	COUNTY		PAGE
1 Hybarger, David C.	NAMED	22	M	I.W.				
2 " Laura T.	Wife	16	F	1/16	1897	Pontotoc		49

TRIBAL ENROLLMENT OF PARENTS

NAME OF FATHER	YEAR	COUNTY	NAME OF MOTHER	YEAR	COUNTY
1 John Hybarger		Non Citz.	Minerva Hybarger	Dead	Non Citz.
2 Jas. W. Chapman		Adopt. Chickasaw	Harriet E.G. Chapman		Pontotoc

(NOTES)

No. 2 On Chickasaw roll as Laura T. Chapman.   *(No. 1 Dawes' Roll No. 176)*

P.O. Maxwell, I.T. 12/12/02   Aug. 7/99.

RESIDENCE: Choctaw Nation COUNTY					CARD NO.			
POST OFFICE: Citra, I.T.					FIELD NO.			
NAME	RELATION-SHIP TO PERSON FIRST NAMED	AGE	SEX	BLOOD	TRIBAL ENROLLMENT			
					YEAR	COUNTY		PAGE
1 Sealey, Louisa	NAMED	28	F	Full	1897	Pontotoc		97
2 Wright, Wilson	Son	2	M	"				
3 " Thomas	Son	3	M	"				
4 " Davis	Son	8mo	M	"				

TRIBAL ENROLLMENT OF PARENTS

NAME OF FATHER	YEAR	COUNTY	NAME OF MOTHER	YEAR	COUNTY
1 *(Illegible)* Sealey	Dead	Chick Roll	*(Name Illegible)*	Dead	Chick Roll
2 Dick Wright		Chick resid'g in Choc. Nation	No. 1		
3 Dillard Wright			No. 1		
4 " "			No. 1		

Chickasaw Enrollment Cards 1898-1914
Chickasaw by Blood   Volume V

(NOTES)

No. 2 On Chickasaw Roll, Page 90, as Wilson Wright
No. 1 on 1893 Chickasaw Pay Roll No. 2 page 202, as *(illegible)*
No. 3 Born Oct. 15, 1899; Enrolled Nov. 21, 1902   *(No. 3 Dawes' Roll No. 4215)*
No. 4 Born Mch. 14, 1902; Enrolled Nov. 21, 1902.*(No. 4 Dawes' Roll No. 4216)*

P.O. Allen, I.T. 11/21/02.   Aug. 7, 1899.

RESIDENCE: Pickens **COUNTY** — **CARD NO.**
POST OFFICE: Paul's Valley, I.T. — **FIELD NO.**

	NAME	RELATION-SHIP TO PERSON FIRST NAMED	AGE	SEX	BLOOD	TRIBAL ENROLLMENT		
						YEAR	COUNTY	PAGE
1	Paul, William H.		22	M	1/4	1897	Pickens	16
2	" Victoria May	Wife	22	F	I.W.			
3	" ~~Samuel G.~~	~~Son~~	~~6wks~~	M	~~1/8~~			
4	" William George	Son	2mo	"	1/8			
5	" Victoria	Dau	2mo	F	1/8			

TRIBAL ENROLLMENT OF PARENTS

	NAME OF FATHER	YEAR	COUNTY	NAME OF MOTHER	YEAR	COUNTY
1	Sam Paul	Dead	Pickens	Sarah Paul (I.W.)	1897	Pickens
2	J.T. Rosser		Non Citizen	Emma E. John		Non Citizen
3	~~No. 1~~			~~No. 2~~		
4	No. 1			No. 2		
5	No. 1			No. 2		

(NOTES)

No. 1 on 1897 Roll as W.H. Paul
No. 4 Enrolled February 1, 1901.
No. 1 transferred from Chickasaw Card #445 to this card Aug. 4, 1899
No. 1 Also known as "Buck Paul"
No. 5 Born July 21, 1902; Enrolled Sept. 1?, 1902
No. 3 Died Dec. 15, 1899; Proof of death filed Oct. 25, 1902
No. 2 Enrolled Aug. 4, 1899   *(No. 2 Dawes' Roll No. 554)*
No. 1   "   Sept. 14, 1898.
No. 3   "   Dec. 14, 1899.

43

Chickasaw Enrollment Cards 1898-1914
Chickasaw by Blood   Volume V

RESIDENCE: Choctaw Nation ~~COUNTY~~   CARD NO.

POST OFFICE: Utica, Ind. Ter.   FIELD NO.

NAME	RELATION-SHIP TO PERSON	AGE	SEX	BLOOD	TRIBAL ENROLLMENT		
					YEAR	COUNTY	PAGE
1 Hillhouse, Walter	FIRST NAMED	27	M	Full	1897	Chick residing in Choctaw Nation	14
2 " Ellen	Wife	16	F	1/2			

TRIBAL ENROLLMENT OF PARENTS

NAME OF FATHER	YEAR	COUNTY	NAME OF MOTHER	YEAR	COUNTY
1 Harmon Hillhouse	Dead	Chick Roll	Lizzie Hillhouse	Dead	Chick Roll
2 Nelson Lewis	"	Choctaw Roll	Martha Lewis	"	" "

(NOTES)

No. 2 On 1896 Choctaw Roll Page 96, No. 8218, Blue Co. as Ellen Lewis.
Transferred to Chickasaw Roll by Dawes Com.
No. 2 Transferred to Choctaw Card No. 5503, Oct. 2, 1902.

Aug. 14/99.

RESIDENCE: Panola   COUNTY   CARD NO.

POST OFFICE: Silo, Ind. Ter.   FIELD NO.

NAME	RELATION-SHIP TO PERSON FIRST	AGE	SEX	BLOOD	TRIBAL ENROLLMENT		
					YEAR	COUNTY	PAGE
1 ~~Shirley, Lizzie~~	NAMED	~~17~~	~~F~~	~~Full~~	~~1897~~	~~Panola~~	~~5~~
2 " Willie	Dau	6mo	"	1/2			
3 " ~~Lillie~~	"	~~6mo~~	"	~~1/2~~			

TRIBAL ENROLLMENT OF PARENTS

NAME OF FATHER	YEAR	COUNTY	NAME OF MOTHER	YEAR	COUNTY
1 ~~Sim Colbert~~		~~Panola~~	~~Rhoda Colbert~~	~~Dead~~	~~Panola~~
2 Sam Shirley		Non Citz.	No. 1		
3 " "		" "	~~No. 1~~		

(NOTES)

No. 1 on Chickasaw Roll as Lizzie Colbert
No. 1 Died Sept. 17th 1899. Proof of Death filed Nov. 6, 1902.
No. 3 Died Sept. 1899. Proof of Death filed Nov. 6, 1902.
No. 2 Ward of A.W. Seecraft, Colbert, I.T. See his letter of 12/17/02
No. 1 Died Sept. 17, 1899; Enrollment cancelled *(remainder illegible)*
No. 3 " Sept. 1899. *(remainder illegible)*

Aug. 14/99

RESIDENCE: Pickens COUNTY						CARD NO.		
POST OFFICE: Ardmore, Ind. Ter.						FIELD NO.		
NAME	RELATION-SHIP TO PERSON FIRST NAMED	AGE	SEX	BLOOD	TRIBAL ENROLLMENT			
					YEAR	COUNTY	PAGE	
1 Chivers, Maud A.	NAMED	22	F	1/16				
2 " Jennie A.	Dau	8mo	"	1/32				
3 " Charles Eynon	Son	2wks	M	1/32				

TRIBAL ENROLLMENT OF PARENTS

	NAME OF FATHER	YEAR	COUNTY	NAME OF MOTHER	YEAR	COUNTY
1	Chas. Le Flore		Choctaw Roll	Angie G. Le Flore	Dead	Chick Roll
2	Edgar E. Chivers		Intermarried	No. 1		
3	" " "		"	No. 1		

(NOTES)

No. 1 on 1896 Choctaw Roll, Page 206, No. 8289, Atoka Co, as Maud A. Le Flore.
   Transferred to Chickasaw Roll by Dawes Com.
   Husband on Card No. D.246
No. 2 Affidavit of Birth to be supplied. Filed Nov. 4/99
No. 3 Enrolled April 17, 1901.

Aug. 14/99.

CANCELLED Stamped across card

RESIDENCE: Blue COUNTY						CARD NO.		
POST OFFICE: Blue, Ind. Ter.						FIELD NO.		
NAME	RELATION-SHIP TO PERSON FIRST NAMED	AGE	SEX	BLOOD	TRIBAL ENROLLMENT			
					YEAR	COUNTY	PAGE	
1 Wiley, Robert	NAMED	20	M	Full	P.R. 1893	Blue	53 No. 557	

TRIBAL ENROLLMENT OF PARENTS

	NAME OF FATHER	YEAR	COUNTY	NAME OF MOTHER	YEAR	COUNTY
1	Forbes Wiley	Dead	Chickasaw Roll	Bacey Wiley	Dead	Blue

(NOTES)

On Page 53, No. 557. 1893 Pay Roll, Blue Co, Choctaw Nation. Transferred to Chickasaw Roll by Dawes Com.

8/14/99

CANCELLED Stamped across card

RESIDENCE: Blue   **COUNTY**
POST OFFICE: Utica, Ind. Ter.

CARD NO.
FIELD NO.

NAME	RELATION-SHIP TO PERSON	AGE	SEX	BLOOD	TRIBAL ENROLLMENT		
					YEAR	COUNTY	PAGE
1 Holden, John	FIRST NAMED	65	M	Full	1896	(Choc. Dist.) Chickasaw Roll	74

TRIBAL ENROLLMENT OF PARENTS

NAME OF FATHER	YEAR	COUNTY	NAME OF MOTHER	YEAR	COUNTY
1 Yakatubbe	Dead	Panola	Chaokle	Dead	Panola

(NOTES)
Enrolled on Page 74, Chickasaw Roll

8/14/99.

RESIDENCE: Choctaw Nation   ~~COUNTY~~
POST OFFICE: Utica, Ind. Ter.

CARD NO.
FIELD NO.

NAME	RELATION-SHIP TO PERSON	AGE	SEX	BLOOD	TRIBAL ENROLLMENT		
					YEAR	COUNTY	PAGE
1 Holden, McKenzie	FIRST NAMED	38	M	Full	1897	Chick residing in Choctaw Nation	74

TRIBAL ENROLLMENT OF PARENTS

NAME OF FATHER	YEAR	COUNTY	NAME OF MOTHER	YEAR	COUNTY
1 Ya-ca-tubbee	Dead	Panola	Cha-ok-le	Dead	Chick Roll

(NOTES)
Wife on Choctaw Card No. 3384.

Aug. 14/99.

RESIDENCE: Pontotoc   **COUNTY**
POST OFFICE: Willey, Ind. Ter.

CARD NO.
FIELD NO.

NAME	RELATION-SHIP TO PERSON FIRST	AGE	SEX	BLOOD	TRIBAL ENROLLMENT		
					YEAR	COUNTY	PAGE
1 Fillmore, Julia	NAMED	16	F	Full	1897	Pontotoc	59
2 Fillmore, Benjamin	Bro	19	M	"	97	"	59

TRIBAL ENROLLMENT OF PARENTS

NAME OF FATHER	YEAR	COUNTY	NAME OF MOTHER	YEAR	COUNTY
1 Sam Fillmore	Dead	Pontotoc	Silvey Fillmore	Dead	Pontotoc
2 " "	"	"	" "	"	"

(NOTES)

No. 1 On Page 268, No. 17532, Choctaw Roll, Blue Co.
Transferred to Chickasaw Roll by Dawes Com. at Durant, I.T. Aug. 13, 1899.
No. 1 On 1897 Chickasaw Roll as Julia Perkens
No. 2 "   "   "   " Benjamin Filmore

RESIDENCE: Chickasaw Nation COUNTY					CARD NO.		
POST OFFICE: Durwood, Ind. Ter.					FIELD NO.		
NAME	RELATION-SHIP TO PERSON FIRST NAMED	AGE	SEX	BLOOD	TRIBAL ENROLLMENT		
					YEAR	COUNTY	PAGE
1 Orr, James A.	NAMED	47	M	I.W.			
2 " Harriet	Wife	16	F	1/2	1897	Tishomingo	32

TRIBAL ENROLLMENT OF PARENTS

NAME OF FATHER	YEAR	COUNTY	NAME OF MOTHER	YEAR	COUNTY
1 Cunningham Orr	Dead	(Illegible)	Nancy L. Youngblood		(Illegible)
2 Jim Wolfe	"	Tishomingo	Ellen McLish		(Illegible)

(NOTES)

No. 1 See decision of June 13 '04.   (No. 1 Dawes' Roll No. 414)

No. 1 was denied by Dawes Commission in 1896, Chickasaw Case #145. No appeal. Applied under name of Andy Orr.
Application made in 1896 was by reason of his marriage to Sallie Colbert, was not married to No. 2 until
March 25, 1899. - 8-15-99;
Children of No. 1 on Chick R.15
No. 2 Transferred from Chickasaw Card 634 at Durant, I.T.
Mother of No. 2 Ellen McLish, widow of Jim Wolfe, was never on Choctaw Rolls, although her parents were
Cherokees.

P.O. (Illegible), IT. 11/10/02.   8-15-99

RESIDENCE: Choctaw Nation COUNTY					CARD NO.		
POST OFFICE: Durant, Ind. Ter.					FIELD NO.		
NAME	RELATION-SHIP TO PERSON FIRST NAMED	AGE	SEX	BLOOD	TRIBAL ENROLLMENT		
					YEAR	COUNTY	PAGE
1 Cobb, Frances	NAMED	19	F	1/2			
2 " Annie	Dau	1	"	1/4			
3 " Clarance	Son	1mo	M	1/4			

TRIBAL ENROLLMENT OF PARENTS

NAME OF FATHER	YEAR	COUNTY	NAME OF MOTHER	YEAR	COUNTY
1 Fred Robinson			Salina Robinson		Chickasaw Roll
2 Charley Cobb			No. 1		

3	" "			No. 1		

(NOTES)

No. 1 On Blue Co 1896 Roll, No. 2847, Transferred to Chickasaw Roll by Dawes Com at Durant, I.T. Aug. 19/99
No. 3 Enrolled Sept. 18th 1900

8-18-99

CANCELLED Stamped across card

RESIDENCE: Blue **COUNTY**   **CARD NO.**

POST OFFICE: Durant, Ind. Ter.   **FIELD NO.**

NAME	RELATION-SHIP TO PERSON FIRST NAMED	AGE	SEX	BLOOD	TRIBAL ENROLLMENT		
					YEAR	COUNTY	PAGE
1 Conn, Minnie J.	NAMED	24	F	1/2			
2 " Agnes	Dau	2	"	1/4			
3 Robinaon, James	Son	1	M	1/4			
4 " Billy	"	4	"	1/4			
5 Conn, Edna	Dau	2mo	F	1/4			
6 " Mary E.	"	1mo	"	1/4			

TRIBAL ENROLLMENT OF PARENTS

	NAME OF FATHER	YEAR	COUNTY	NAME OF MOTHER	YEAR	COUNTY
1	Fred Robinson		Non Citz	Salina Robinson	Dea	Chickasaw Roll
2	John Conn		" "	No. 1		
3	Jake Robinson		" "	No. 1		
4	" "		" "	No. 1		
5	John Conn		" "	No. 1		
6	" "		" "	No. 1		

(NOTES)

No. 1 On Page 280, No. 10894, Blue Co., Choctaw Roll as Janie Roberson
No. 3 " " " " 10896 " " " " " James "
No. 4 " " " " 10897 " " " " " Billy "

  Transferred to Chickasaw Roll by Dawes Commission at Durant, I.T. 8-15-99
No. 5 Enrolled May 24th 1900
No. 6 Enrolled July 10th 1901

CANCELLED Stamped across card

RESIDENCE: Blue   COUNTY   CARD NO.

POST OFFICE: Durant, Ind. Ter.   FIELD NO.

NAME	RELATION-SHIP TO PERSON FIRST NAMED	AGE	SEX	BLOOD	TRIBAL ENROLLMENT		
					YEAR	COUNTY	PAGE
1 Robinson, Jesse	NAMED	21	M	1/2			
2 " Sarah	Wife	19	F	I.W.			
3 " Finnie	Dau	9mo	"	1/8			
4 " Walter	Son	1mo	M	1/8			

TRIBAL ENROLLMENT OF PARENTS

	NAME OF FATHER	YEAR	COUNTY	NAME OF MOTHER	YEAR	COUNTY
1	Fred Robinson		Non Citz	Salina Robinson	Dead	Chick Roll
2	(Illegible) Miller			Julia Miller		
3	No. 1			No. 2		
4	No. 1			No. 2		

(NOTES)

No. 1 on Blue Co 1896 Roll, No. 10898 Page 280 as Jesse Roberson;
   Transferred to Chickasaw Roll at Durant I.T. 8/18/99
No. 2 on Blue Co, 1896 Roll, No. 14988 Page 398, Transferred to Chickasaw Roll at Durant I.T. 8/18/99
No. 4 Enrolled January 15, 1901.

8-18-99

CANCELLED Stamped across card

RESIDENCE: Choctaw Nation   COUNTY   CARD NO.

POST OFFICE: Durant, Ind. Ter.   FIELD NO.

NAME	RELATION-SHIP TO PERSON FIRST NAMED	AGE	SEX	BLOOD	TRIBAL ENROLLMENT		
					YEAR	COUNTY	PAGE
1 Mullens, Tempy	NAMED	18	F	1/4			
2 " Lewis	Son	3	M	1/8			
3 " Claude	"	9mo	"	1/8			
4 " Marvin Allen	"		"	1/8			

TRIBAL ENROLLMENT OF PARENTS

	NAME OF FATHER	YEAR	COUNTY	NAME OF MOTHER	YEAR	COUNTY
1	Fred Robinson		Non-Citz	Salina Robinson	Dead	Chick Roll
2	Jasper Mullens		" "	No. 1		
3	" "		" "	No. 1		
4	" "		" "	No. 1		

(NOTES)

(All notations illegible)   Aug. 14/99.

CANCELLED Stamped across card

RESIDENCE: Choctaw Nation COUNTY					CARD NO.			
POST OFFICE: Durant, Ind. Ter.					FIELD NO.			
NAME	RELATION-SHIP TO PERSON FIRST	AGE	SEX	BLOOD	TRIBAL ENROLLMENT			
					YEAR	COUNTY		PAGE
1 Robinson, William	NAMED	18	M	1/4				

TRIBAL ENROLLMENT OF PARENTS

NAME OF FATHER	YEAR	COUNTY	NAME OF MOTHER	YEAR	COUNTY
1 Fred Robinson		Non-Citizen	Salina Robinson	Dead	Chick Roll

(NOTES)

(All notations illegible)

CANCELLED Stamped across card

Aug. 15/99.

RESIDENCE: Blue COUNTY					CARD NO.			
POST OFFICE: Durant, Ind. Ter.					FIELD NO.			
NAME	RELATION-SHIP TO PERSON FIRST	AGE	SEX	BLOOD	TRIBAL ENROLLMENT			
					YEAR	COUNTY		PAGE
1 Vail, John F.	NAMED	53	M	I.W.				

TRIBAL ENROLLMENT OF PARENTS

NAME OF FATHER	YEAR	COUNTY	NAME OF MOTHER	YEAR	COUNTY
1 William Vail			Rebecca Vail		

(NOTES)

(All notations illegible)

RESIDENCE: Pickens COUNTY					CARD NO.			
POST OFFICE: Willis, Ind. Ter.					FIELD NO.			
NAME	RELATION-SHIP TO PERSON FIRST	AGE	SEX	BLOOD	TRIBAL ENROLLMENT			
					YEAR	COUNTY		PAGE
1 Hays, John Benjamin	NAMED	23	M	1/32	1897	Pickens		12
2 " Annie	Wife	17	F	I.W.				
3 " Buna	Dau	?	"	1/64				
4 " Alice	"	?	"	1/64				

TRIBAL ENROLLMENT OF PARENTS

NAME OF FATHER	YEAR	COUNTY	NAME OF MOTHER	YEAR	COUNTY
1 Jesse S. Hays	I.W.	Pickens	*(Illegible)* Hays		Pickens
2 Frank Gill		Non Citz	Lucy Gill		Non citz
3 No. 1			No. 2		

4	No. 1			No. 2		

(NOTES)

No. 1 Transferred from Chickasaw Care 1018
No. 1 On 1897 Roll as Ben Hays
No. 3 Enrolled July 16th 1900
No. 4 Born July 14th 1902; Enrolled July 19, 1902

RESIDENCE: Panola *COUNTY*   *CARD NO.*

POST OFFICE: Colbert, Ind. Ter.   *FIELD NO.*

NAME	RELATION-SHIP TO PERSON FIRST NAMED	AGE	SEX	BLOOD	TRIBAL ENROLLMENT		
					YEAR	COUNTY	PAGE
1 Ned, Watson	NAMED	22	M	Full	1897	Pon. and Pickens	95

TRIBAL ENROLLMENT OF PARENTS

	NAME OF FATHER	YEAR	COUNTY	NAME OF MOTHER	YEAR	COUNTY
1	*(Illegible)* Nws	Dead	Chick Roll	Becky Ned	Dead	Chick Roll

(NOTES)

(All notations illegible)   Aug. 18/99.

RESIDENCE: Choctaw Nation ~~*COUNTY*~~   *CARD NO.*

POST OFFICE: Sterrett, I.T.   *FIELD NO.*

NAME	RELATION-SHIP TO PERSON FIRST NAMED	AGE	SEX	BLOOD	TRIBAL ENROLLMENT		
					YEAR	COUNTY	PAGE
1 Moore, Joseph C.	NAMED	64	M	1/4			
2 " Mary A.	Wife	62	F	I.W.			
3 " Harvey A.	Son	21	M	1/8			
4 " Edna	Dau	?	F	1/8			

TRIBAL ENROLLMENT OF PARENTS

	NAME OF FATHER	YEAR	COUNTY	NAME OF MOTHER	YEAR	COUNTY
1	Colbert Moore	Dead	Adoption	Fannie Moore	Dead	Adoption
2	Chas B. Murray	"	Non Citizen	Margaret Murray	"	Non Citizen
3	No. 1			No. 2		
4	No. 1			No. 2		

(NOTES)

Nos. 1, 2, 3, and 4 Admitted by U.S. Court, Ardmore, I.T. May 27, 1899
   As to residence see testimony of No. 1.
(Other notations illegible)

DENIED CITIZENSHIP BY THE CHOCTAW AND
CHICKASAW CITIZENSHIP COURT

Aug. 16, 1899

Chickasaw Enrollment Cards 1898-1914
Chickasaw by Blood   Volume V

RESIDENCE: Choctaw Nation ~~COUNTY~~					CARD NO.			
POST OFFICE: Durant, I.T.					FIELD NO.			
NAME	RELATIONSHIP TO PERSON FIRST NAMED	AGE	SEX	BLOOD	TRIBAL ENROLLMENT			
					YEAR	COUNTY	PAGE	
1 Durant, Melvina	NAMED	42	F	1/2				
2 " Lena	Dau	20	"	1/4				
3 " Ethelbert	Son	17	M	1/4				
4 " Martha	Dau	15	F	1/4				
5 " Juanita	"	12	"	1/4				
6 " Clint	Son	10	M	1/4				
7 " Florence	Dau	5	F	1/4				

TRIBAL ENROLLMENT OF PARENTS

	NAME OF FATHER	YEAR	COUNTY	NAME OF MOTHER	YEAR	COUNTY
1	V.D. Durant		Choctaw Roll	Kitty Durant	Dead	Chick Roll
2	Pier Durant		" "	No. 1		
3	" "		" "	No. 1		
4	" "		" "	No. 1		
5	" "		" "	No. 1		
6	" "		" "	No. 1		
7	" "		" "	No. 1		

(NOTES)

No. 1 on 1896 Choctaw Roll, Page 84, No. 3516. Blue Co.
No. 2 " 1896 " " " 84, " 3517, " "
No. 3 " 1896 " " " 84, " 3518, " " as Bud Durant.
No. 4 " 1896 " " " 84, " 3519, " "
No. 5 " 1896 " " " 84, " 3520, " "
No. 6 " 1896 " " " 84, " 3521, " "
No. 7 " 1896 " " " 84, " 3522, " "
All transferred to Chickasaw Roll by Dawes Commission

Aug. 15. 1899.

CANCELLED Stamped across card
Transferred to Choctaw Card No. 5452.
Oct. 20, 1902

52

RESIDENCE: Panola COUNTY   CARD NO.

POST OFFICE: Colbert, I.T.   FIELD NO.

	NAME	RELATIONSHIP TO PERSON FIRST NAMED	AGE	SEX	BLOOD	TRIBAL ENROLLMENT		
						YEAR	COUNTY	PAGE
1	Moore, Harvey B	NAMED	55	M	1/4			
2	" Eva A	Wife	48	F				
3	" Colbert J	Son	21	M	1/8			
4	Bacon, Ollie	Dau	18	F	1/8			
5	Moore, Gertrude	"	16	"	1/8			
6	" John F.	Son	13	M	1/8			

TRIBAL ENROLLMENT OF PARENTS

	NAME OF FATHER	YEAR	COUNTY	NAME OF MOTHER	YEAR	COUNTY
1	Colbert Moore	Dead	Adoption	Fannie Moore	Dead	Adoption
2	James Terry	"	Non Citizen	Elvira Terry	"	Non Citizen
3	No. 1			No. 2		
4	No. 1			No. 2		
5	No. 1			No. 2		
6	No. 1			No. 2		

(NOTES)

No. 1 admitted by U.S. Court at Ardmore, May 27, 1899 as Harvey V. Moore

No. 2   "   "   "   "   "   "   "   "   " Mrs. Eva Moore

No. 3   "   "   "   "   "   "   "   "   " C.J. Moore

No. 4   "   "   "   "   "   "   "   "

No. 5   "   "   "   "   "   "   "   "   " (Name Illegible)

No. 6   "   "   "   "   "   "   "   "   " Fred Moore

As to residence see testimony of No. 1

Judgement of U.S. Ct. admitting Nos. 1 to 6 incl. vacated and set aside by decree of C.C.C.C. Dec' 17, '02

Nos. 1 to 6 incl. now in C.C.C.C. Case (illegible)

March 2, 1907, Decision of Commissioner of Nov. 1, 1906 denying No. 2 affirmed by Department (illegible)

For child of No. 5 see N.B. (Apr 26-06) #370

Aug. 16, 1899.

All DENIED CITIZENSHIP BY THE CHOCTAW AND
CHICKASAW CITIZENSHIP COURT

RESIDENCE: Choctaw Nation	**COUNTY**	**CARD NO.**
POST OFFICE: Sterrett. I.T.		**FIELD NO.**

	NAME	RELATIONSHIP TO PERSON FIRST NAMED	AGE	SEX	BLOOD	TRIBAL ENROLLMENT		
						YEAR	COUNTY	PAGE
1	Moore, John F.		56	M	1/4			
2	" Mary T.	Wife	36	F	I.W.			
3	" Colbert R.	Son	18	M	1/8			
4	" Adalia	Dau	17	F	1/8			
5	" John A.	Son	15	M	1/8			
6	" Christopher W.	"	13	"	1/8			

TRIBAL ENROLLMENT OF PARENTS

	NAME OF FATHER	YEAR	COUNTY	NAME OF MOTHER	YEAR	COUNTY
1	Colbert Moore	Dead	Adopted White	Fannie Moore	Dead	Adopted White
2	A.R. Hockersmith	"	Non Citizen	Susan Hockersmith	"	Non Citizen
3	No. 1			No. 2		
4	No. 1			No. 2		
5	No. 1			No. 2		
6	No. 1			No. 2		

(NOTES)

Admitted by U.S. Court, Ardmore, I.T. May 27, 1899
As to residence see testimony of No. 1
No. 3 was admitted as Colbert Moore
No. 5 " " " Alfred "
No. 6 " " " Wyatt "
No. 1 died Nov. 1900; Proof of death filed Nov. 22. 1902
For child of No. 3 see N.B. (Apr. 26-06) #369
(Other notations illegible)

Aug. 16, '99.

DENIED CITIZENSHIP BY THE CHOCTAW AND
CHICKASAW CITIZENSHIP COURT

RESIDENCE: Choctaw Nation	~~**COUNTY**~~	**CARD NO.**
POST OFFICE: Lehigh, I.T.		**FIELD NO.**

	NAME	RELATIONSHIP TO PERSON FIRST NAMED	AGE	SEX	BLOOD	TRIBAL ENROLLMENT		
						YEAR	COUNTY	PAGE
1	Crabtree, Johnathan L.		66	M	I.W.			

TRIBAL ENROLLMENT OF PARENTS						
NAME OF FATHER	YEAR	COUNTY	NAME OF MOTHER	YEAR	COUNTY
1 Anderson Crabtree	Dead	Non Citizen	Eliz. Crabtree	Dead	Non Citizen

(NOTES)

Admitted by U.S. Court, Ardmore, I.T. May 27, 1899.
as to residence see his testimony
Admitted as an intermarried Chickasaw, as J.L. Crabtree.
(Other notations illegible)

Aug. 16, 1899

RESIDENCE: Choctaw Nation   ~~COUNTY~~   CARD NO.

POST OFFICE: Sterrett, I.T.   FIELD NO.

NAME	RELATION-SHIP TO PERSON FIRST NAMED	AGE	SEX	BLOOD	TRIBAL ENROLLMENT		
					YEAR	COUNTY	PAGE
1 Clayton, Mary M.	NAMED	26	F				
2 " Clara E.	Dau	3	"				
3 " Joe Steele	Son	3mo	M				
4 " Thelma	Dau	3	F				
5 " Mary Berry	"	8mo	"				

TRIBAL ENROLLMENT OF PARENTS						
NAME OF FATHER	YEAR	COUNTY	NAME OF MOTHER	YEAR	COUNTY
1 Joseph C. Moore		Adoption	Mary A. Moore	I.W.	Choc. Nation
2 John S. Clayton	I.W.	Choc Nation	No. 1		
3 "	"	" "	No. 1		
4 "	"	" "	No. 1		
5 "	"	" "	No. 1		

(NOTES)

Admitted to U.S. Court at Ardmore, I.T. May 27, 1899
As to residence see testimony of John S. Clayton
Also see testimony of Joseph C. Moore
Husband of No. 1 enrolled on Chickasaw Card D.250
No. 3 died September 1900; Proof of death filed Nov. 22, 1902.
No. 5 Born March 29, 1902; Enrolled Nov. 22, 1902.
No. 4 Enrolled June 23, 1900
No. 3   "   Dec. 14, 1899
       Name of No. 1 is Meda M. Clayton, see letter #5146 filed in this cae.
(Other notations illegible)

DISMISSED   Aug. 16, 1899.

DENIED CITIZENSHIP BY THE CHOCTAW AND
CHICKASAW CITIZENSHIP COURT

Chickasaw Enrollment Cards 1898-1914
Chickasaw by Blood   Volume V

RESIDENCE: Pontotoc   COUNTY   CARD NO.

POST OFFICE: Dibble, I.T.   FIELD NO.

	NAME	RELATION-SHIP TO PERSON FIRST NAMED	AGE	SEX	BLOOD	TRIBAL ENROLLMENT		
						YEAR	COUNTY	PAGE
1	Womack, John C.	NAMED	41	M	I.W.			
2	" Lillian B.	Wife	23	F				
3	" Gladys	Dau	3	"				
4	" Charles Bird	Son	6mo	M				
5	" John C. Jr.	"	6mo	"				

TRIBAL ENROLLMENT OF PARENTS

	NAME OF FATHER	YEAR	COUNTY	NAME OF MOTHER	YEAR	COUNTY
1	Charley Womack		Non Citizen	Sarah Womack		Non Citizen
2	Jno, S, Layman		" "	Hattie Layman		Adoption
3	No. 1			No. 2		
4	No. 1			No. 2		
5	No. 1			No. 2		

(NOTES)

Admitted by U.S. Court at Ardmore, I.T., May 27, 1899

No. 1 admitted as J.C. Womack

No. 2 "   " Mrs. J.C. "

As to residence see testimony of No. 1

No. 4 Enrolled June 23, 1900

No. 5 Enrolled Aug. 1901

No. 2 is daughter of John S. Laymon on Chickasaw Card #D.273.

(Other notations illegible)

P.O. Minco, I.T. 12/30/02.   Aug. 16, 1899.

DISMISSED

DENIED CITIZENSHIP BY THE CHOCTAW AND
CHICKASAW CITIZENSHIP COURT

RESIDENCE: Panola   COUNTY   CARD NO.

POST OFFICE: Blue, I.T.   FIELD NO.

	NAME	RELATION-SHIP TO PERSON FIRST NAMED	AGE	SEX	BLOOD	TRIBAL ENROLLMENT		
						YEAR	COUNTY	PAGE
1	Cox, Missouri C.	NAMED	37	F	I.W.			
2	Capel, Stanley	Son	17	M				
3	" Minnie	Dau	15	F				

Chickasaw Enrollment Cards 1898-1914
Chickasaw by Blood   Volume V

	TRIBAL ENROLLMENT OF PARENTS					
NAME OF FATHER	YEAR	COUNTY	NAME OF MOTHER	YEAR	COUNTY
1	John Smith		Non Citizen	Narcissa Smith		Non Citizen
2	John ? Capel	Dead	Adoption	No. 1		
3	" " "	"	"	No. 1		

(NOTES)

All admitted by U.S. Court at Ardmore, May 27, 1899.
No. 1   "   as Mrs. Zue Capel Cox
As to residence see testimony of No. 1
(Other notations illegible)

Aug. 10, 1899.

DENIED CITIZENSHIP BY THE CHOCTAW AND
CHICKASAW CITIZENSHIP COURT

RESIDENCE: Choctaw Nation   ~~COUNTY~~   CARD NO.
POST OFFICE: Lehigh, I.T.   FIELD NO.

	NAME	RELATION-SHIP TO PERSON FIRST NAMED	AGE	SEX	BLOOD	TRIBAL ENROLLMENT		
						YEAR	COUNTY	PAGE
1	Crabtree, James M.	NAMED	40	M				
2	" Luvina C.	Wife	27	F	I.W.			
3	" Mary M.	Dau	14	"				
4	" Juanita M.	"	10	"				
5	" Allie B.	"	8	"				
6	" Laura E.	"	5	"				
7	" Emma A.	"	3	"				
8	" Clara M.	"	3 2/3	"				

	TRIBAL ENROLLMENT OF PARENTS					
NAME OF FATHER	YEAR	COUNTY	NAME OF MOTHER	YEAR	COUNTY
1	J.L. Crabtree		Non Citizen	Mildred A. Crabtree	Dead	Chickasaw
2	A.J. Harris	Dead	" "	Elizabeth Harris		Non Citizen
3	No. 1			Billie Crabtree		" "
4	No. 1			No. 2		
5	No. 1			No. 2		
6	No. 1			No. 2		
7	No. 1			No. 2		
8	No. 1			No. 2		

(NOTES)

Admitted by U.S. Court, Ardmore, I.T. May 27, 1899.   Refused Nov. 1 - 1905
As to residence see testimony of No. 1   Recent forwarded to Department Nov. 5 - 1906.

No. 1 was admitted as J.M. Crabtree
No. 2 "   "   " Lavinia C. "
No. 3 "   "   " Minnie   "
No. 4 "   "   " Juanita "
No. 8 was born subsequent to filing of original application. Sept. 2, 1896
No. 8 Born Nov. 8, 1898; Enrolled July 26, 1902.
No. 3 is wife of A.J. Harris, non citizen. Evidence of marriage filed Jany. 3, 1903.
For children of No. 3 see N.B. Act April 26, 1906, No. 362; For child of No. 2 see Act N.B. April 26, 1906, No. 363
Aug. 16, 1899.

DISMISSED

DENIED CITIZENSHIP BY THE CHOCTAW AND

CHICKASAW CITIZENSHIP COURT

RESIDENCE: Choctaw Nation	~~COUNTY~~				CARD NO.			
POST OFFICE: Sterrett, I.T.					FIELD NO.			
NAME	RELATION-SHIP TO PERSON FIRST NAMED	AGE	SEX	BLOOD	TRIBAL ENROLLMENT			
					YEAR	COUNTY		PAGE
1 ~~Crabtree, Allen B. DEAD~~	NAMED	42	M					
2 " Mattie	Wife	39	F	I.W.				
3 " James Lee	Son	20	M					
4 " Abbie	Dau	16	F					
5 " Wesley	Son	14	M					
6 " Nora	Dau	12	F					
7 " Eddie	Son	10	M					
8 " Charlie	"	5	"					
9 " L.D.	"	3	"					
10 " Berta	Gr.Dau	2	F					
11 " Gerie	Gr.Dau	2	"					
12 " William Franklin	Gr.Son	6wks	M					
13 " Ben Allen	" "	6wks	"					
14 Carlisle, Ollie May	" Dau	1	F					

TRIBAL ENROLLMENT OF PARENTS

	NAME OF FATHER	YEAR	COUNTY	NAME OF MOTHER	YEAR	COUNTY	
1	~~Johnathan Crabtree~~		~~White man~~	~~Mildred Crabtree~~	~~Dead~~	~~Non Citizen~~	
2	John Smith	Dead	Non Citizen	Narcissa Smith		" "	
3	No. 1			No. 2			
4	No. 1			No. 2			
5	No. 1			No. 2			

6	No. 1			No. 2		
7	No. 1			No. 2		
8	No. 1			No. 2		
9	No. 1			No. 2		
10	No. 3			May Crabtree		Non Citizen
11	No. 3			" "		" "
12	(No. 3)			(May Crabtree)		(Non Citizen)
13	(")			(" ")		(" ")
14	(R.L. Carlisle)			(No. 4)		

(NOTES)

Admitted by U.S. Court. Ardmore, I.T. May 27, 1899

No. 1 was admitted as A.B. Crabytree - as to residence see testimony of Joseph C. Moore.

No. 1 died Dec. 2, 1900; Proof of death filed 7/9-'01.

No. 4 is wife of R.L. Carlisle, a non citizen; evidence of marriage filed Dec. 1, 1902.

Full given name of No. 3 is James Lee Crabtree. See his letter in G.O. files #17104-1902.

No. 3 is now the husband of May Crabtree, non citizen. Evidence of marriage filed Oct.ber 9, 1902.

No. 10 born Sept. 9, 1900; Enrolled Oct. 9, 1902.

No. 11   "   "   "   "   "   " "   "

No. 12   "   Aug. 20, 1902;   "   "   "   "

No. 14   "   Feby. 25, 1902;   "   Dec. 1,   "

Father of No. 12 is No. 3. Mother is May Crabtree, non Citz.

Father of No. 13 is No. 3. Mother is May Crabtree, non Citz.

Father of No. 14 is R.L. Carlisle; Mother is No. 4,

No. 2 denied by C.C.C.C. as Mattie A. Driver or Mattie Crabtree.

7   "   "   "   " Ed. Crabtree or Eddie Crabtree.

8   "   "   "   " Charles or Charley   "

4   "   "   "   " Abbie Carlisle or Abbie Crabtree.

DENIED CITIZENSHIP BY THE CHOCTAW AND
DISMISSED   ## CHICKASAW CITIZENSHIP COURT

	RESIDENCE: Choctaw Nation ~~COUNTY~~			CARD NO.			
	POST OFFICE: Sterrett, I.T.			FIELD NO.			

NAME	RELATION-SHIP TO PERSON FIRST NAMED	AGE	SEX	BLOOD	TRIBAL ENROLLMENT		
					YEAR	COUNTY	PAGE
1 Moore, John C.		29	M				

TRIBAL ENROLLMENT OF PARENTS							
NAME OF FATHER	YEAR	COUNTY	NAME OF MOTHER		YEAR	COUNTY	
1 John C. Moore		Adoption	Mary A. Moore		I.W.	Choct. Nation	

(NOTES)

Admitted by U.S. Court at Ardmore, I.T., May 27. 1899,
as to residence see his testimony
No. 1 is the husband of Mary Ellen Moore on Choctaw Card #372.

Aug. 16, 1899.

DENIED CITIZENSHIP BY THE CHOCTAW AND
CHICKASAW CITIZENSHIP COURT

RESIDENCE: Choctaw Nation ~~COUNTY~~					CARD NO.			
POST OFFICE: Sterrett, I.T.					FIELD NO.			
	NAME	RELATION-SHIP TO PERSON FIRST NAMED	AGE	SEX	BLOOD	TRIBAL ENROLLMENT		
						YEAR	COUNTY	PAGE
1	McVergh, Susie		25	F				
2	" Guy	Son	6	M				
3	" Arthur	"	4	"				
4	" William M.	"	2mo	"				
5	" Frank G.	"	2	"				

TRIBAL ENROLLMENT OF PARENTS

	NAME OF FATHER	YEAR	COUNTY	NAME OF MOTHER	YEAR	COUNTY
1	Jno. F. Moore		Adoption	Mary Moore	I.W.	Choc. Nation
2	Geo. D. McVergh	I.W.	Choc. Nation	No. 1		
3	"	"	"	No. 1		
4	"	"	"	No. 1		
5	"	"	"	No. 1		

(NOTES)

Admitted to U.S. Court at Ardmore I.T., May 27, 1899.
As to residence see his testimony. Also see testimony of Joseph C. Moore.
Husband of No. 1 enrolled on Chickasaw Card D.249.
No. 5 enrolled June 23, 1900.
No. 4 " Dec. 16, 1899.
(Other notations illegible)

Aug. 16, 1899.

DENIED CITIZENSHIP BY THE CHOCTAW AND
CHICKASAW CITIZENSHIP COURT

DISMISSED

RESIDENCE: Tishomingo	COUNTY	CARD NO.

POST OFFICE: Tishomingo, I.T.				FIELD NO.			

	NAME	RELATION-SHIP TO PERSON FIRST NAMED	AGE	SEX	BLOOD	TRIBAL ENROLLMENT		
						YEAR	COUNTY	PAGE
1	Murray, William H.	NAMED	29	M	I.W.			
2	" Alice H.	Wife	24	F	1/8	1897	Pontotoc	20
3	" Massena Bancroft	Son	1wk	M	1/16			
4	" Johnston	"	2mo	M	1/16			

TRIBAL ENROLLMENT OF PARENTS

	NAME OF FATHER	YEAR	COUNTY	NAME OF MOTHER	YEAR	COUNTY
1	U.D.T. Murray		Non Citiz.	Eliz. Murray	Dead	Non Citizen
2	J.S. Hearrell	Dead	" "	Martha A. Hearrell	"	Pontotoc
3	No. 1			No. 2		
4	No. 1			No. 2		

(NOTES)

No. 2 on Chickasaw Roll as "Hewald" *(No. 1 Dawes' Roll No. 177)*
No. 3 Enrolled January 10, 1901.
No. 4 Born July 21, 1902; enrolled Oct. 2, 1902. *(No. 4 Dawes' Roll No. 4217)*

Nida, I.T. 10/03-02. Aug. 16, 1899.

RESIDENCE: Pickens COUNTY				CARD NO.			
POST OFFICE: Woodville, I.T.				FIELD NO.			

	NAME	RELATION-SHIP TO PERSON FIRST NAMED	AGE	SEX	BLOOD	TRIBAL ENROLLMENT		
						YEAR	COUNTY	PAGE
1	Christian, Ed	NAMED	21	M	1/8	1897	Pickens	12

TRIBAL ENROLLMENT OF PARENTS

	NAME OF FATHER	YEAR	COUNTY	NAME OF MOTHER	YEAR	COUNTY
1	John Christian	Dead	Non Citizen	Ellen Christian now Moore		Pickens

(NOTES)

Also on page 13.
Admitted by Dawes Commission Case #267. No appeal.
Wife of No. 1 enrolled on Chickasaw Card #1171.
No. 1 is now in the penitentiary.

Aug. 16, 1899.

RESIDENCE: Pontotoc COUNTY		CARD NO.	

Chickasaw Enrollment Cards 1898-1914
Chickasaw by Blood   Volume V

POST OFFICE: Emmet, I.T.   FIELD NO.

	NAME	RELATION-SHIP TO PERSON FIRST NAMED	AGE	SEX	BLOOD	TRIBAL ENROLLMENT		
						YEAR	COUNTY	PAGE
1	Hunnicutt, Thomas M.	NAMED	19	M	I.W.			
2	" Daisy	Wife	18	F	1/8	1897	Pontotoc	50
3	" Calvin H.	Son	3mo	M	1/16			

TRIBAL ENROLLMENT OF PARENTS

	NAME OF FATHER	YEAR	COUNTY	NAME OF MOTHER	YEAR	COUNTY
1	John Hunnicutt		Non Citizen	Nancy Hunnicutt		Non Citizen
2	J.B. Hearrell	Dead	"	Martha A. Proffitt	1897	Pontotoc
3	No. 1			No. 2		

(NOTES)

No. 2 transferred from Chickasaw Card No. 693, at Durant, I.T. Aug. 17, 1899.
No. 2 on 1897 Roll as Daisy Hewald
No. 3 born May 20, 1902; Enrolled Aug. 28, 1902.

P.O. Sterrett, I.T. 11/10/02.   Aug. 17, 1899.

RESIDENCE: Tishomingo COUNTY   CARD NO.
POST OFFICE: Emet, I.T.   FIELD NO.

	NAME	RELATION-SHIP TO PERSON FIRST NAMED	AGE	SEX	BLOOD	TRIBAL ENROLLMENT		
						YEAR	COUNTY	PAGE
1	Blocker, Abner M	NAMED	24	M	I.W.			
2	" Ada	Wife	17	F	1/8	1897	Pontotoc	50
3	" Hallie J.	Dau	2mo	F	1/16			
4	" Abner	Son	3wks	M	1/16			

TRIBAL ENROLLMENT OF PARENTS

	NAME OF FATHER	YEAR	COUNTY	NAME OF MOTHER	YEAR	COUNTY
1	W.M. Blocker	Dead	Non Citizen	Josephine Blocker		Non Citizen
2	J.B. Hearrell	"	" "	Martha A. Hearrell	Dead	Pontotoc
3	No. 1			No. 2		
4	No. 1			No. 2		

(NOTES)

No. 2 on 1897 Roll as "Hewald"
No. 3 Enrolled Aug. 18, 1900.
No. 4 Born February 4, 1902; Enrolled February 24, 1902.
No. 1 died January 11, 1902; Proof of death filed March 4, 1902.

                                                    Aug. 17, 1899.

RESIDENCE: Choctaw Nation ~~COUNTY~~   CARD NO.

Chickasaw Enrollment Cards 1898-1914
Chickasaw by Blood Volume V

FIELD NO.

NAME	RELATION-SHIP TO PERSON FIRST NAMED	AGE	SEX	BLOOD	TRIBAL ENROLLMENT		
					YEAR	COUNTY	PAGE
1 Durant, Sophia	NAMED	48	F	1/4			
2 " Burnetta A.	Dau	21	"	1/8			
3 " Zogare	Soon	15	M	1/8			
4 Clark, Justin T.	Gr.Son	3mo	M	1/16			

TRIBAL ENROLLMENT OF PARENTS

NAME OF FATHER	YEAR	COUNTY	NAME OF MOTHER	YEAR	COUNTY
1 David Carender	Dead	Non Citizen	Annie Carender	Dead	Chick. Roll
2 Joe Durant	"	Choc. Roll	No. 1		
3 " "	"	" "	No. 1		
4 T.A. Clark		Non Citizen	No. 2		

(NOTES)

No. 1 on 1896 Choctaw Roll, Page 83, No. 3464, Jackson Co., as Sophia Durant
No. 2 " 1896   "   "   " 83 " 3466   "   "   " B.A.   "
No. 3 " 1896   "   "   " 83 " 3468   "   "   " Zosiah   "
No. 4 born March 30, 1902; Enrolled July 22, 1902.
No. 2 is now the wife of J.A. Clark, a non Citizen; Evidence of marriage requested 7/22, '02. Filed Aug. 14, 1902.
Aug. 18, 1899.

CANCELLED Stamped across card
Transferred to Choctaw Card #5453
Oct. 20, 1902.

RESIDENCE: Choctaw Nation COUNTY   CARD NO.

FIELD NO.

NAME	RELATION-SHIP TO PERSON FIRST NAMED	AGE	SEX	BLOOD	TRIBAL ENROLLMENT		
					YEAR	COUNTY	PAGE
1 Gray, Cordelia	NAMED	19	F	1/8			
2 " Roy	Son	2	M	1/16			
3 " Cordelia Amelia	Dau	1mo	F	1/16			
4 " Ollie Bernetta	"	1mo	"	1/16			

TRIBAL ENROLLMENT OF PARENTS

NAME OF FATHER	YEAR	COUNTY	NAME OF MOTHER	YEAR	COUNTY
1 Durant	Dead	Choc. Roll	Sophia Durant		Chickasaw
2 (Name Illegible)		Non Citizen	No. 1		
3 " "		" "	No. 1		
4 " "		" "	No. 1		

(NOTES)

No. 1 on 1896 Choctaw Roll, Page 83, No. 3467, Jackson Co., as Cordelia Durant

No. 3 Enrolled Aug. 22, 1900.

No. 4 Born Oct. 19, 1901; Enrolled Nov. 21, 1901.

Aug. 18, 1899.

CANCELLED Stamped across card

Transferred to Choctaw Card #5454.

Oct. 20, 1902.

RESIDENCE: Jackson COUNTY					CARD NO.		
POST OFFICE: Bennington, I.T.					FIELD NO.		
NAME	RELATION-SHIP TO PERSON FIRST NAMED	AGE	SEX	BLOOD	TRIBAL ENROLLMENT		
					YEAR	COUNTY	PAGE
1 Durant, Albert P.		38	M	1/8			

TRIBAL ENROLLMENT OF PARENTS							
NAME OF FATHER	YEAR	COUNTY	NAME OF MOTHER		YEAR	COUNTY	
1 Joe Durant	Dead	Choc. Roll	Sophia Durant			Chickasaw	

(NOTES)

On 1896 Choctaw Roll, Page 83, No. 3462, Jackson County, as A.P. Durant.

Aug. 18, 1899.

CANCELLED Stamped across card

Transferred to Choctaw Card No. *(illegible)*

RESIDENCE: Choctaw Nation ~~COUNTY~~					CARD NO.		
POST OFFICE: Bennington, I.T.					FIELD NO.		
NAME	RELATION-SHIP TO PERSON FIRST NAMED	AGE	SEX	BLOOD	TRIBAL ENROLLMENT		
					YEAR	COUNTY	PAGE
1 Durant, Morgan J.	NAMED	27	M	1/8			
2 " Carmine	Wife	18	F	I.W.			
3 " *(Illegible)* U.	Son	9mo	M	1/16			
4 " Oliver H.	"	2mo	M	1/16			

TRIBAL ENROLLMENT OF PARENTS							
NAME OF FATHER	YEAR	COUNTY	NAME OF MOTHER		YEAR	COUNTY	
1 Joe Durant	Dead	Choc Roll	Sophia Durant			Chickasaw	
2 ?.W. Caruthers	"	Non Citizen	Mollie Caruthers			Non Citizen	
3 No. 1			No. 2				
4 No. 1			No. 2				

(NOTES)

No. 1 on 1896 Choctaw Roll, Page 83, No. 3465, Jackson County, as M.J. Durant. Evidence of marriage of parents to be supplied. Filed January 5, 1900.

No. 3 Affidavit of birth to be supplied. Filed Nov. 4, 1899.

Transferred to Chickasaw Roll by Dawes Commission

No. 4 enrolled Dec. 3, 1900.

Aug. 18, 1899.

CANCELLED Stamped across card

Transferred to Choctaw Card No. 5456

	RESIDENCE: Panola COUNTY					CARD NO.			
	POST OFFICE: Colbert, I.T.					FIELD NO.			
	NAME	RELATION-SHIP TO PERSON FIRST NAMED	AGE	SEX	BLOOD	TRIBAL ENROLLMENT			
						YEAR	COUNTY	PAGE	
1	Wigand, Bogistar C.		64	M	I.W.				

	TRIBAL ENROLLMENT OF PARENTS							
	NAME OF FATHER	YEAR	COUNTY	NAME OF MOTHER	YEAR	COUNTY		
1	Chas. Wigand	Dead	Non Citizen	Catherine Wigand	Dead	Non Citizen		

(NOTES)

Admitted by U.S. Court, Ardmore, I.T., May 27, 1899.

As to residence, see his testimony.

Dec. 6, 1899. See if application was made to Commission in 1896 - Yes: on Chickasaw Case #203.

Aug. 18, 1899.

	RESIDENCE: Choctaw Nation ~~COUNTY~~					CARD NO.			
	POST OFFICE: Jackson, I.T.					FIELD NO.			
	NAME	RELATION-SHIP TO PERSON FIRST NAMED	AGE	SEX	BLOOD	TRIBAL ENROLLMENT			
						YEAR	COUNTY	PAGE	
1	Bills, Robert C.	NAMED	35	M	I.W.				
2	" Sarah	Wife	19	F	1/4				

	TRIBAL ENROLLMENT OF PARENTS							
	NAME OF FATHER	YEAR	COUNTY	NAME OF MOTHER	YEAR	COUNTY		
1	G.C. Bills		Non Citizn	Nannie E. Bills	Dead	Non Citizen		
2	Wm. Le Flore		Choc. Roll	Rosa Le Flore		Chickasaw		

(NOTES)

No. 2 on 1896 Choctaw Roll, Page 202, No. 8111, Jackson Co, as Sarah Le Flore

Aug. 21, 1899.

CANCELLED Stamped across card

RESIDENCE: Choctaw Nation   ~~COUNTY~~   CARD NO.

POST OFFICE: Jackson, I.T.   FIELD NO.

NAME	RELATION-SHIP TO PERSON FIRST NAMED	AGE	SEX	BLOOD	TRIBAL ENROLLMENT		
					YEAR	COUNTY	PAGE
1 Le Flore, Rosanna	NAMED	45	F	1/4			
2 " William W.	Son	21	M	1/8			
3 " Jencey	Dau	15	F	1/8			
4 " Jorilla	"	12	"	1/8			
5 " Josephine	"	12	"	1/8			
6 " David A.	Son	10	M	1/8			
7 " Thomas J.	"	2	"	1/8			

TRIBAL ENROLLMENT OF PARENTS

	NAME OF FATHER	YEAR	COUNTY	NAME OF MOTHER	YEAR	COUNTY
1	William Wilson	Dead	Choctaw	Ellen Wilson	Dead	Chickasaw
2	William Le Flore		"	No. 1		
3	" "		"	No. 1		
4	" "		"	No. 1		
5	" "		"	No. 1		
6	" "		"	No. 1		
7	" "		"	No. 1		

(NOTES)

No. 1 on 1896 Choctaw Roll, Page 202, No. 8109, Jackson Co, as Rose Le Flore
No. 2 "   "   "   "   "   "   "   8112,   "   "   " Willie W. Le Flore
No. 3 "   "   "   "   "   "   "   8116,   "   "
No. 4 "   "   "   "   "   "   "   8114,   "   "   " Joulla Le Flore
No. 5 "   "   "   "   "   "   "   8115,   "   "   " David   "
No. 6 "   "   "   "   "   "   "   8117,   "   "
No. 7 Affidavit of birth to be supplied; Filed Nov. 4, 1899.
June 26, 1902; No. 2 is now the husband of Daisy Le Flore on Chickasaw Card #D.358.

Aug. 21, 1899.

CANCELLED Stamped across card
Transferred to Choctaw Card No. 5449
Oct. 20, 1902

Chickasaw Enrollment Cards 1898-1914
Chickasaw by Blood   Volume V

RESIDENCE: Choctaw Nation   ~~COUNTY~~   CARD NO.

POST OFFICE: Jackson, I.T.   FIELD NO.

NAME	RELATION-SHIP TO PERSON FIRST NAMED	AGE	SEX	BLOOD	TRIBAL ENROLLMENT		
					YEAR	COUNTY	PAGE
1 Le Flore, Michael W.	NAMED	24	M	1/8			

TRIBAL ENROLLMENT OF PARENTS

NAME OF FATHER	YEAR	COUNTY	NAME OF MOTHER	YEAR	COUNTY
1 Wm Le Flore		Choctaw	Rosanna Le Flore		Chickasaw

(NOTES)

On 1896 Choctaw Roll, Page 202, No. 8119, Jackson Co.
Transferred to Chickasaw Roll by Dawes Commission
On Roll as Michael Le Flore
Also on 1896 Choctaw Roll, Page 202, No. 8153.

Aug. 24, '99.

CANCELLED Stamped across card
Transferred to Choctaw *(remainder illegible)*

RESIDENCE: Choctaw Nation   ~~COUNTY~~   CARD NO.

POST OFFICE: Blue, I.T.   FIELD NO.

NAME	RELATION-SHIP TO PERSON FIRST NAMED	AGE	SEX	BLOOD	TRIBAL ENROLLMENT		
					YEAR	COUNTY	PAGE
1 Capin, Silmer	NAMED	45	F				

TRIBAL ENROLLMENT OF PARENTS

NAME OF FATHER	YEAR	COUNTY	NAME OF MOTHER	YEAR	COUNTY
1 Joel Shacubbee	Dead	Choc. Roll	Lottie	Dead	Chickasaw

(NOTES)

On 1896 Choctaw Roll as Silan Kapen, Page 189, No. 7636, Blue Co.
Transferred to Chickasaw Roll by Dawes Commission

Aug. 24, 1899.

CANCELLED Stamped across card
Transferred to Choctaw Card No. *(illegible)*

Chickasaw Enrollment Cards 1898-1914
Chickasaw by Blood   Volume V

RESIDENCE: Choctaw Nation   ~~COUNTY~~   CARD NO.

POST OFFICE: Blue, I.T.   FIELD NO.

NAME	RELATION-SHIP TO PERSON FIRST NAMED	AGE	SEX	BLOOD	TRIBAL ENROLLMENT		
					YEAR	COUNTY	PAGE
1 King, Mary A.	NAMED	19	F	1/4			
2 " Louisa	Dau	2	"	1/8			

TRIBAL ENROLLMENT OF PARENTS

NAME OF FATHER	YEAR	COUNTY	NAME OF MOTHER	YEAR	COUNTY
1 Norman Capin	Dead	Choctaw	Silmer Capin		Chickasaw
2 Chas. King	"	"	No. I		

(NOTES)

No. I on 1896 Choctaw Roll as Mary King, Page 189, No. 7634, Blue Co.
Transferred to Chickasaw Roll by Dawes Coommission

Aug. 24, '99.

CANCELLED Stamped across card
Transferred to Choctaw Card No. 5479

RESIDENCE: Choctaw Nation   COUNTY   CARD NO.

POST OFFICE: Caddo, I.T.   FIELD NO.

NAME	RELATION-SHIP TO PERSON FIRST NAMED	AGE	SEX	BLOOD	TRIBAL ENROLLMENT		
					YEAR	COUNTY	PAGE
1 Jones, Betsey	NAMED	39	F	Full			

TRIBAL ENROLLMENT OF PARENTS

NAME OF FATHER	YEAR	COUNTY	NAME OF MOTHER	YEAR	COUNTY
1 Lih-to-sh-to-te	Dead	Chick Roll	Sho-la-he-ye	Dead	Chickasaw

(NOTES)

On 1896 Choctaw Roll, Page 178, No. 7240, Blue Co, as Betsey Jones;
Transferred to Chickasaw Roll by Dawes Commission.

Aug. 23, 1899.

CANCELLED Stamped across card
Transferred to Choctaw Card No. *(illegible)*

RESIDENCE: Choctaw Nation	~~COUNTY~~				CARD NO.			
POST OFFICE: Caddo, I.T.					FIELD NO.			

NAME	RELATION-SHIP TO PERSON FIRST NAMED	AGE	SEX	BLOOD	TRIBAL ENROLLMENT		
					YEAR	COUNTY	PAGE
1 Jones, Nat		12	M	1/4			

TRIBAL ENROLLMENT OF PARENTS							
NAME OF FATHER	YEAR	COUNTY	NAME OF MOTHER	YEAR	COUNTY		
1 William Jones	Dead	Choctaw	Amelia Jones		Chickasaw		

(NOTES)

On 1896 Choctaw Roll, Page 176, No. 7160.
Transferred to Chickasaw Roll by Dawes Commission.

Aug. 25, 1899.

CANCELLED Stamped across card

RESIDENCE: Choctaw Nation	~~COUNTY~~				CARD NO.			
POST OFFICE: Blue, I.T.					FIELD NO.			

NAME	RELATION-SHIP TO PERSON FIRST NAMED	AGE	SEX	BLOOD	TRIBAL ENROLLMENT		
					YEAR	COUNTY	PAGE
1 Houston, Martha		40	F	Full			
2 Loving, Edward	Son	11	M	1/2			

TRIBAL ENROLLMENT OF PARENTS							
NAME OF FATHER	YEAR	COUNTY	NAME OF MOTHER	YEAR	COUNTY		
1 Allen Tishkilla	Dead	Chick Dist.	(Name Illegible)	Dead	Chickasaw		
2 Louis loving	"	Choctaw	No. 1				

(NOTES)

No. 1 On 1896 Choctaw Roll, Blue Co, No. 9423, as Martha McCann
No. 2 " 1896 " " " " " 8219
Both transferred to Chickasaw Roll by Dawes Commission
Husband of No. 1 on Choctaw Card No. 3372.
No. Ticket is sued for No. 12. Enrolled Aug. 25, 1899.
Original ticket issued 8/14, '99,

CANCELLED Stamped across card
Transferred to Choctaw Card No.

Chickasaw Enrollment Cards 1898-1914
Chickasaw by Blood   Volume V

RESIDENCE: Choctaw Nation COUNTY	CARD NO.
POST OFFICE: Caddo, I.T.	FIELD NO.

NAME	RELATION-SHIP TO PERSON FIRST NAMED	AGE	SEX	BLOOD	TRIBAL ENROLLMENT		
					YEAR	COUNTY	PAGE
1 Frazier, William	NAMED	30	M	1/2			

TRIBAL ENROLLMENT OF PARENTS

NAME OF FATHER	YEAR	COUNTY	NAME OF MOTHER	YEAR	COUNTY
1 Daniel Frazier	Dead	Choc. Roll	Ho-lo-a-ha-ke	Dead	Chick Roll

(NOTES)

On 1896 Choctaw Roll, No. 4408, Blue Co., transferred to Chickasaw Roll by Dawes Commission.
Wife and child on Choctaw Card No. 3716.

No ticket issued.
Enrolled Aug. 25, 1899.
Original ticket issued 9/22, '99.

CANCELLED Stamped across card
Transferred to Choctaw Card No. *(illegible)*

RESIDENCE: Choctaw Nation COUNTY	CARD NO.
POST OFFICE: Caddo, I.T.	FIELD NO.

NAME	RELATION-SHIP TO PERSON FIRST NAMED	AGE	SEX	BLOOD	TRIBAL ENROLLMENT		
					YEAR	COUNTY	PAGE
1 Robinson, Raymond	NAMED	9	M	1/2			
2 " Sallie	Sister	6	F	1/2			

TRIBAL ENROLLMENT OF PARENTS

NAME OF FATHER	YEAR	COUNTY	NAME OF MOTHER	YEAR	COUNTY
1 Loving Robinson		Choc. Roll	Minerva Robinson	Dead	Chick. Roll
2 "		" "	" "	"	" "

(NOTES)

No. 1 on 1896 Choctaw Roll No. 10901, Blue Co, as Raymond Robinson.
No. 2 on 1896 Choctaw Roll No. 10902, Blue Co, as Sallie Roberson
Both transferred to Chickasaw Roll by Dawes Commission.

Aug. 25, '99.
Original ticket issued Aug. 23, 1899.

CANCELLED Stamped across card
Transferred to Choctaw Card No. 5495.

RESIDENCE: Choctaw Nation ~~COUNTY~~					CARD NO.		
POST OFFICE: Owl, I.T.					FIELD NO.		

NAME	RELATION-SHIP TO PERSON FIRST NAMED	AGE	SEX	BLOOD	TRIBAL ENROLLMENT		
					YEAR	COUNTY	PAGE
1 Roberts, Sloan	NAMED	13	M	Full			

	TRIBAL ENROLLMENT OF PARENTS						
NAME OF FATHER	YEAR	COUNTY	NAME OF MOTHER	YEAR	COUNTY		
1 Lewis Benton		Chick. Roll	Alice Bond		Chick Roll		

(NOTES)

On 1893 Choctaw Pay Roll, Page 91, No. 907, Atoka Co, as Slone Roberts;
Transferred to Chickasaw Roll by Dawes Commission.

Aug. 28, '99.

CANCELLED Stamped across card
Transferred to Choctaw Card No. 5474

RESIDENCE: Choctaw Nation ~~COUNTY~~					CARD NO.		
POST OFFICE: Owl, I.T.					FIELD NO.		

NAME	RELATION-SHIP TO PERSON FIRST NAMED	AGE	SEX	BLOOD	TRIBAL ENROLLMENT		
					YEAR	COUNTY	PAGE
1 Bond, Lizzie	NAMED	19	F	Full			
2 " Uuice[sic]	Dau	1	"	1/2			
3 Churchman, Mertie May	Dau	6mo	"	1/2			

	TRIBAL ENROLLMENT OF PARENTS						
NAME OF FATHER	YEAR	COUNTY	NAME OF MOTHER	YEAR	COUNTY		
1 Larsen Roberts	Dead	Chick Roll	Kelisey Roberts		Chick Roll		
2 Reed Bond		Choc Roll	No. 1				
3 Thomas Churchman		Non Citizen	No. 1				

(NOTES)

No. 1 on 1893 Pay Roll, Choctaw Nation, Page 29, No. 301, Atoka Co, as Elizabeth Roberts.
No. 1 now the wife of Thomas Churchman, non Citizen; Evidence of marriage filed June 28, 1902.
Husband on Choctaw card No. 3980.
No. 2 Affiodavit of birth to be supplied.
No. 3 born Dec. 28, 1901; Enrolled June 28, 1902.

Aug. 28, 1899.

CANCELLED Stamped across card
Transferred to Choctaw Card No. 5473.

Chickasaw Enrollment Cards 1898-1914
Chickasaw by Blood Volume V

RESIDENCE: Choctaw Nation ~~COUNTY~~					CARD NO.		
POST OFFICE: Antlers, I.T.					FIELD NO.		

NAME	RELATION-SHIP TO PERSON FIRST NAMED	AGE	SEX	BLOOD	TRIBAL ENROLLMENT		
					YEAR	COUNTY	PAGE
1 Wade, Thomas		31	M	1/2			

TRIBAL ENROLLMENT OF PARENTS

NAME OF FATHER	YEAR	COUNTY	NAME OF MOTHER	YEAR	COUNTY
1 Simon Wade	Dead	Choctaw	Nancy Peter	Dead	Chick Roll

(NOTES)

On 1896 Choctaw Roll, Page 366, No. 13985, Atoka County
Transferred to Chickasaw Roll by Dawes Commission
Wife and Children on Choctaw Card No. 3999.

Aug. 28, 1899

CANCELLED Stamped across card
Transferred to Choctaw Card No. *(Illegible)*

RESIDENCE: Pontotoc COUNTY					CARD NO.		
POST OFFICE: Waupaunucka[sic], I.T.					FIELD NO.		

NAME	RELATION-SHIP TO PERSON FIRST NAMED	AGE	SEX	BLOOD	TRIBAL ENROLLMENT		
					YEAR	COUNTY	PAGE
1 James, Eloise		7	F	1/2	1897	Pontotoc	59
2 " Rufus	Bro	4	M	1/2	1897	"	59

TRIBAL ENROLLMENT OF PARENTS

NAME OF FATHER	YEAR	COUNTY	NAME OF MOTHER	YEAR	COUNTY
1 Rufus James	Dead	Chick Roll	Mattie James		Shawnee Indian
2 " "	"	" "	" "		" "

(NOTES)

No. 1 on Ieshatubby Roll of 1893, where Rufus James, now deceased, and two children, not named, were enrolled.
No. 1 on 1897 Roll, Page 59, as Eleeris James
No. 1 on Chickasaw Roll as Eleeris James
No. 2 "   "   "   " Ruphus "
Mother of above children on Chickasaw Card R.6
Lyman D. Worcester is legal guardian of Nos. 1 and 2
See copy of guardianship papers filed July 11, 1903.

Aug. 28, '99.

Chickasaw Enrollment Cards 1898-1914
Chickasaw by Blood   Volume V

RESIDENCE: Pontotoc   COUNTY   CARD NO.
POST OFFICE: Wapanucka[sic], I.T.   FIELD NO.

	NAME	RELATION-SHIP TO PERSON FIRST NAMED	AGE	SEX	BLOOD	TRIBAL ENROLLMENT		
						YEAR	COUNTY	PAGE
1	Mosely, Sarah	NAMED	30	F	Full			
2	" Ida	Son?[sic]	9	F	1/2			
3	" Ara	"	4	"	1/2			
4	" Annie	"	3mo	"	1/2			

TRIBAL ENROLLMENT OF PARENTS

	NAME OF FATHER	YEAR	COUNTY	NAME OF MOTHER	YEAR	COUNTY
1	Jim Hillhouse	Dead	Chick Roll	Lucy Hillhouse	Dead	Chick Roll
2	William Mosely		Choc. Roll	No. 1		
3	" "		" "	No. 1		
4	" "		" "	No. 1		

(NOTES)
No. 1 is found on Maytubby Roll, 3rd District, 1893 payment as Mrs. Wm Mosely.
No. 2 on 1893 Choctaw Pay Roll, Page 77, No. 803, Atoka Co, as Ida Mosly
Transferred to Chickasaw Roll by Dawes Commission
Nos. 3-4 Affidavits of birth to be supplied. Filed Nov. 4, 1899.
William Mosely on Choctaw Card No. 4014.

Aug. 28, '99.

RESIDENCE: Choctaw Nation   COUNTY   CARD NO.
POST OFFICE: Mayhew, I.T.   FIELD NO.

	NAME	RELATION-SHIP TO PERSON FIRST NAMED	AGE	SEX	BLOOD	TRIBAL ENROLLMENT		
						YEAR	COUNTY	PAGE
1	Belvin, Melissa	NAMED	50	F	3/4			
2	Frazier, Rosa	G.D.	9	"	3/16			

TRIBAL ENROLLMENT OF PARENTS

	NAME OF FATHER	YEAR	COUNTY	NAME OF MOTHER	YEAR	COUNTY
1	Tecumseh Lata	Dead	Chick Roll	Sho-pa-yo-key	Dead	Chick Roll
2	Joe Frazier	"	Chick Roll	Emily Frazier	"	" "

(NOTES)
No. 1 on 1896 Choctaw Roll, Page 37, No. 1510, Jackson Co, as Melissie Belvin
No. 2 on 1893 Pay Roll, Page 15, No. 169, Cedar Co.
Both transferred to Chickasaw Roll by Dawes Commission.

Aug. 28, 1899.

CANCELLED Stamped across card
Transferred to Choctaw Card No. *(illegible)*

73

Chickasaw Enrollment Cards 1898-1914
Chickasaw by Blood   Volume V

RESIDENCE: Choctaw Nation ~~COUNTY~~					CARD NO.			
POST OFFICE: Atoka, I.T.					FIELD NO.			

NAME	RELATION-SHIP TO PERSON FIRST NAMED	AGE	SEX	BLOOD	TRIBAL ENROLLMENT		
					YEAR	COUNTY	PAGE
1 Wilson, John		45	M	1/4			

TRIBAL ENROLLMENT OF PARENTS

NAME OF FATHER	YEAR	COUNTY	NAME OF MOTHER	YEAR	COUNTY
1 William Wilson	Dead	Choc. Roll	Ellen Wilson	Dead	Chick Roll

(NOTES)

on 1896 Choctaw Roll, Page 370, No. 14121, Jacks Fork Co.
Transferred to Chickasaw Roll by Dawes Commission.

Aug. 30, 1899.

CANCELLED Stamped across card
Transferred to Choctaw Card No. 5469.

RESIDENCE: Choctaw Nation ~~COUNTY~~					CARD NO.			
POST OFFICE: Atoka, I.T.					FIELD NO.			

NAME	RELATION-SHIP TO PERSON FIRST NAMED	AGE	SEX	BLOOD	TRIBAL ENROLLMENT		
					YEAR	COUNTY	PAGE
1 Peter, Alexander		22	M	1/2			

TRIBAL ENROLLMENT OF PARENTS

NAME OF FATHER	YEAR	COUNTY	NAME OF MOTHER	YEAR	COUNTY
1 Simon Peter	Dead	Choctaw	Nancy Peter	Dead	Chick Roll

(NOTES)

On 1896 Choctaw Roll Page 2691, No. 10042, Atoka Co.
Transferred to Chickasaw Roll by Dawes Commission.

Aug. 31, 1899.

CANCELLED Stamped across card
Transferred to Choctaw Card No. 5468

RESIDENCE: Pontotoc COUNTY					CARD NO.			
POST OFFICE: Conway, I.T.					FIELD NO.			

NAME	RELATION-SHIP TO PERSON FIRST NAMED	AGE	SEX	BLOOD	TRIBAL ENROLLMENT		
					YEAR	COUNTY	PAGE
1 Walton, Davis		56	M	Full	1896	On 1893 and not on 1896 Chick	97

TRIBAL ENROLLMENT OF PARENTS					
NAME OF FATHER	YEAR	COUNTY	NAME OF MOTHER	YEAR	COUNTY
1 *(Name Illegible)*	Dead	Pontotoc	*(Name Illegible)*		Pontotoc

(NOTES)

On 1893 Pay Roll, No. 2, Page 236
No. 1 on Chickasaw Roll as Davis Walton.

Aug. 31, 1899.

RESIDENCE: Choctaw Nation	*COUNTY*				*CARD NO.*		
POST OFFICE: Atoka, I.T.					*FIELD NO.*		

NAME	RELATION-SHIP TO PERSON FIRST	AGE	SEX	BLOOD	TRIBAL ENROLLMENT		
					YEAR	COUNTY	PAGE
1 Holson, Julia	NAMED	37	F	1/2			

TRIBAL ENROLLMENT OF PARENTS					
NAME OF FATHER	YEAR	COUNTY	NAME OF MOTHER	YEAR	COUNTY
1 Ellis Folsom	Dead	Choctaw	Selina Folsom	Dead	Chick Roll

(NOTES)

On 1893 Choctaw Pay Roll, Page 56, No. 590, Blue Co.
Transferred to Chickasaw Roll by Dawes Commission.

Aug. 31, 1899.

CANCELLED Stamped across card
Transferred to Choctaw Card No. 5467

RESIDENCE: Pontotoc	*COUNTY*				*CARD NO.*		
POST OFFICE: Conway, I.T.					*FIELD NO.*		

NAME	RELATION-SHIP TO PERSON FIRST	AGE	SEX	BLOOD	TRIBAL ENROLLMENT		
					YEAR	COUNTY	PAGE
1 Nutt, William E.	NAMED	32	M	I.W.			

TRIBAL ENROLLMENT OF PARENTS					
NAME OF FATHER	YEAR	COUNTY	NAME OF MOTHER	YEAR	COUNTY
1 Thompson Nutt		Non Citizen	Ma? Nutt	Dead	Non Citizen

(NOTES)

See his testimony
See enrollment of wife, Annie Burris or Annie Cosby
No. 1 is husband of Annie Crosby on Chickasaw Card #77.
See evidence of marriage with papers herein.
Affidavits of J.E. Fussell and Alice Fussell as to the marriage between No. 1 and Annie Crosby filed Oct. 10, 1902.
Certified copy of divorce proceedings between No. 1 and former wife filed April 8, 1903.

11/12/02 P.O. Oakman, I.T.   Sept. 1, 1899.

75

Chickasaw Enrollment Cards 1898-1914
Chickasaw by Blood   Volume V

RESIDENCE: Choctaw Nation   ~~COUNTY~~   CARD NO.

POST OFFICE: Limestone, I.T.   FIELD NO.

NAME	RELATION-SHIP TO PERSON FIRST NAMED	AGE	SEX	BLOOD	TRIBAL ENROLLMENT		
					YEAR	COUNTY	PAGE
1 Thurlow, Harmon C.	NAMED	45	M	I.W.			
2 " Joseph	Son	12	"	1/8			
3 " Josephine	Dau	10	F	1/8			
4 " Louisa	"	8	"	1/8			
5 " Sylvina E.	"	4	"	1/8			

TRIBAL ENROLLMENT OF PARENTS

	NAME OF FATHER	YEAR	COUNTY	NAME OF MOTHER	YEAR	COUNTY
1	Amos Thurlow		Non Citizen	Sylvina Thurlow	Dead	Non Citizen
2	No. 1			Sophia Thurlow	"	Chick Roll
3	No. 1			" "	"	" "
4	No. 1			" "	"	" "
5	No. 1			" "	"	" "

(NOTES)

No. 1 is now the husband of Lucinda Wade, on Choctaw Card #5466, January 22, 1902

No. 1 License and certificate exhibited, found satisfactory not not in condition to be filed.

No. 5 on 1896 Choctaw Roll as Eliza Thurlow

All but No. 1 are on 1896 Choctaw Roll, Page 325

No. 2 on 1896 Roll No. 12469.   No. 3 on 1896 Roll, No. 12470

No. 4 " 1896 " " 12471   No. 5 " 1896 " " 12472

No. 1 " 1896 " " 15112 as Hermon C. Thurlow.

No. 1 Admitted as an intermarried Choctaw and No. 5 as a Choctaw by blood, by Dawes Commission in 1896;
   See Choctaw Case #285.

Sept. 1, 1899.

CANCELLED Stamped across card
Transferred to Choctaw Card No. 5463

RESIDENCE: Choctaw Nation   ~~COUNTY~~   CARD NO.

POST OFFICE: Owl, I.T.   FIELD NO.

NAME	RELATION-SHIP TO PERSON FIRST NAMED	AGE	SEX	BLOOD	TRIBAL ENROLLMENT		
					YEAR	COUNTY	PAGE
1 Hawley, Arthur E.	NAMED	26	M	I.W.			
2 " Lizzie	Wife	16	F	1/2	1897	Chick resid'g in Choc. N. 3rd Dist.	75
3 " Alice	Dau	4mo	"	1/4			
4 " Lydia	Dau	1mo	"	1/4			

Chickasaw Enrollment Cards 1898-1914
Chickasaw by Blood   Volume V

	TRIBAL ENROLLMENT OF PARENTS					
NAME OF FATHER	YEAR	COUNTY	NAME OF MOTHER	YEAR	COUNTY
1	Edward Hawley		Non Citizen	Jane Hawley		Non Citizen
2	Wm E. Colley		Intermarried	Lucy Colley	Dead	Pontotoc
3	No. 1			No. 2		
4	No. 1			No. 2		

(NOTES)

No. 2 on 1897 Roll as Lizzie Colly   *(No. 1 Dawes' Roll No. 178)*
No. 3 Enrolled May 24, 1900
No. 4 Enrolled May 29, 1901
No. 2 first enrolled on Card 116 with father Sept. 3, 1898.

Sept. 1, 1899.

RESIDENCE: Choctaw Nation   ~~COUNTY~~   CARD NO.
POST OFFICE: Atoka, I.T.   FIELD NO.

NAME	RELATION-SHIP TO PERSON FIRST NAMED	AGE	SEX	BLOOD	TRIBAL ENROLLMENT		
					YEAR	COUNTY	PAGE
1	Carnes, Amanda	NAMED	17	F	1/2			

	TRIBAL ENROLLMENT OF PARENTS					
NAME OF FATHER	YEAR	COUNTY	NAME OF MOTHER	YEAR	COUNTY
1	Tillis Carnes	Dead	Choctaw	Phoebe Carnes	Dead	Chick Roll

(NOTES)

On 1893 Choctaw Pay Roll, Page 21, No. 276, Atoka County, as Maudy Carn
Transferred to Chickasaw Roll by Dawes Commission

Sept. 1, 1899

CANCELLED Stamped across card
Transferred to Choctaw Card No. 5462

RESIDENCE: Choctaw Nation   ~~COUNTY~~   CARD NO.
POST OFFICE: Oconee, I.T.   FIELD NO.

NAME	RELATION-SHIP TO PERSON FIRST NAMED	AGE	SEX	BLOOD	TRIBAL ENROLLMENT		
					YEAR	COUNTY	PAGE
1	Shanks, Mary A.	NAMED	42	F	I.W.			
2	" Bonnie L	Dau	6	"				

	TRIBAL ENROLLMENT OF PARENTS					
NAME OF FATHER	YEAR	COUNTY	NAME OF MOTHER	YEAR	COUNTY
1	James Glenn	Dead	Non Citizen	Mary Glenn	Dead	Non Citizen

2	George Shanks		" "	No. 1		

(NOTES)

Admitted by U.S. Court Southern District, March 7, 1898, Case No. 150

As to residence, see testimony of No. 1

No. 2 admitted as Bonny Lyn Shanks

No. 1 wife of George W. Shanks, on Chickasaw Card D.332.

Nos. 1 & 2 denied by Com. in 1896, Case #219.

No. 1 was formerly wife of William McKinney now deceased, a recognized and enrolled citizen of the Chickasaw Nation, who is enrolled upon the 1878 Chickasaw Annuity Roll, Panola County. Her son by said marriage, Oyd McKinney, appears at No. 4647 upon the approved roll of citizens by blood of Chickasaw Nation.

#1-2 - Dismissed Nov. 14, 1904.

P.O. Olney, I.T.   Sept. 2, 1899.

RESIDENCE: Choctaw Nation	COUNTY				CARD NO.		
POST OFFICE: Atoka, I.T.					FIELD NO.		

NAME	RELATION-SHIP TO PERSON FIRST NAMED	AGE	SEX	BLOOD	TRIBAL ENROLLMENT		
					YEAR	COUNTY	PAGE
1 Leader, Silas		19	M	3/4			

TRIBAL ENROLLMENT OF PARENTS

NAME OF FATHER	YEAR	COUNTY	NAME OF MOTHER	YEAR	COUNTY
1 Tecumseh Leader	Dead	Chick Roll	Bicey Leader	Dead	Chick Roll

(NOTES)

On 1896 Choctaw Roll, Page 205, No. 8250, Atoka County.

Transferred to Chickasaw Roll by Dawes Commission.

Sept. 2, 1899.

CANCELLED Stamped across card

Transferred to Choctaw Card No. 5461

RESIDENCE: Choctaw Nation	~~COUNTY~~				CARD NO.		
POST OFFICE: Lehigh, I.T.					FIELD NO.		

NAME	RELATION-SHIP TO PERSON FIRST NAMED	AGE	SEX	BLOOD	TRIBAL ENROLLMENT		
					YEAR	COUNTY	PAGE
1	Parker, David A.	NAMED	44	M	I.W.			
2	" Samuel A.	Son	19	"	1/8			
3	" Robert C.	"	16	"	1/8			
4	" Charles E.	"	12	"	1/8			
5	" Agnes G.	Dau	10	F	1/8			

6	" Douglas A.	Son	4	M	1/8			
7	" Willie May	Grand Dau	1	F	1/16			

TRIBAL ENROLLMENT OF PARENTS

	NAME OF FATHER	YEAR	COUNTY	NAME OF MOTHER	YEAR	COUNTY
1	Sam Parker	Dead	Non Citizen	Emily Parker	Dead	Non Citizen
2	No. 1			Eliz. F. Parker	"	Chickasaw
3	No. 1			" " "	"	"
4	No. 1			" " "	"	"
5	No. 1			" " "	"	"
6	No. 1			" " "	"	"
7	No. 2			Sallie Parker		non citizen

(NOTES)

Admitted by U.S. Court, Ardmore, I.T. May 27, 1902
As to residence see testimony of No. 1
No. 1 Admitted as D.A. Parker
Evidence of marriage between No. 2 and Sallie Wilson filed March 10, 1903.
No. 7 Born Dec. 29. 1901; proof of birth filed March 10, 1903.
(Other notations illegible)

Sept. 2, 1899

DENIED CITIZENSHIP BY THE CHOCTAW AND
CHICKASAW CITIZENSHIP COURT

DISMISSED

RESIDENCE: Pickens ***COUNTY***					***CARD NO.***			
POST OFFICE: Ardmore, I.T					***FIELD NO.***			
	NAME	RELATION-SHIP TO PERSON FIRST NAMED	AGE	SEX	BLOOD	TRIBAL ENROLLMENT		
						YEAR	COUNTY	PAGE
1	Pate, George W.		22	M	I.W.			
2	" Ora P.	Wife	17	F	1/64			
3	" Url Ray	Son	3mo	M	1/128			

TRIBAL ENROLLMENT OF PARENTS

	NAME OF FATHER	YEAR	COUNTY	NAME OF MOTHER	YEAR	COUNTY
1	Wash Pate	Dead	Non Citizen	Nancy C. Page		Non Citizen
2	C.C. Balthrop		Intermarried	Susanna M. Balthrop		Chickasaw
3	No. 1			No. 2		

(NOTES)

No. 2 Admitted by U.S. Court, Southern District, March 10, 1898, Case No. 16, as Pearl Balthrop

No. 3 Enrolled April 10, 1902
No. 2 Enrolled Sept. 22, 1898
reenrolled Sept. 4, 1899.

Sept. 4, 1899.

RESIDENCE: COUNTY					CARD NO.		
POST OFFICE: Hartshorne, I.T.					FIELD NO.		

NAME	RELATION-SHIP TO PERSON FIRST NAMED	AGE	SEX	BLOOD	TRIBAL ENROLLMENT		
					YEAR	COUNTY	PAGE
1 Watkins, Sallie	NAMED	38	F	Full	1896	Tobucksy	98

TRIBAL ENROLLMENT OF PARENTS							
NAME OF FATHER	YEAR	COUNTY	NAME OF MOTHER		YEAR	COUNTY	
1 Mastatubbee	Dead	Tobucksy	Lucy		Dead	Tobucksy	

(NOTES)

On 1896 Choctaw Roll, page 98, No. 4052, Tobucksy Co, as Sallie Frazier.

9/4/99.

CANCELLED Stamped across card

RESIDENCE: Cherokee Nation ~~COUNTY~~					CARD NO.		
POST OFFICE: Bragg					FIELD NO.		

NAME	RELATION-SHIP TO PERSON FIRST NAMED	AGE	SEX	BLOOD	TRIBAL ENROLLMENT		
					YEAR	COUNTY	PAGE
1 Fallin, Jesse	NAMED	9	M	1/2	1893		
2 McLish, Ollie	Sister	13	F	1/2	1897	Choc. N. 1st Dist.	70

TRIBAL ENROLLMENT OF PARENTS							
NAME OF FATHER	YEAR	COUNTY	NAME OF MOTHER		YEAR	COUNTY	
1 Geo. Fallin		Cherokee	Lena Fallin		Dead	Chickasaw	
2 Israel McLish		Choc. Citizen	Lena Fallin		"	"	

(NOTES)

No. 1 on Ioshatubby, 1893 Pay Roll as one of the children of George Fallin.

Father is a Cherokee; See if children are on the Cherokee Roll.

No. 2 is duplicate enrollment of Ollie M. McLish on Chickasaw Card #12.

No. 2 on Chickasaw Roll as Ollie M. McLish.

No. 1 is on Cherokee Doubtful Card #D.1001; on 1890 Cherokee Roll, Delaware Dist. #1124.

See testimony of George Fallen taken March taken March 12, 1902.

No. 1 was refused enrollment in the Cherokee Nation by the Commission July 16, 1902; The action of the Commission was approved by the Secretary of the Interior August 1, 1901.

Sept. 6, 1899.

RESIDENCE: Pickens   COUNTY   CARD NO.
POST OFFICE: Ara   FIELD NO.

NAME	RELATION-SHIP TO PERSON FIRST NAMED	AGE	SEX	BLOOD	TRIBAL ENROLLMENT		
					YEAR	COUNTY	PAGE
1 Jones, James Milton	NAMED	25	M	I.W.			
2 " Sallie	Wife	16	F	1/2	1897	Pontotoc	49
3 " William Sammy E.	Son	1mo	M	1/4			

TRIBAL ENROLLMENT OF PARENTS

NAME OF FATHER	YEAR	COUNTY	NAME OF MOTHER	YEAR	COUNTY
1 Wm E. Jones		Non Citizen	Nancy A. Jones		Non Citizen
2 Isaac Thomas	Dead	Chick Roll	Harriett Burnett	1897	Pontotoc
3 No. 1			No. 2		

(NOTES)

No. 2 on 1897 Roll as Sallie Thomas
No. 3 Enrolled June 3, 1901.

Sept. 12, 1899.

RESIDENCE: Pontotoc   COUNTY   CARD NO.
POST OFFICE: Stonewall   FIELD NO.

NAME	RELATION-SHIP TO PERSON FIRST NAMED	AGE	SEX	BLOOD	TRIBAL ENROLLMENT		
					YEAR	COUNTY	PAGE
1 Beakley, George F.	NAMED	22	M	I.W.			
2 Beakley, Mary B.	Wife	15	F	1/4	1897	Pontotoc	73

TRIBAL ENROLLMENT OF PARENTS

NAME OF FATHER	YEAR	COUNTY	NAME OF MOTHER	YEAR	COUNTY
1 W.B. Beakley		Non Citizen	Bettie Beakley	Dead	U.S. Citizen
2 Daniel Sullivan		I.W.	Margaret Sullivan	"	Chick Roll

(NOTES)

See his testimony.
No. 2 transferred from Card #332.
No. 2 on 1897 Roll as Mary B. Sullivan
No. 2 died Oct. or Nov, 1900; Proof of death filed Ocy. 28, 1902; additional proof filed Dec. 23 '02.
No. 1 in U.S. Penitentiary at Fort Leavenworth, Kansas Aug. 10, 1904
No. 2 Hereon dismissed under order of the Commission to the Five Civilized Tribes of March 31, 1905,

P.O. Ardmore I.T. 2/26/03   Sept. 12, 1899.

Chickasaw Enrollment Cards 1898-1914
Chickasaw by Blood   Volume V

RESIDENCE: Tobucksey COUNTY					CARD NO.		
POST OFFICE: Alderson, I.T.					FIELD NO.		

NAME	RELATION-SHIP TO PERSON FIRST NAMED	AGE	SEX	BLOOD	TRIBAL ENROLLMENT		
					YEAR	COUNTY	PAGE
1 Colbert, Ely[sic]	NAMED	31	F	Full			
2 " Emily	Dau	10	F	"			

	TRIBAL ENROLLMENT OF PARENTS						
NAME OF FATHER	YEAR	COUNTY	NAME OF MOTHER	YEAR	COUNTY		
1 *(Illegible)*Colbert	Dead	Gaines	Julia Colbert	Dead	San Bois		
2 *(Illegible)*Thompson		*(Illegible)*	No. 1				

(NOTES)
No. 1 on Choctaw Roll as Aly Colbert, P.R. Gaines Co, P. 8, #79
No. 2 " " " P.8 #80 " " " " " " "

Sept. 5, 1899.

CANCELLED Stamped across card
Transferred to Choctaw Card No. 5466

RESIDENCE: Pontotoc COUNTY					CARD NO.		
POST OFFICE: *(Illegible)*					FIELD NO.		

NAME	RELATION-SHIP TO PERSON FIRST NAMED	AGE	SEX	BLOOD	TRIBAL ENROLLMENT		
					YEAR	COUNTY	PAGE
1 Randolph, Thomas M.	NAMED	26	M	I.W.			
2 " Nellie P.	Wife	23	F	3/8	1896	Pickens	12
3 Hill, Mamie	S.Dau	5	F	3/16	1897	"	13
4 Randolph, *(Illegible)*	Son	6wks	M	3/16			

	TRIBAL ENROLLMENT OF PARENTS						
NAME OF FATHER	YEAR	COUNTY	NAME OF MOTHER	YEAR	COUNTY		
1 H.C. Randolph		Non Citizen	M.J. Randolph		Non Citizen		
2 Overton Love		Pickens	Harriet Love	Dead	Non Citizen		
3 O.L. Hill	Dead	Non Citizen	No. 2				
4 No. 1			No. 2				

(NOTES)
See his testimony.
No. 2 & 3 transferred from Card #1733
No. 4 Enrolled December 26, 1900.

Sept. 14, 1899

Chickasaw Enrollment Cards 1898-1914
Chickasaw by Blood   Volume V

RESIDENCE: Tobucksy   COUNTY   CARD NO.
POST OFFICE: S. Canadian   FIELD NO.

NAME	RELATION-SHIP TO PERSON FIRST NAMED	AGE	SEX	BLOOD	TRIBAL ENROLLMENT		
					YEAR	COUNTY	PAGE
1 Lane, Joseph C.	NAMED	53	M	I.W.			
2 " ~~Martha~~	~~Wife~~	~~32~~	F	~~1/8~~			
3 Winchester, Luther E.	Son	14	M	1/16			
4 ~~Lane, Dick Alice~~	~~Dau~~	4	F	~~1/16~~			
5 " Ima J.	"	2	"	1/16			
6 " ~~Eva~~	~~"~~	~~3mo~~	~~"~~	~~1/16~~			

TRIBAL ENROLLMENT OF PARENTS

	NAME OF FATHER	YEAR	COUNTY	NAME OF MOTHER	YEAR	COUNTY
1	Wm Lane		Non Cit	Peggy A. Lane		Non Citizen
2	~~Allen Lee~~		~~Pontotoc~~	~~Lucy Lee~~		~~Pontotoc~~
3	Alfred Winchester		Non Citz.	No. 2		
4	~~No. 1~~			~~No. 2~~		
5	No. 1			No. 2		
6	~~No. 1~~			~~No. 2~~		

(NOTES)

No. 6 Died June 1, 1900. Enrollment cancelled by Dept. *(remainder illegible)*
No. 2 on Ishatubby Chickasaw Roll as Marthey Lane
No. 3 "   "   "   " Not named, but indicated by figures.
No. 6 Enrolled May 24, 1900.
No. 2 died April 14, 1900; See affidavit of Wiley Adams and J.G. Smith, filed July 29, '01.
No. 2 Affidavit of husband filed August 6, 1901
Evidence of birth of No. 5 received and filed May 24, 1902.
No. 4 Proof of birth received and filed Oct. 15. 1902   *(No. 4 Dawes' Roll No. 4218)*
No. 6 died June 1, 1900; proof of death filed Dec. 16, 1902

Sept. 14, 1899.

RESIDENCE: Pickens   COUNTY   CARD NO.
POST OFFICE: Winnekah   FIELD NO.

NAME	RELATION-SHIP TO PERSON FIRST NAMED	AGE	SEX	BLOOD	TRIBAL ENROLLMENT		
					YEAR	COUNTY	PAGE
1 Miller, Jim C.	NAMED	20	M	I.W.			

TRIBAL ENROLLMENT OF PARENTS

	NAME OF FATHER	YEAR	COUNTY	NAME OF MOTHER	YEAR	COUNTY
1	Jesse Miller	Dead	Non Citizen	Mary Miller	Dead	Non Citizen

Chickasaw Enrollment Cards 1898-1914
Chickasaw by Blood   Volume V

Admitted by Dawes Commission, Case #102, as J.C. Miller.

Sept. 15, 1899.

RESIDENCE: Panola   COUNTY   CARD NO.

POST OFFICE: Colbert, I.T.   FIELD NO.

NAME	RELATION-SHIP TO PERSON FIRST NAMED	AGE	SEX	BLOOD	TRIBAL ENROLLMENT		
					YEAR	COUNTY	PAGE
1 Bacon, William J.	NAMED	28	M	A.W.	1897	Panola	P.R.#2 8
2 " Frances Belle	Dau	15mo	F	"			
3 " Robert	Son	5mo	M	"			
4 " Henry Clinton	Son	3	M	adopted white	1896	Panola	12
5 " Belle	Wife	26	F	I.W.			

TRIBAL ENROLLMENT OF PARENTS

	NAME OF FATHER	YEAR	COUNTY	NAME OF MOTHER	YEAR	COUNTY
1	Wm H. Bacon		Non Citizen	Elizabeth Bacon	Dead	Non Citizen
2	No. 1			Belle Bacon		" "
3	No. 1		" "			" "
4	No. 1		" "			" "
5	No. 1		" "			" "

Nos. 1,2,3,4 See Decision of June 10 '04 in Jacket 9-1408.
No. 5 enrolled by Department
    On 1897 *(Illegible)* Pay Roll, Page 8, No. 256 as Billy Bacon
Put his child, Henry C. Bacon, on his card
Son of Wm H. Bacon, adopted by Chickasaws
No. 1 the father of Henry Clinton Bacon, on Chickasaw Card No. 1407.
No. 1 Son of Wm Henderson Bacon, Chickasaw Card #1408
No. 2 enrolled Oct. 4, 1901. Evidence of marriage of parents filed Oct. 4, 1901.
No. 3 born February 11, 1902; enrolled July 29, 1902
No. 4 transferred from Chickasaw Card No. 1407
No. D 174 from which #1407 was transferred was made Octl 14/98.
Descendants of Harvey Bacon adopted by Chickasaw Indians in *(illegible)*

P.O. Hanton, I.T.   Oct. 10, 1899.

RESIDENCE:	COUNTY				CARD NO.			
POST OFFICE:					FIELD NO.			

NAME	RELATION-SHIP TO PERSON FIRST NAMED	AGE	SEX	BLOOD	TRIBAL ENROLLMENT		
					YEAR	COUNTY	PAGE
1 Colbert, Ben	NAMED	39	M	Full			

TRIBAL ENROLLMENT OF PARENTS

	NAME OF FATHER	YEAR	COUNTY	NAME OF MOTHER	YEAR	COUNTY
1	Jim Colbert	Dead	Chickasaw	(Illegible) Colbert	Dead	Chickasaw

(NOTES)

On 1896 Choctaw Roll, Jacks Fork Co, Page 72, No. 3049
Transferred to Chickasaw Roll by Dawes Commission
(Illegible) inquiry is made concerning his name, address
William Anderson, Pontotoc, I.T.

Nov. 15, 1899

CANCELLED Stamped across card
Transferred to Choctaw Card No. (illegible)

RESIDENCE: Sans Bois	COUNTY				CARD NO.			
POST OFFICE: Featherstone, I.T.					FIELD NO.			

NAME	RELATION-SHIP TO PERSON FIRST NAMED	AGE	SEX	BLOOD	TRIBAL ENROLLMENT		
					YEAR	COUNTY	PAGE
1 Carney, Jincy	NAMED	23	F	1/2			
2 " Morton	Bro	21	M	1/2			
3 " William Dead	"	10	"	1/2			
4 " George	"	9	"	1/2			
5 " Adeline	Sister	7	F	1/2			
6 Bascomb, Lena	Dau	4mo	"	1/4			

TRIBAL ENROLLMENT OF PARENTS

	NAME OF FATHER	YEAR	COUNTY	NAME OF MOTHER	YEAR	COUNTY
1	Wallace Carney		Choc. Freedman	Susan Carney	Dead	Chickasaw
2	" "		" "	" "	"	"
3	" "		" "	Anne Carney	"	"
4	" "		" "	" "	"	"
5	" "		" "	" "	"	"
6	Charles Bascomb		Choc. Roll	No. 1		

(NOTES)

All on 1896 Choctaw Pay Roll, Page 21, No's. 2085, 2086, 2087, 2089 and 2090 respectively.
   Transferred to Chickasaw Roll by Dawes Commission.
Wallace Carney, father of Nos. 1,2,3,4 and 5 on Choctaw Freedman Card No. 786.

No. 3 on 1896 Choctaw Roll as Wm Carney
No. 1 is now the wife of Charles Bascom on Choctaw Card #3730. Feb'y. 14, 1901.
    Evidence of marriage to be supplied. Filed March 24, 1901.
No. 6 enrolled March 6, 1901.
The notation as to No. 3 being dead is an error. See letter of Wallace Carney March 18, 1901.

Nov. 16, 1899.

CANCELLED Stamped across card
Transferred to Choctaw Card No. 546?

RESIDENCE: Pontotoc COUNTY					CARD NO.			
POST OFFICE: Connorville, I.T.					FIELD NO.			
NAME	RELATION-SHIP TO PERSON FIRST NAMED	AGE	SEX	BLOOD	TRIBAL ENROLLMENT			
					YEAR	COUNTY		PAGE
1 Alexander, Betsy	NAMED	25	F	Full	1897	Pontotoc		56
TRIBAL ENROLLMENT OF PARENTS								
NAME OF FATHER	YEAR	COUNTY		NAME OF MOTHER		YEAR	COUNTY	
1 *(Name Illegible)*	Dead	Chickasaw		*(Name Illegible)*		Dead	Chickasaw	

(NOTES)
No. 1 died March ?, 1900; Proof of death filed July 15, 1901.

Dec. 8, 1899.

CANCELLED Stamped across card
Died prior to Sept. 25, '02.

RESIDENCE: Pontotoc COUNTY					CARD NO.			
POST OFFICE: Jesse, I.T.					FIELD NO.			
NAME	RELATION-SHIP TO PERSON FIRST NAMED	AGE	SEX	BLOOD	TRIBAL ENROLLMENT			
					YEAR	COUNTY		PAGE
1 Cicin	NAMED	50	F	Full	1897	Pontotoc		51
TRIBAL ENROLLMENT OF PARENTS								
NAME OF FATHER	YEAR	COUNTY		NAME OF MOTHER		YEAR	COUNTY	
1 *(Name Illegible)*	Dead	Chickasaw		*(Name Illegible)*		Dead	Chickasaw	

(NOTES)

Dec. 8, 1899.

Chickasaw Enrollment Cards 1898-1914
Chickasaw by Blood   Volume V

RESIDENCE: Pontotoc COUNTY   CARD NO.

POST OFFICE: Connorville, I.T.   FIELD NO.

| NAME | RELATION-SHIP TO PERSON FIRST NAMED | AGE | SEX | BLOOD | TRIBAL ENROLLMENT | | |
					YEAR	COUNTY	PAGE
1 Underwood, Mollie	NAMED	24	F	Full	1897	Pontotoc	54
2 Grayson, Rena	Dau	7mo	"	"			

TRIBAL ENROLLMENT OF PARENTS

NAME OF FATHER	YEAR	COUNTY	NAME OF MOTHER	YEAR	COUNTY
1 Gabriel Underwood		Chickasaw	*(Illegible)* Underwood	Dead	Chickasaw
2 Felix Grayson	1897	Pontotoc	No. 1		

(NOTES)

On 1897 Roll as Mollie Fulsom

No. 2 Enrolled Aug. 14, 1901

Is not No. 1 a duplicate of No. 1 on Chickasaw Card #907?

See copy of letter from G.D. Rodgers herein dated Nov. 12, 1902.

P.O. Seems now to be Jesse I.T.   Dec. 8, 1899.

RESIDENCE: Pontotoc COUNTY   CARD NO.

POST OFFICE: Viola, I,T   FIELD NO.

| NAME | RELATION-SHIP TO PERSON FIRST NAMED | AGE | SEX | BLOOD | TRIBAL ENROLLMENT | | |
					YEAR	COUNTY	PAGE
1 Hotubby, Malinda	NAMED	76	F	Full	1897	Pontotoc	74

TRIBAL ENROLLMENT OF PARENTS

NAME OF FATHER	YEAR	COUNTY	NAME OF MOTHER	YEAR	COUNTY
1 John Hotubby	Dead	Chickasaw	Julia Hotubby		Chickasaw

(NOTES)

Written on a separate piece of paper:

Withhold issuance of Citizenship Certificate to No. 1. See letter File No. 4667.

On 1896 Roll as Malinda Holubby

No. 1 on 1893 Chickasaw Pay Roll No. 2, Page 103, as Lindy Hotubby.

RESIDENCE: **COUNTY** **CARD NO.**
POST OFFICE: Ravia, I.T. **FIELD NO.**

	NAME	RELATION-SHIP TO PERSON FIRST NAMED	AGE	SEX	BLOOD	TRIBAL ENROLLMENT YEAR	COUNTY	PAGE
1	Allen, *(Illegible)*		36	F	Full	1897	Tishomingo	27

TRIBAL ENROLLMENT OF PARENTS

	NAME OF FATHER	YEAR	COUNTY	NAME OF MOTHER	YEAR	COUNTY
1	Doctor Allen	Dead	Chickasaw	Shimonaya	Dead	Chickasaw

(NOTES)

No other information could be obtained.
P.O. Troy I.T. 3/20/06 Granted Apr. 25, 1906 Dec. 9, 1897.

RESIDENCE: Tishomingo **COUNTY** **CARD NO.**
POST OFFICE: Dougherty, I.T. **FIELD NO.**

	NAME	RELATION-SHIP TO PERSON FIRST NAMED	AGE	SEX	BLOOD	TRIBAL ENROLLMENT YEAR	COUNTY	PAGE
1	Gilbert, Lucy		27	F	Full	1897	Tishomingo	31
2	" Ida	Dau	10	"	"	1897	"	31
3	" Lela	"	6	"	"	1897	"	31
4	" Jennie	"	4	"	"	1897	"	31
5	" Elpha M	"	2	"	"			

TRIBAL ENROLLMENT OF PARENTS

	NAME OF FATHER	YEAR	COUNTY	NAME OF MOTHER	YEAR	COUNTY
1	Chillin Alexander	Dead	Tishomingo	Carrie Alexander		Tishomingo
2	Esias Gilbert	"	"	No. 1		
3	" "	"	"	No. 1		
4	" "	"	"	No. 1		
5	" "	"	"	No. 1		

(NOTES)

Surnames on 1897 Roll as Bilbert.
(Other notations illegible)

CANCELLED Stamped across card

RESIDENCE: Tishomingo COUNTY					CARD NO.		
POST OFFICE: Dougherty, I.T.					FIELD NO.		

	NAME	RELATION-SHIP TO PERSON FIRST NAMED	AGE	SEX	BLOOD	TRIBAL ENROLLMENT		
						YEAR	COUNTY	PAGE
1	Brown, Jerome	NAMED	24	M	Full	1897	Tishomingo	31
2	" Lizzie	Dau	3	F	"			
3	" Benjamin F.	Son	6mo	M	1/2			
4	" Mary	Wife	25	F	I.W.			

TRIBAL ENROLLMENT OF PARENTS

	NAME OF FATHER	YEAR	COUNTY	NAME OF MOTHER	YEAR	COUNTY
1	Charley Brown	Dead	Tishomingo	Malinda Brown	Dead	Tishomingo
2	No. 1			Emily "	"	"
3	No. 1			Mary Brown		Non Citizen
4	L.B. York		non citizen	Rosie York		non citizen

(NOTES)

No. 3 Enrolled July 20, 1900
No. 4 placed hereon August 18, 1905, application having been made by her for enrollment June 13, 1900, at
    Colbert, Indian Territory

Dec. 9, 1899.

RESIDENCE: Choctaw Nation ~~COUNTY~~					CARD NO.		
POST OFFICE: Krebbs, I.T.					FIELD NO.		

	NAME	RELATION-SHIP TO PERSON FIRST NAMED	AGE	SEX	BLOOD	TRIBAL ENROLLMENT		
						YEAR	COUNTY	PAGE
1	Jefferson, Simon	NAMED	17	M	Full	1897	Chick resid'g in Choc. Nation	69

TRIBAL ENROLLMENT OF PARENTS

	NAME OF FATHER	YEAR	COUNTY	NAME OF MOTHER	YEAR	COUNTY
1	Isham Jefferson	Dead	Chickasaw	Jinsey Jefferson	Dead	Chickasaw

(NOTES)

CANCELLED Stamped across card
No. 1 duplicate of No. 1 on Chick *(remainder illegible)*

RESIDENCE: Choctaw Nation   COUNTY   CARD NO.

POST OFFICE: Atoka, I.T.   FIELD NO.

NAME	RELATION- SHIP TO PERSON	AGE	SEX	BLOOD	TRIBAL ENROLLMENT		
					YEAR	COUNTY	PAGE
1 Tumbler, Willie	FIRST NAMED	26	M	1/2	1896	Atoka County Choctaw Roll	12457

TRIBAL ENROLLMENT OF PARENTS

NAME OF FATHER	YEAR	COUNTY	NAME OF MOTHER	YEAR	COUNTY
1 Jesse Tumbler	Dead	Atoka	Mosley Tumbler	Dead	Chick Dist.

(NOTES)

No. 1 transferred from Choctaw Card #4258
Wife and child enrolled on Choctaw Card #4258

March 6, 1900.

CANCELLED Stamped across card
Transferred to Choctaw Card No. 5463
Oct. 20, 1902

RESIDENCE: Choctaw Nation   COUNTY   CARD NO.

POST OFFICE: Goodland, I.T.   FIELD NO.

NAME	RELATION- SHIP TO PERSON	AGE	SEX	BLOOD	TRIBAL ENROLLMENT		
					YEAR	COUNTY	PAGE
1 Lawechubbe, Rhoda	FIRST NAMED	49	F	Full	1896	Choctaw Roll Kiamitia Co.	8101
2 " Lewis	Son	16	M	"	"	Choctaw Roll Kiamitiz Co.	8102

TRIBAL ENROLLMENT OF PARENTS

NAME OF FATHER	YEAR	COUNTY	NAME OF MOTHER	YEAR	COUNTY
1 Garland		Unknown	Liza Garland	Dead	Chickasaw
2 Lawechubbe, William	1896	Choctaw Roll Kiamitia Co.	No. 1		

(NOTES)

William Lawechubbe, husband of No. 1 and father of No. 2 enrolled on Choctaw Card 5322

March 6, 1900.

CANCELLED Stamped across card
and transferred *(remainder illegible)*

RESIDENCE: Tishomingo COUNTY						CARD NO.		
POST OFFICE: Tishomingo, I.T.						FIELD NO.		

NAME	RELATION-SHIP TO PERSON FIRST NAMED	AGE	SEX	BLOOD	TRIBAL ENROLLMENT		
					YEAR	COUNTY	PAGE
4 ~~Watkins, James~~	NAMED	24	M	~~Full~~	~~1896~~	~~Pontotoc~~	~~59~~

TRIBAL ENROLLMENT OF PARENTS

NAME OF FATHER	YEAR	COUNTY	NAME OF MOTHER	YEAR	COUNTY
4 ~~Noah Watkins~~	~~Dead~~	~~Pontotoc~~	~~(Illegible) Watkins~~	~~Dead~~	~~Pontotoc~~

(NOTES)

No. 1 died in December, 1901. Enrollment cancelled by Department *(remainder illegible)*

June 14, 1900.

RESIDENCE: Pontotoc COUNTY						CARD NO.		
POST OFFICE: Holder, I.T.						FIELD NO.		

NAME	RELATION-SHIP TO PERSON FIRST NAMED	AGE	SEX	BLOOD	TRIBAL ENROLLMENT		
					YEAR	COUNTY	PAGE
1 Burris, William	NAMED	17	M	Full	1896	Pickens	18
2 " Eben	Bro	12	M	"	1896	"	18

TRIBAL ENROLLMENT OF PARENTS

NAME OF FATHER	YEAR	COUNTY	NAME OF MOTHER	YEAR	COUNTY
1 Saffren Burris	Dead	Pickens	Martha Burris	Dead	Pickens
2 " "	"	"	" "	"	"

(NOTES)

John B. Chastine, Oakland, I.T. is the Guardian of No's 1 & 2.
No. 1 Also on Chickasaw Roll, Pickens Co, Page 24, as Billie Burris
No. 2 " " " " " " " "
No. 1 " " " " 18 " Willie Burris.

June 14, 1900.

RESIDENCE: Pontotoc COUNTY						CARD NO.		
POST OFFICE: Chickasha, I.T.						FIELD NO.		

NAME	RELATION-SHIP TO PERSON FIRST NAMED	AGE	SEX	BLOOD	TRIBAL ENROLLMENT		
					YEAR	COUNTY	PAGE
1 Minor, Thos. J, Jr.	NAMED	9	M	1/2			
2 " Sarah Lucy	Sis.	1	F	1/2			

Chickasaw Enrollment Cards 1898-1914
Chickasaw by Blood   Volume V

TRIBAL ENROLLMENT OF PARENTS						
NAME OF FATHER	YEAR	COUNTY	NAME OF MOTHER	YEAR	COUNTY
1 Thomas J. Miner		Non Citizen	Sarah Miner	Dead	Court Citizen
2 " " "		" "	" "	"	" "

(NOTES)

No. 1 denied by Commission *(remainder illegible)*   *(No. 1 Dawes' Roll No. 4940)*
(Notation illegible)
No. 1 admitted by U.S. Court, Southern District Ind. Ter., in case of Sarah Seeley, et al, vs. Chickasaw Nation
June 9, 1900, in Court Case No. 156.
No. 2 Enrolled on proper birth affidavits   *(No. 2 Dawes' Roll No. 4983)*
(Other notations illegible)
No. 2 Granted Oct. 3, 1905.

See Choctaw Card No. 3321, and
Chickasaw Card #C.208.   June 15, 1900.

RESIGNENCE: Creek Nation   ~~COUNTY~~   CARD NO.
POST OFFICE: Bearden, I.T.   FIELD NO.

NAME	RELATION-SHIP TO PERSON FIRST NAMED	AGE	SEX	BLOOD	TRIBAL ENROLLMENT		
					YEAR	COUNTY	PAGE
1 Chief, Louena	NAMED	40	F	Full	1896	Pontotoc	45
2 Anderson, Lena	Dau	19	F	"	"	"	"
3 " Lottie	"	15	F	"	"	"	"

TRIBAL ENROLLMENT OF PARENTS						
NAME OF FATHER	YEAR	COUNTY	NAME OF MOTHER	YEAR	COUNTY
1 Amokolonubbi	Dead	Pontotoc	Lonatauah	Dead	Pontotoc
2 Tom Anderson	"	Creek Roll	No. 1		
3 " "	"	" "	No. 1		

(NOTES)

No. 1 on 1896 Chickasaw Roll as Irena Chief
No. 2 " " " " " Zina Anderson
No. 3 " " " " " Lottie Anderson
No. 1 is the wife of James Chief on Chickasaw Freedman Card #121
Nos. 1, 2 & 3 Enrolled Sept. 6, 1900, subject to approval of Commission
No. 3 died July 6, 1901. Proof of death filed with the records of the Creek Enrollment Division. Sept. 6, 1901.
No's 2 and 3 enrolled as Citizens of the Creek Nation on Creek Roll Card #3893 Dec. 12, 1901.
No. 2 on final roll, Creek Nation, as Luia Richardson, Creek Card #3944.
No. 3 on final Creek Roll Card #3944.

                                        Muskogee, I.T.
                                        Sept. 6, 1900.

Chickasaw Enrollment Cards 1898-1914
Chickasaw by Blood   Volume V

RESIDENCE: Pontotoc   COUNTY   CARD NO.
POST OFFICE: Connorville, I.T.   FIELD NO.

NAME	RELATION-SHIP TO PERSON FIRST NAMED	AGE	SEX	BLOOD	TRIBAL ENROLLMENT		
					YEAR	COUNTY	PAGE
1 Greenwood, Setphen	NAMED	17	M	3/4	1897	Pontotoc	55
2 " Jensie	Wife	23	F	1/2	1897	"	56
3 " Sela	Dau	3mo	F	5/8			

TRIBAL ENROLLMENT OF PARENTS

	NAME OF FATHER	YEAR	COUNTY	NAME OF MOTHER	YEAR	COUNTY
1	Hogen Greenwood	1897	Pontotoc	Mahala Greenwood	1897	Pontotoc
2	Ellis Carnes	Dead	Choc. Roll	Wincey Carnes	Dead	Chick Roll
3	No. 1			No. 2		

(NOTES)

No. 1 Enrolled on Chickasaw Card #235, Sept. 6, 1898 and transferred to this Card Dec. 3, 1900.
No. 2 Enrolled on Chickasaw Card #758 as Gincy Carnes Sept. 29, 1898 and transferred to this Card Dec. 3, 1900.
No. 2 on Chickasaw Roll as Gincy Carns
No. 3 Enrolled December 3, 1900.

Dec. 3, 1900

RESIDENCE: Choctaw Nation   ~~COUNTY~~   CARD NO.
POST OFFICE: Simpson, I.T.   FIELD NO.

NAME	RELATION-SHIP TO PERSON FIRST NAMED	AGE	SEX	BLOOD	TRIBAL ENROLLMENT		
					YEAR	COUNTY	PAGE
1 Tuskatomby, James	NAMED	26	M	1/2	1893	Tishomingo	P.R.#1 132
2 " Hattie	Dau	4 1/2	F	1/4			
3 " Willie	Son	2	M	1/4			
4 " Clara	Dau	2mo	F	1/4			
5 " Orlena	Wife	22	"	I.W.			

TRIBAL ENROLLMENT OF PARENTS

	NAME OF FATHER	YEAR	COUNTY	NAME OF MOTHER	YEAR	COUNTY
1	Tushalounubby	Dead	Tishomingo	Lottie Wilson	Dead	Non Citizen
2	No. 1	1893	"	Orlena Tushkalomby		" "
3	No. 1	"	"	" "		" "
4	No. 1			" "		" "
5	F.C. Hagwood		Non Citizen	Mary J. Hagwood		" "

(NOTES)

Testimony taken in this case under the name of James Tuskalounubby at Atoka, I.T. June 7, 1900.
    See additional testimony of No. 1 taken at Muskogee, I.T. Oct. 21, 1902.

See testimony of No. 5 taken at Tishomingo, I.T. Nov. 6, 1902.
Evidence of marriage requested Nov. 14, 1902.
No. 1 was listed on Chickasaw Card #1252, Oct. 14, 1909 and
transferred to this card as James Tushatomby Dead. 2, 1900.
No, 1 is the husband of Olena Tuskalomby, non Citizen.   *(No. 1 Dawes' Roll No. 4946)*
No. 2 Born April 16, 1898; Enrolled Nov. 10, 1902   *(No. 2 Dawes' Roll No. 4947)*
No. 3 Born Dec. 16, 1900; Enrolled Nov. 10, 1902   *(No. 3 Dawes' Roll No. 4948)*
No. 4 Born Sept. 14, 1902; Enrolled Nov. 10, 1902   *(No. 4 Dawes' Roll No. 4949)*
No. 1 on 1893 roll as Jim Tuskatomby   *(No. 5 Dawes' Roll No. 593)*
No. 1 also known as James Brown. See testimony of Oct. 21, 1902.

P.O. Palmer I.T. 6/20/02   Dec. 5, 1900.

RESIDENCE: Gaines *COUNTY*				CARD No.			
POST OFFICE: Wilburton, I.T.				FIELD No.			
NAME	RELATION-SHIP TO PERSON FIRST NAMED	AGE	SEX	BLOOD	TRIBAL ENROLLMENT		
					YEAR	COUNTY	PAGE
1 Sturnbaugh, Lula	NAMED	20	F	Full			
2 " Helen Maud	Dau	3wks	F	1/2			

	TRIBAL ENROLLMENT OF PARENTS						
NAME OF FATHER	YEAR	COUNTY	NAME OF MOTHER	YEAR	COUNTY		
1 Chas. Davis	Dead	Chickasaw	Louisiana Davis	Dead	Chickasaw		
2 Harry Sturnbaugh		Non Citizen	No. 1				

(NOTES)

On Iskatubby Pay Roll as Lula Davis.
As to parents, see her testimony and that of Louisa Hargis, her Aunt.
No. 1 was listed for enrollment Sept. 9, 1899 on Chickasaw Card #D.277
and transferred and enrolled on this Card Dec. 2, 1900.
No. 2 Enrolled January 3, 1901.

Dec. 5, 1900.

RESIDENCE: Pontotoc *COUNTY*				CARD No.			
POST OFFICE: Wiley, I.T.				FIELD No.			
NAME	RELATION-SHIP TO PERSON FIRST NAMED	AGE	SEX	BLOOD	TRIBAL ENROLLMENT		
					YEAR	COUNTY	PAGE
1 John, Stephen	NAMED	35	M	Full	1897	Pontotoc	57
2 " Hannah	Wife	32	F	1/2	1897	"	57
3 " Nancy	Dau	9	F	3/4	1897	"	57
4 " Amanda	Dau	6	F	3/4	1897	"	57

5	" Tecumseh	Son	4	M	3/4	1897	"	57
6	" Mary	Dau	2	F	3/4	1897	"	57
7	" Edward	Son	2mo	M	3/4			
8	Noel, Willie	Ward	9	M	1/2	1897	Pontotoc	95
9	" Freeman	Ward	6	M	1/2	1897	"	95

TRIBAL ENROLLMENT OF PARENTS

	NAME OF FATHER	YEAR	COUNTY	NAME OF MOTHER	YEAR	COUNTY
1	John Tucknatubby	Dead	Pontotoc	Lucy Pucknatubby	Dead	Pontotoc
2	Thomas Wright	Dead	Tishomingo	Phe-la-ney	Dead	Seminole Citz.
3	No. 1			No. 2		
4	No. 1			No. 2		
5	No. 1			No. 2		
6	No. 1			No. 2		
7	No. 1			No. 2		
8	Easmon Keel	1897	Pontotoc	Sophia Keel	Dead	Pontotoc
9	" "	"	"	" "	"	"

(NOTES)

No. 9 on Chickasaw Roll as Aphrions Keel
No. 8 also on page 58, Pontotoc Co, as Jack Keel
No. 9 " " " " " " " Fice "
Nos. 1, 8 and 9 were enrolled Sept. 30, 1898, which Card has been Cancelled and ⟨Card-9-891⟩
    applicants transferred to this Card Dec. 7, 1900
No's 2 to 7, inclusive, were listed for enrollment Sept. 30, 1898, on Chickasaw Card #D.103, which is cancelled and
    Applicants transferred to this card Dec. 7, 1900.

Dec. 7, 1900.

RESIDENCE: Choctaw Nation	~~COUNTY~~		CARD NO.			
POST OFFICE: Caddo, I.T.			FIELD NO.			

NAME	RELATION-SHIP TO PERSON FIRST NAMED	AGE	SEX	BLOOD	TRIBAL ENROLLMENT		
					YEAR	COUNTY	PAGE
1 Miller, Norman	NAMED	24	M	I.W.			
2 " Sophia	Wife	19	F	1/2	1897	Chick resid'g in Choc. Nat. 3rd Dist.	74
3 " Stephen *(Illegible)*	Son	5wks	M	1/4			

TRIBAL ENROLLMENT OF PARENTS

	NAME OF FATHER	YEAR	COUNTY	NAME OF MOTHER	YEAR	COUNTY
1	Stephen V. Miller		Non Citizen	Sarah Miller		Non Citizen
2	Peter Maytubby		Chickasaw	Tobitha Maytubby		White woman
3	No. 1			No. 2		

(NOTES)

No. 2 on Chickasaw Roll as Sophia Maytubby
No. 2 was enrolled on Chickasaw Card #1242, Oct. 14, 1898.
and transferred to this card with her husband. Dec. 10, 1900.
No. 3 enrolled Sept. 4, 1901.

Dec. 10, 1900.

RESIDENCE: Tishomingo	COUNTY				CARD NO.			
POST OFFICE: Reagan, I.T.					FIELD NO.			
	NAME	RELATIONSHIP TO PERSON FIRST NAMED	AGE	SEX	BLOOD	TRIBAL ENROLLMENT YEAR	COUNTY	PAGE
1	McKellop, William		20	M	1/2	1893	Pickens	158
2	" William L.	Son	5mo	M	1/4			

TRIBAL ENROLLMENT OF PARENTS

	NAME OF FATHER	YEAR	COUNTY	NAME OF MOTHER	YEAR	COUNTY
1	Joseph M. McKellop	1895	Creek Roll	Alena McKellop	Dead	Chickasaw
2	No. 1			Beulah McKellop		Non Citizen

(NOTES)

No. 1 also on Creek Census Card #1535
No. 1 elects for self and child to be finally enrolled as Citizens of the Chickasaw Nation - Dec. 2, 1901.
No. 1 is in U.S. Jail at Ardmore, I.T.
No. 2 born June 26, 1901.
Evidence of marriage of No. 1 and Beulah McKellop filed Dec. 4, 1901.
No. 1 and his wife are separated. See testimony of Beulah McKellop of May 18, 1903.
(Other notations illegible)

Ardmore, I.T.
Dec. 4, 1901.

RESIDENCE: Chickasaw Nation	~~COUNTY~~				CARD NO.			
POST OFFICE: Waupanucka, I.T.					FIELD NO.			
	NAME	RELATIONSHIP TO PERSON FIRST NAMED	AGE	SEX	BLOOD	TRIBAL ENROLLMENT YEAR	COUNTY	PAGE
1	Francis, B.L.		40	M	I.W.	1896	Pontotoc	81
2	" Katie	Wife	24	F	1/2	1896	"	59
3	" Percy	Son	2	M	1/4	1896	"	59
4	" Bertram	Son	18days	M	1/4			

TRIBAL ENROLLMENT OF PARENTS

	NAME OF FATHER	YEAR	COUNTY	NAME OF MOTHER	YEAR	COUNTY
1	Miller Francis		Non Citizen	Mary A. Francis		Non Citizen

Chickasaw Enrollment Cards 1898-1914
Chickasaw by Blood   Volume V

2	Solomon Goforth	1897	Chick resid'g in Choc. N. 2nd Dist	Caroline Goforth	Dead	Choc Roll
3	No. 1			No. 2		
4	No. 1			No. 2		

(NOTES)

Marriage License to be forwarded to Muskogee Office. Rec'd Sept. 12, 1898.   *(No. 1 Dawes' Roll No. 491)*

No. 3 on Chickasaw Roll as "Pearcy";   *(No. 2 Dawes' Roll No. 4219)*

Evidence of birth received and filed Mch. 6, 1902.   *(No. 3 Dawes' Roll No. 4220)*

No. 4 Enrolled Aug. 31, 1901.   *(No. 4 Dawes' Roll No. 4221)*

Nos. 1, 2, 3 and 4 originally enrolled on Choctaw Card #23; transferred to this card Oct. 10, 1902.

Sept. 3, 1898.

RESIDENCE: Chickasaw Nation   ~~COUNTY~~   CARD NO.

POST OFFICE: Waupunucka   FIELD NO.

NAME	RELATIONSHIP TO PERSON FIRST NAMED	AGE	SEX	BLOOD	TRIBAL ENROLLMENT		
					YEAR	COUNTY	PAGE
1	Goforth, Eli P.	NAMED	41	M	3/8	1896	Pontotoc	57
2	" Sophina	Wife	36	F	Full	1896	"	57
3	" Charlotte	Dau	14	"	11/16	1896	"	57
4	" Bessie	"	12	"	11/16	1896	"	57
5	" Odelia	"	10	"	11/16	1896	"	57
6	" Solomon	Son	8	M	11/16	1896	"	57
7	" William	"	6	"	11/16	1896	"	57
8	" Grover C.	"	4	"	11/16	1896	"	57
9	" E.P., Jr.	"	3	"	11/16	1896	"	57
~~10~~	~~" Louvinia~~	~~Dau~~	~~1~~	~~F~~	~~11/16~~	~~1896~~	~~"~~	~~57~~
~~11~~	~~" Francis E.~~	~~"~~	~~2mo~~	~~"~~	~~11/16~~			
12	Goforth, Ruth	"	2mo	"	11/16			
13	" Louisa	Mother	17	F	3/4			

TRIBAL ENROLLMENT OF PARENTS

	NAME OF FATHER	YEAR	COUNTY	NAME OF MOTHER	YEAR	COUNTY
1	Wm Goforth	Dead	Chick Roll	Louisa Goforth		Choc resid'g in Chick. Dist.
2	Robinson Mahaley	"	Choc. Roll	Melissa	Dead	Choc. Roll
3	No. 1			No. 2		
4	No. 1			No. 2		
5	No. 1			No. 2		
6	No. 1			No. 2		
7	No. 1			No. 2		

8	No. 1				No. 2		
9	No. 1				No. 2		
~~10~~	~~No. 1~~				~~No. 2~~		
~~11~~	~~No. 1~~				~~No. 2~~		
12	No. 1				No. 2		
13	Dan McCoy	Dead	Choctaw Roll	Rebecca		Dead	Choctaw Roll

(NOTES)

No's. 1,2,3,4,5,6,7,8,9,10,11 and 12 originally enrolled on Choctaw Card #24. Transferred to this card Oct. 11, 1902.

No. 10 died in May 1899; Proof of death filed Nov. 10, 1902.   *(No. 1 Dawes' Roll No. 4222)*

No. 11 " " Oct. 1899; " " " " " 10, 1902.   *(No. 2 Dawes' Roll No. 4223)*

No. 13 on 1896 Chickasaw Roll, Pontotoc Co, Page 57. Originally enrolled on   *(No. 3 Dawes' Roll No. 4224)*

    Choctaw Card #24 and transferred to this card Sept. 11, 1903.   *(No. 4 Dawes' Roll No. 4225)*

No. 1 on Chickasaw Roll as "E.P."   *(No. 5 Dawes' Roll No. 4226)*

No. 7 " " " " "William Jr."   *(No. 6 Dawes' Roll No. 4227)*

No. 10 " " " " "Luvinia"   *(No. 7 Dawes' Roll No. 4228)*

No. 11 Enrolled Oct. 6, 1899.   *(No. 8 Dawes' Roll No. 4229)*

No. 12 Born March 11, 1902; Enrolled May 26. 1902.   *(No. 9 Dawes' Roll No. 4230)*

    (No. 12 Dawes' Roll No. 4231)   *(No. 13 Dawes' Roll No. 4910)*

P.O. Fillmore I.T. 8/12/02.   Sept. 3, 1898.

RESIDENCE: Chickasaw Nation   ~~COUNTY~~   CARD NO.

POST OFFICE: Conway, I.T.   FIELD NO.

NAME	RELATION-SHIP TO PERSON FIRST NAMED	AGE	SEX	BLOOD	TRIBAL ENROLLMENT		
					YEAR	COUNTY	PAGE
1 Perry, Annie	NAMED	24	F	1/2	1896	Pontotoc	47
2 " Tandy F.	Son	7	M	1/4	1896	"	47
3 " Juanita	Dau	4	F	1/4	1896	"	47
4 " Minnie	"	2	"	1/4	1896	"	47
5 " Lillie M	"	6mo	"	1/4			
6 " Roxy	"	4mo	"	1/4			
7 " Theodore Mosely	Son	3mo	M	1/4			

TRIBAL ENROLLMENT OF PARENTS

	NAME OF FATHER	YEAR	COUNTY	NAME OF MOTHER	YEAR	COUNTY
1	Tandy Walker	1897	Chick Roll	Adeline Wade	Dead	Choctaw Roll
2	Geo H. Perry		" "	No. 1		
3	" " "		" "	No. 1		
4	" " "		" "	No. 1		
5	" " "		" "	No. 1		
6	" " "		" "	No. 1		

7	" " "		" "	No. 1	

(NOTES)

No. 1 is the wife of Geo. H. Perry on Chickasaw Card #127   (No. 1 Dawes' Roll No. 4232)
No. 2 on Chickasaw Roll as Andy F. Perry   (No. 2 Dawes' Roll No. 4233)
No. 3 "   "   " " Jaunita "   (No. 3 Dawes' Roll No. 4234)
No. 5 evidence of birth received and filed Feby 28, 1902.   (No. 4 Dawes' Roll No. 4235)
No. 6 enrolled July 14, 1900.   (No. 5 Dawes' Roll No. 4236)
No. 7 Born June 22, 1902; Enrolled Sept. 19, 1902.   (No. 6 Dawes' Roll No. 4237)
No. 1 to 7 inclusive originally enrolled on Choctaw Card #25.   (No. 7 Dawes' Roll No. 4238)
     Transferred to this card Oct. 11, 1902.

Sept. 3, 1898.

RESIGNED: Chickasaw Nation   ~~COUNTY~~   CARD NO.
POST OFFICE: Viola, I.T.   FIELD NO.

NAME	RELATIONSHIP TO PERSON FIRST NAMED	AGE	SEX	BLOOD	TRIBAL ENROLLMENT		
					YEAR	COUNTY	PAGE
1 Cravatt, Allen W.		42	M	1/2	1896	Pontotoc	54

TRIBAL ENROLLMENT OF PARENTS

	NAME OF FATHER	YEAR	COUNTY	NAME OF MOTHER	YEAR	COUNTY
1	Wm Cravatt	Dead	Cick Roll	(Name Illegible)	Dead	Choc Roll

(NOTES)

Husband of Katie Cravatt, Chickasaw Roll, Card #139.   (No. 1 Dawes' Roll No. 4239)
No. 1 originally enrolled on Choctaw Card #26. Transferred to this card Oct. 11, 1902.

Sept. 3, 1898

RESIDENCE: Chickasaw Nation   ~~COUNTY~~   CARD NO.
POST OFFICE: Center, I.T.   FIELD NO.

	NAME	RELATIONSHIP TO PERSON FIRST	AGE	SEX	BLOOD	TRIBAL ENROLLMENT		
						YEAR	COUNTY	PAGE
1	Cofer, Bettie	NAMED	26	F	1/2	1896	Pontotoc	41
2	" Andrew Jackson	Son	9	M	1/4	1896	"	"
3	" Emma Lena	Dau	7	F	1/4	1896	"	"
4	" Geo Edward	Son	3	M	1/4	1896	"	"
5	" Jesse Freeman	"	5mo	"	1/4			
6	" Virgil Lee	"	2mo	"	1/4			

TRIBAL ENROLLMENT OF PARENTS

	NAME OF FATHER	YEAR	COUNTY	NAME OF MOTHER	YEAR	COUNTY
1	Geo. Johnson	Dead	Chick Roll	Elizabeth Cocheron	1896	Atoka CCR Page 70

2	G.F. Cofer		Non Citizen		No. I		
3	" " "		" "		No. I		
4	" " "		" "		No. I		
5	" " "		" "		No. I		
6	" " "		" "		No. I		

(NOTES)

No. I on Chickasaw Roll as Bettie Coffer
No. 2 "   "   "   "   A.G.   "
No. 3 "   "   "   "   E.L.   "
No. 4 "   "   "   "   Edward "
No. 5 Evidence of birth received and filed July 25, 1902.
No. 6 Enrolled May 24, 1900.
No's. I to 6 incl. originally enrolled on Choctaw Card #29.
    Transferred to this card Oct. II, 1902.

(No. I Dawes' Roll No. 4240)
(No. 2 Dawes' Roll No. 4241)
(No. 3 Dawes' Roll No. 4242)
(No. 4 Dawes' Roll No. 4243)
(No. 5 Dawes' Roll No. 4244)
(No. 6 Dawes' Roll No. 4245)

P.O. Tuttle, I.T. 8/2-04

Sept. 5, 1898.

RESIDENCE: Chickasaw Nation   ~~COUNTY~~   CARD NO.
POST OFFICE: Waupunucka, I.T.   P.O. Byrne I.T. 2/22/03 FIELD NO.

	NAME	RELATION-SHIP TO PERSON FIRST NAMED	AGE	SEX	BLOOD	TRIBAL ENROLLMENT		
						YEAR	COUNTY	PAGE
1	James, McKee	NAMED	48	M	1/2	1896	Pontotoc	51
2	" Rhoena	Wife	40	F	Full	1896	"	"
3	" Edward W.	Son	19	M	3/4	1896	"	"
4	" Mary Ann	Dau	18	F	3/4	1896	"	"
5	" Benj. D.	Son	14	M	3/4	1896	"	"
6	" Frank	"	12	"	3/4	1896	"	"
7	" Jesse	"	10	"	3/4	1896	"	"
8	" Elsie H.	Dau	17	F	3/4	1896	"	"

TRIBAL ENROLLMENT OF PARENTS

	NAME OF FATHER	YEAR	COUNTY	NAME OF MOTHER	YEAR	COUNTY
1	Robison James	Dead	Chick Roll	Mary James	Dead	Gaines
2	David Perkins	"	Choctaw "	Elsie Perkins		Blue Co.
3	No. I			No. 2		
4	No. I			No. 2		
5	No. I			No. 2		
6	No. I			No. 2		
7	No. I			No. 2		
8	No. I			No. 2		

Chickasaw Enrollment Cards 1898-1914
Chickasaw by Blood   Volume V

(NOTES)

No. 3 on Chickasaw Roll as Edward *(No. 1 Dawes' Roll No. 4246)*

No. 4 " " " " Mary *(No. 2 Dawes' Roll No. 4247)*

Placed on Choctaw Card #4451 with husband Stephen B. Taylor; Sept. 4, 1899.

No. 7 on Chickasaw Roll as Jessie *(No. 5 Dawes' Roll No. 4248)*

No's. 1,2,3,4,5,6 and 7 originally on Choctaw Card #62 *(No. 6 Dawes' Roll No. 4249)*

Transferred to this card Oct. 11, 1902. *(No. 7 Dawes' Roll No. 4250)*

No. 3 died Aug. 9, 1902. See affidavit of No. 1 filed Nov. 20, 1902.

No. 8 originally enrolled on Choctaw card #62. Transferred to this card May 14, 1903.

See testimony of that date.

Sept. 7, 1898.

RESIDENCE: Atoka COUNTY					CARD NO.		
POST OFFICE: Allen, I.T.					FIELD NO.		
NAME	RELATION-SHIP TO PERSON FIRST NAMED	AGE	SEX	BLOOD	TRIBAL ENROLLMENT		
					YEAR	COUNTY	PAGE
1 Wolfe, Alum	NAMED	12	M	1/2	1893	Pontotoc	226
2 " Chiminayne	Sis	10	F	1/2	"	"	"

TRIBAL ENROLLMENT OF PARENTS

	NAME OF FATHER	YEAR	COUNTY	NAME OF MOTHER	YEAR	COUNTY
1	Moses Wolfe		Chick Roll	Rachel Wolfe		CCR #21 Atoka 486
2	" "		" "	" "		" "

(NOTES)

Nos. 1 and 2 on 1893 Chickasaw Pay Roll No. s Page226 *(No. 1 Dawes' Roll No. 4251)*

No. 2 on Chickasaw Roll as "Chimmie" *(No. 2 Dawes' Roll No. 4252)*

Originally enrolled on Choc. Card #67; Transferred to this card Oct. 11, 1902.

Surname of both on 1896 Roll as Wolf.

Sept. 7, 1898.

RESIDENCE: Chickasaw Nation ~~COUNTY~~					CARD NO.		
POST OFFICE:					FIELD NO.		
NAME	RELATION-SHIP TO PERSON FIRST NAMED	AGE	SEX	BLOOD	TRIBAL ENROLLMENT		
					YEAR	COUNTY	PAGE
1 Conner, James O.	NAMED	41	M	I.W.	1896	Pickens	78
2 " Ada	Wife	37	F	1/2	1896	"	14
3 Shelton, Myrtle C.	S.Dau	12	"	1/4	1896	"	14

101

TRIBAL ENROLLMENT OF PARENTS						
NAME OF FATHER	YEAR	COUNTY	NAME OF MOTHER	YEAR	COUNTY	
1 Thos. H. Conner		Non Citizen	Elizabeth A. Conner		Non Citizen	
2 Calvin Colbert	Dead	Chick Roll	Emma Colbert	Dead	Choc. Roll	
3 Doctor Shelton	"	Non Citizen	No. 2			

(NOTES)

No. 1 on Chickasaw Roll as James O'Conner.   *(No. 1 Dawes' Roll No. 525)*
  Admitted by Dawes Commission; Case No. 35.
No. 2 on Chickasaw Roll as Ida B. Bonner; also on Chickawaw Roll   *(No. 2 Dawes' Roll No. 4253)*
  Page 96, as Ada O'Connor
No. 3 on Chickasaw Roll as Myrtle Shelton.   *(No. 3 Dawes' Roll No. 4254)*
No's. 1, 2 and 3 Originally enrolled on Choctaw Card #79.
  Transferred to this Card Oct. 11, 1902.

Sept. 12, 1898.

RESIDENCE: Chickasaw Nation   ~~COUNTY~~   CARD NO.

POST OFFICE: Rush Springs, I.T.   FIELD NO.

NAME	RELATION-SHIP TO PERSON FIRST	AGE	SEX	BLOOD	TRIBAL ENROLLMENT		
					YEAR	COUNTY	PAGE
1 Reynolds, Charles A.	NAMED	34	M	I.W.	1896	Pickens	79
2 " ~~Katie~~	~~Wife~~	~~25~~	F	~~1/2~~	~~1896~~	"	~~24~~
3 " Willie	Son	9	M	1/4	1896	"	24
4 " Frank	"	7	"	1/4	1896	"	24
5 " Seldan	"	5	"	1/4	1896	"	24
6 " Ethel A.	Dau	4	F	1/4	1896	"	24
7 " ~~Lillie May~~	"	~~15mo~~	"	~~1/4~~	~~1896~~	"	~~24~~

TRIBAL ENROLLMENT OF PARENTS						
NAME OF FATHER	YEAR	COUNTY	NAME OF MOTHER	YEAR	COUNTY	
1 J.B. Reynolda		Non Citizen	Louisa Reynolda		Non Citizen	
2 ~~Levi Perry~~	~~Dead~~	~~Chick Roll~~	~~Ellen Perry~~	~~Dead~~	~~Chick Roll~~	
3 No. 1			No. 2			
4 No. 1			No. 2			
5 No. 1			No. 2			
6 No. 1			No. 2			
7 ~~No. 1~~			~~No. 2~~			

(NOTES)

No. 1 admitted as an intermarried Chickasaw and No's 2,3,4,5 and 6 as   *(No. 1 Dawes' Roll No. 526)*
  Chickasaws by blood, by Dawes Commission in 1896, in Chickasaw Case #77. No appeal.
No. 6 on Chickasaw Roll as "Ethel Reynolds"
No. 7 "   "   " " "Lillie M. " "

Chickasaw Enrollment Cards 1898-1914
Chickasaw by Blood   Volume V

No's 1 to 7 inclusive originally enrolled on Choctaw Card #103, transferred to this card Oct. 11, 1902.
No. 2 died March 15, 1899; Proof of death file Oct. 20, 1902.
No. 7 died in July, 1899; Proof of death filed Oct. 20, 1902.

Sept. 13, 1898.

RESIDENCE: Chickasaw Nation   ~~COUNTY~~   CARD NO.
POST OFFICE: Purcell, I.T.   FIELD NO.

	NAME	RELATION-SHIP TO PERSON FIRST NAMED	AGE	SEX	BLOOD	TRIBAL ENROLLMENT		
						YEAR	COUNTY	PAGE
1	Perry, Joseph	NAMED	39	M	1/2	1896	Pontotoc	62
2	" Matilda	Wife	39	F	1/4	1896	"	62
3	" Charles E.	Son	16	M	3/8	1896	"	62
4	" Joel F.	"	15	"	3/8	1896	"	62
5	" Lela A.	Dau	13	F	3/8	1896	"	62
6	" James W.	Son	5	M	3/8	1896	"	62
7	" *(Illegible)* May	Dau	3	F	3/8	1896	"	62
8	" Mildrid Catherine	"	7mo	"	3/8			

TRIBAL ENROLLMENT OF PARENTS

	NAME OF FATHER	YEAR	COUNTY	NAME OF MOTHER	YEAR	COUNTY
1	Morgan Perry	Dead	Chic Roll	Elizabeth Perry		
2	Charles E. Eastman	"	Non Citizen	Betsey Eastman		
3	No. 1			No. 2		
4	No. 1			No. 2		
5	No. 1			No. 2		
6	No. 1			No. 2		
7	No. 1			No. 2		
8	No. 1			No. 2		

(NOTES)

No. 2 on Chickasaw Roll as "Malila"
No. 7 "   "   " " "C.M."
No. 8 Evidence of birth received received[sic] and filed Feb'y 15, 1902.
No's 1 to 8 inclusive originally enrolled on Choctaw Card #107.
    Transferred to this card Oct. 11, 1902.
(No. 6 Dawes' Roll No. 4260)   *(No. 7 Dawes' Roll No. 4261)*

(No. 1 Dawes' Roll No. 4235)
(No. 2 Dawes' Roll No. 4236)
(No. 3 Dawes' Roll No. 4237)
(No. 4 Dawes' Roll No. 4238)
(No. 5 Dawes' Roll No. 4239)
(No. 8 Dawes' Roll No. 4262)
Sept. 13, 1898.

Chickasaw Enrollment Cards 1898-1914
Chickasaw by Blood   Volume V

RESIDENCE: Chickasaw Nation ~~COUNTY~~					CARD NO.			
POST OFFICE: Purcell, I.T.					FIELD NO.			

NAME	RELATION-SHIP TO PERSON FIRST NAMED	AGE	SEX	BLOOD	TRIBAL ENROLLMENT		
					YEAR	COUNTY	PAGE
1 Hamblin, Charley M.	NAMED	23	M	1/8	1896	Panola	5

TRIBAL ENROLLMENT OF PARENTS

NAME OF FATHER	YEAR	COUNTY	NAME OF MOTHER	YEAR	COUNTY
1 H.C. Hamblin		Non Citizen	Mollie Hamblin	Dead	Choc. Roll

(NOTES)

No. 1 originally enrolled on Choctaw Card #129.
   Transferred to this card Oct. 13, 1902.

(No. 1 Dawes' Roll No. 4263)

Sept. 14, 1898.

RESIDENCE: Chickasaw Nation ~~COUNTY~~					CARD NO.			
POST OFFICE: Wynnewood, I.T.					FIELD NO.			

NAME	RELATION-SHIP TO PERSON FIRST NAMED	AGE	SEX	BLOOD	TRIBAL ENROLLMENT		
					YEAR	COUNTY	PAGE
1 Walner, Lula	NAMED	43	F	1/4	1896	Pontotoc	60
2 " Susan V.	Dau	14	"	1/8	1896	"	60
3 " Acca	"	12	"	1/8	1896	"	60
4 " Julia	"	10	"	1/8	1896	"	60
5 " Hugh	Son	5	M	1/8	1896	"	60

TRIBAL ENROLLMENT OF PARENTS

NAME OF FATHER	YEAR	COUNTY	NAME OF MOTHER	YEAR	COUNTY
1 Wiley Stewart	Dead	Non Citizen	Nancy F. Stewart		Blue
2 John H. Walner	1897	Pontotoc Co. Chick. Roll	No. 1		
3 " " "	"	"	No. 1		
4 " " "	"	"	No. 1		
5 " " "	"	"	No. 1		

(NOTES)

No. 1 the wife of John H. Walner, Chickasaw Roll Card No. 370
No. 4 on Chickasaw Roll as "Lula D. Walner"
Nos. 1 to 5 inclusive originally enrolled on Choc Card #91
   Transferred to this card Oct. 13, 1902.   *(No. 4 Dawes' Roll No. 4267)*

(No. 1 Dawes' Roll No. 4264)
(No. 2 Dawes' Roll No. 4265)
(No. 3 Dawes' Roll No. 4266)
(No. 5 Dawes' Roll No. 4268)

Chickasaw Enrollment Cards 1898-1914
Chickasaw by Blood   Volume V

RESIDENCE: Chickasaw Nation   COUNTY   CARD NO.
POST OFFICE: Wynnewood, I.T.   FIELD NO.

NAME	RELATION-SHIP TO PERSON FIRST NAMED	AGE	SEX	BLOOD	TRIBAL ENROLLMENT		
					YEAR	COUNTY	PAGE
1 Jennings, Henrietta L	NAMED	42	F	1/4	1896	Pontotoc	60
2 " Daisy	Dau	18	"	1/8	1896	"	60
3 " Themia	"	17	"	1/8	1896	"	60
4 " ~~Kutchentubby~~	~~Son~~	~~15~~	~~M~~	~~1/8~~	~~1896~~	~~"~~	~~60~~
5 " Louina	Dau	13	F	1/8	1896	"	60
6 " Alvers	Son	10	M	1/8	1896	"	60
7 " James	"	8	"	1/8	1896	"	60
8 " John	"	5	"	1/8	1896	"	60
9 " R.W.	Husband	42	"	I.W.	1896	"	60

TRIBAL ENROLLMENT OF PARENTS

	NAME OF FATHER	YEAR	COUNTY	NAME OF MOTHER	YEAR	COUNTY
1	Jim Colbert	Dead	Chic Roll	Themins Colbert		Atoka
2	No. 9			No. 1		
3	No. 9			No. 1		
4	~~No. 9~~			~~No. 1~~		
5	No. 9			No. 1		
6	No. 9			No. 1		
7	No. 9			No. 1		
8	No. 9			No. 1		
9	John Jennings	Dead	Non Citizen	Elmira Jennings		Non Citizen

(NOTES)

No. 1 on Chickasaw Roll as H.L. Jennings Wife of R.W. Jennings, Choctaw Doubtful Card No. D.19.
No. 3 "   "   " " Themia "   (No. 1 Dawes' Roll No. 4269)
No. 4 "   "   " " D.T.   "   (No. 2 Dawes' Roll No. 4270)
No. 7 "   "   " " Jane   "   (No. 3 Dawes' Roll No. 4271)
No. 9 "   "   " " R.W. Jennings.   (No. 5 Dawes' Roll No. 4272)
No. 9 transferred from Card No. D.19 Nov. 26, 1898.   (No. 6 Dawes' Roll No. 4273)
No's 1 to 9 inclusive originally enrolled on Choctaw Card #135; (No. 7 Dawes' Roll No. 4274)
        Transferred to this card Oct. 13, 1902.   (No. 8 Dawes' Roll No. 4275)
No. 3 was married on Jan'y 12, 1903 to (Illegible) Harrington Burris, Chick. Card No. 659
No. 4 died Aug. 31, 1899; Proof of death filed Oct. 25, 1902.

Sept. 14, 1898

Chickasaw Enrollment Cards 1898-1914
Chickasaw by Blood   Volume V

RESIDENCE: Chickasaw Nation ~~COUNTY~~					CARD NO.		
POST OFFICE: Paul's Valley, I.T.					FIELD NO.		

NAME	RELATION-SHIP TO PERSON FIRST NAMED	AGE	SEX	BLOOD	TRIBAL ENROLLMENT		
					YEAR	COUNTY	PAGE
1 Fleming, Willie Hampton	NAMED	7	M	1/16	1896	Tishomingo	29

TRIBAL ENROLLMENT OF PARENTS

NAME OF FATHER	YEAR	COUNTY	NAME OF MOTHER	YEAR	COUNTY
1 Wm B. Fleming	Dead	Non Citizen	Minnie Fleming		Choc. resid'g in Chick. Dist.

(NOTES)

No. 1 on Chickasaw Roll as "Hamp Flemmings"   *(No. 1 Dawes' Roll No. 4276)*
No. 1 originally enrolled on Choctaw Card #145.
   Transferred to this Card Oct. 13, 1902.

Sept. 15, 1898.

RESIDENCE: Chickasaw Nation COUNTY					CARD NO.		
POST OFFICE: Paul's Valley, I.T.					FIELD NO.		

NAME	RELATION-SHIP TO PERSON FIRST NAMED	AGE	SEX	BLOOD	TRIBAL ENROLLMENT		
					YEAR	COUNTY	PAGE
1 Dennis, A.B.	NAMED	37	M	I.W.			
2 " ~~Sallie~~	~~Wife~~	~~37~~	F	~~1/2~~	~~1896~~	~~Pickens~~	~~17~~
3 " Jessie	Dau	13mo	"	1/4	1896	"	86
4 Ard. Emet	S.Son	11	M	1/4	1896	"	17
5 " Maud Lena	" Dau	8	F	1/4	1896	"	16
6 " Albert Devro	" Son	5	M	1/4	1896	"	16

TRIBAL ENROLLMENT OF PARENTS

NAME OF FATHER	YEAR	COUNTY	NAME OF MOTHER	YEAR	COUNTY
1 John Dennis	Dead	Non Citizen	Delilah Dennis	Dead	Non Citizen
2 ~~Stone Thomas~~	"	~~Chick Roll~~	~~Hettie Jenkins~~	"	~~Choc. Roll~~
3		No. 1	No. 2		
4 Albert E. Ard	Dead	Non Citizen	No. 2		
5 " " "	"	" "	No. 2		
6 " " "	"	" "	No. 2		

(NOTES)

No. 1 appears on page 78, 1896 Chickasaw Roll, Pickens Co., as Kenny Dennis.
No's 1 and 2 admitted by Dawes Commission, Case No. 38, No appeal taken.
No. 3 on Chickasaw Roll, Registered under Act of Legislature, July 31, 1897.
No. 5 "   "   " as Maude Ard.
No. 6 "   "   " " Devora "

106

Chickasaw Enrollment Cards 1898-1914
Chickasaw by Blood   Volume V

No's 1,2,4,5 and 6 admitted as Chickasaws in 1896, Chickasaw Case #38. No appeal.
Marriage papers on file with Dawes Commission in Case No. 38, Chick. Nation
Certified copies of marriage License and Certificate to be furnished
No's 1 to 6, inclusive, originally enrolled on Choc. Card #151
    Transferred to this card Oct. 13, 1902.
Clarinda Ard of Elmore, I.T. is legal guardian of Nos. 4, 5, & 6. July 13, 1903.
No. 2 died July 2, 1899; Proof of death filed Oct. 27, 1902.
Affidavit of Malinda Brown as to birth of No. 3 filed Jan. 14, 1903.
Affidavit of Sallie Featherstone and Altha Paul as to birth of No. 3 filed Feb. 4/03,

Sept. 15, 1898.

	NAME	RELATION-SHIP TO PERSON FIRST NAMED	AGE	SEX	BLOOD	TRIBAL ENROLLMENT		
						YEAR	COUNTY	PAGE
1	Bond, Galloway	NAMED	17	M	3/4	1896	Pontotoc	47
2	" Jesse	Bro	15	"	3/4	1896	"	47

RESIDENCE: Chickasaw Nation ~~COUNTY~~   CARD NO.
POST OFFICE: Center, I.T.   FIELD NO.

TRIBAL ENROLLMENT OF PARENTS

	NAME OF FATHER	YEAR	COUNTY	NAME OF MOTHER	YEAR	COUNTY
1	Sampson Bond	Dead	Choc Roll	Melvina Johnson		Choc. resid'g in Chick Dist.
2	" "	"	" "	" "		"

(NOTES)

No. 2 on Chickasaw Roll as Jessie
No's 1 and 2 originally enrolled on Choctaw Card #160.
    Transferred to this card Oct. 13, 1902.

(No. 1 Dawes' Roll No. 4277)
(No. 2 Dawes' Roll No. 4278)

Sept. 15, 1898.

RESIDENCE: Chickasaw Nation ~~COUNTY~~   CARD NO.
POST OFFICE: Ardmore, I.T.   FIELD NO.

	NAME	RELATION-SHIP TO PERSON FIRST NAMED	AGE	SEX	BLOOD	TRIBAL ENROLLMENT		
						YEAR	COUNTY	PAGE
1	Colbert, Walter	NAMED	33	M	1/8	1896	Pickens	16
2	" Czarina M.	Dau	14mo	F	1/16			
3	" Walter Cerera	Son	7days	M	1/16			

TRIBAL ENROLLMENT OF PARENTS

	NAME OF FATHER	YEAR	COUNTY	NAME OF MOTHER	YEAR	COUNTY
1	Jim Colbert	Dead	Chick Roll	(Illegible)Colbert		Chick Roll

Chickasaw Enrollment Cards 1898-1914
Chickasaw by Blood   Volume V

2	No. 1			Henrietta C. Colbert	1897	Intermarried Chick Roll
3	No. 1			" " "	1897	" "

(NOTES)

No. 1 Husband of Henrietta C. Colbert, Chickasaw Roll, Card No. 613   *(No. 1 Dawes' Roll No. 4279)*

No. 2 was born July 30, 1897, and enrolled on Chickasaw Card #613, Sept. 24, 1898. *(No. 2 Dawes' Roll No. 4280)*
  Tranferred to Choctaw Card #279, Feby. 4, 1902.

No. 3 was born Sept. 15, 1898, and enrolled on Chick. Card #613, Sept. 24, 1898.   *(No. 3 Dawes' Roll No. 4281)*
  Transferred to Choctaw Card No. 279, Feby. 4, 1902.

Evidence of marriage between No. 1 and Henrietta C. Juzan, filed 2/27/02.

No's. 1, 2, & 3 originally enrolled on Choctaw Card #279, and transferred to this card Oct. 13, 1902.

Sept. 24, 1898.

RESIDENCE: Chickasaw Nation   ~~COUNTY~~   CARD NO.

POST OFFICE: Tishomingo, I.T.   FIELD NO.

NAME		RELATION-SHIP TO PERSON FIRST NAMED	AGE	SEX	BLOOD	TRIBAL ENROLLMENT		
						YEAR	COUNTY	PAGE
1	Harris, R.M.		48	M	1/8	1896	Tishomingo	38
2	" Jennie	Wife	29	F	3/8	1896	"	38
3	" Dixie	Dau	5	F	1/4	1896	"	38
4	" Halley	"	3	F	1/4	1896	"	38
5	" Robert Maxwell	Son	3wks	M	1/4			

TRIBAL ENROLLMENT OF PARENTS

	NAME OF FATHER	YEAR	COUNTY	NAME OF MOTHER	YEAR	COUNTY
1	Joe D. Harris	Dead	Chick Roll	Catherine Nail Harris	Dead	Choctaw Roll
2	Wyatt	"	Non Citizen	*(Name Illegible)*	"	" "
3	No. 1			No. 2		
4	No. 1			No. 2		
5	No. 1			No. 2		

(NOTES)

No. 1 is father of children on Chickasaw Card #617

No. 2 enrolled January 19, 1901.

No's 1 to 5 inclusive originally enrolled on Choctaw Card #281.
  Transferred to this card October 13, 1902.

Sept. 26, 1898.

Chickasaw Enrollment Cards 1898-1914
Chickasaw by Blood   Volume V

RESIDENCE: Chickasaw Nation	COUNTY				CARD NO.		
POST OFFICE: Hickory, I.T.					FIELD NO.		

NAME	RELATION-SHIP TO PERSON FIRST NAMED	AGE	SEX	BLOOD	TRIBAL ENROLLMENT		
					YEAR	COUNTY	PAGE
1 Kay, Fred	NAMED	8	M	1/2	1896	Tishomingo	27

TRIBAL ENROLLMENT OF PARENTS

NAME OF FATHER	YEAR	COUNTY	NAME OF MOTHER	YEAR	COUNTY
1 Charley Kay	Dead	Non Citizen	Minnie Kay	Dead	Choctaw Roll

(NOTES)
No. 1 on Chickasaw Roll as "Fred Key" ward of and lives with
    Newton Galloway Frazier, Chickasaw Roll Card No. 690.
No. 1 originally enrolled on Choctaw Card #299; Transferred to this card Oct. 13, 1902.

Sept. 27, 1898.

RESIDENCE: Tobucksy	COUNTY				CARD NO.		
POST OFFICE: Hartshorne, I.T.					FIELD NO.		

NAME	RELATION-SHIP TO PERSON FIRST NAMED	AGE	SEX	BLOOD	TRIBAL ENROLLMENT		
					YEAR	COUNTY	PAGE
1 Carney, Philip	NAMED	19	M	1/2	1896	Choc. Dist. Chick Roll	71

TRIBAL ENROLLMENT OF PARENTS

NAME OF FATHER	YEAR	COUNTY	NAME OF MOTHER	YEAR	COUNTY
1 William Carney		Chick resid'g in Choc N. 1st Dist.	Silsey Carney	Dead	Choc Roll

(NOTES)
No. 1 on Chickasaw Roll as "Phillip Carney"
No. 1 originally enrolled on Choc Card #302. Transferred to this card Oct. 13, 1902.

Sept. 28, 1898.

RESIDENCE: Chickasaw Nation	~~COUNTY~~				CARD NO.		
POST OFFICE: Waupunuka, I.T.					FIELD NO.		

NAME	RELATION-SHIP TO PERSON FIRST NAMED	AGE	SEX	BLOOD	TRIBAL ENROLLMENT		
					YEAR	COUNTY	PAGE
1 Hawkins, Kingsberry	NAMED	38	M	1/2	1896	Pontotoc	28

TRIBAL ENROLLMENT OF PARENTS

NAME OF FATHER	YEAR	COUNTY	NAME OF MOTHER	YEAR	COUNTY
1 Isum Hawkins	Dead	Choc Roll	E-ma-to-na	Dead	Choc Roll

(NOTES)

No. 1 Husband of Ledicy Hawkins, Chickasaw Roll Card #757

No. 1 originally enrolled on Choc. Card #304 and transferred to this card Oct. 13, 1902.

No. 1 is now separated from Ledicy Hawkins, Chickasaw Card 757 and living
with Mollie Durant, Chickasaw Card #99.

11/6-02 P.O. Byrne, I.T.   Sept. 29, 1898

RESIDENCE: Chickasaw Nation	COUNTY				CARD No.			
POST OFFICE: Hickory, I.T.					FIELD No.			
NAME	RELATION-SHIP TO PERSON FIRST NAMED	AGE	SEX	BLOOD	TRIBAL ENROLLMENT			
					YEAR	COUNTY		PAGE
1 Bradley, Bruce	NAMED	17	M	1/2	1896	Tishomingo		28
2 " Ellen	Dau	2wks	F	1/4				

TRIBAL ENROLLMENT OF PARENTS

NAME OF FATHER	YEAR	COUNTY	NAME OF MOTHER	YEAR	COUNTY
1 John Bradley	Dead	Non Citizen	Jincy Bradley	Dead	Choc Roll
2 No. 1			Ida Bradley		Non Citizen

(NOTES)

No. 1 now the husband of Ida Bradley, non Citizen; evidence of marriage filed Sept. 28, 1901.

No. 2 Enrolled Sept. 28, 1901.

No's 1 and 2 originally enrolled on Choctaw Card #300
ane transferred to this card Oct. 13, 1902.

No. 2 died Oct. 4, 1901; Proof of death filed Nov. 18, 1902.

Sept. 29, 1898.

RESIDENCE: Chickasaw Nation	COUNTY				CARD No.		
POST OFFICE: Wiley, I.T.					FIELD No.		
NAME	RELATION-SHIP TO PERSON FIRST NAMED	AGE	SEX	BLOOD	TRIBAL ENROLLMENT		
					YEAR	COUNTY	PAGE
1 Smith, Wood	NAMED	42	M	I.W.	1896	Pontotoc	81
2 " Serena	Wife	38	F	1/4	1896	"	49
3 " Frank	Son	19	M	1/8	1896	"	49
4 " Mollie	Dau	16	F	1/8	1896	"	49
5 " Birdie	"	14	"	1/8	1896	"	49
6 " Richard	Son	10	M	1/8	1896	"	49
7 " Rector	"	9	"	1/8	1896	"	49
8 " Cheadle	"	5	"	1/8	1896	"	49

9	" Almirena	Dau	3	F	1/8	1896	"	49
10	" Dewey	"	4mo	"	1/8			
11	" Katie	"	3mo	"	1/8			

TRIBAL ENROLLMENT OF PARENTS

	NAME OF FATHER	YEAR	COUNTY	NAME OF MOTHER	YEAR	COUNTY
1	Thomas Smith	Dead	Non Citizen	Letitia Smith	Dead	Non Citizen
2	Thomas Cheadle	"	Chick Roll	Rebecca Cheadle	"	Choc Roll
3	No. 1			No. 2		
4	No. 1			No. 2		
5	No. 1			No. 2		
6	No. 1			No. 2		
7	No. 1			No. 2		
8	No. 1			No. 2		
9	No. 1			No. 2		
10	No. 1			No. 2		
11	No. 1			No. 2		

(NOTES)

No's 1 to 11 inclusive originally enrolled on Choc. Card No. 307; Transferred to this card Oct. 13, 1902.

Certified copy of marriage license and certificate to be supplie.

No. 2 died Nov. 1, 1901; Evidence of death filed January 20, 1902.

No. 1 born Nov. 1, 1901; Enrolled January 20, 1902.

No. 9 Died Oct. 20, 1900; Proof of death filed Aug. 2, 1902.

No. 10 enrolled March 6/99.

See affidavits of M.V. Cheadle and Mary Cheadle relative to the marriage between Nos. 1 and 2 filed April 8, 1903.

P.O. Duncan I.T. 12/29-04   Sept. 29, 1898.

RESIDENCE: Chickasaw Nation	COUNTY				CARD NO.			
POST OFFICE: Sulphur, I.T.					FIELD NO.			

NAME	RELATION-SHIP TO PERSON FIRST NAMED	AGE	SEX	BLOOD	TRIBAL ENROLLMENT		
					YEAR	COUNTY	PAGE
1	Hilton, Charles N.	NAMED	31	M	I.W.			
2	" Minnie	Wife	24	F	1/4	1896	Tishomingo	29
3	Flemmings, Joel	S.Son	5	M	1/8	1896	"	29
4	Hilton, Louia Ruth	Dau	4mo	F	1/8			

TRIBAL ENROLLMENT OF PARENTS

	NAME OF FATHER	YEAR	COUNTY	NAME OF MOTHER	YEAR	COUNTY
1	Wm D. Hilton		Non Citizen	Sarah R. Hilton	Dead	Non Citizen

111

Chickasaw Enrollment Cards 1898-1914
Chickasaw by Blood   Volume V

2	Hamp Willis	Dead	Chick Roll	Delila Willis now Davis		Towson Co. Choc. Roll
3	Will Flemmings	"	Non Citizen	No. 2		
4	No. 1			No. 2		

(NOTES)

No. 2 on Chickasaw Roll as "Minnie Flemmings"   *(No. 1 Dawes' Roll No. 443)*
No. 4 enrolled May 24, 1900.
No's 1,2,3 and 4 originally enrolled on Choctaw Card #311, and
    transferred to this card Oct. 13, 1902.

Sept. 29, '98.

RESICENCE: Chickasaw Nation   ~~COUNTY~~   CARD NO.
POST OFFICE: Wiley, I.T.   FIELD NO.

NAME	RELATION-SHIP TO PERSON FIRST NAMED	AGE	SEX	BLOOD	TRIBAL ENROLLMENT		
					YEAR	COUNTY	PAGE
1 Fillmore, Jacon		28	M	1/2	1896	Pontotoc	59

TRIBAL ENROLLMENT OF PARENTS

NAME OF FATHER	YEAR	COUNTY	NAME OF MOTHER	YEAR	COUNTY
1 Millet Fillmore	Dead	Choc. Roll	Lottie Fillmore	Dead	Choc Roll

(NOTES)

No. 1 Husband of Selan Fillmore, Chickasaw Roll Card #832
No. 1 on Chickasaw Roll as Jacob Filmore
No. 1 originally enrolled on Choctaw Card #317 and transferred to this card Oct. 13, 1902.

RESIDENCE: Chickasaw Nation   ~~COUNTY~~   CARD NO.
POST OFFICE: Tishomingo, I.T.   P.O. Heavener 1/3/03   FIELD NO.

NAME	RELATION-SHIP TO PERSON FIRST NAMED	AGE	SEX	BLOOD	TRIBAL ENROLLMENT		
					YEAR	COUNTY	PAGE
1 Folsome, John		38	M	1/2	1896	Tishomingo	36

TRIBAL ENROLLMENT OF PARENTS

NAME OF FATHER	YEAR	COUNTY	NAME OF MOTHER	YEAR	COUNTY
1 Lorne Folsome		Blue	Rhoda Morris		Choc resid'g in Chick Dist.

(NOTES)

No. 1 on Chickasaw Roll as John Folsome
No. 1 Husband of Catherine Folsome, on Chickasaw Roll Card #805
No. 1 originally enrolled on Choctaw Card #312, and transferred to this card Oct. 13, 1902.

Sept. 29, 1898.

Chickasaw Enrollment Cards 1898-1914
Chickasaw by Blood   Volume V

RESIDENCE: Chickasaw Nation   ~~COUNTY~~   CARD NO.
POST OFFICE: Waupunuka, I.T.   FIELD NO.

NAME	RELATION-SHIP TO PERSON FIRST NAMED	AGE	SEX	BLOOD	TRIBAL ENROLLMENT		
					YEAR	COUNTY	PAGE
1 Fillmore, Silas	NAMED	24	M	3/4	1896	Pontotoc	58

TRIBAL ENROLLMENT OF PARENTS

NAME OF FATHER	YEAR	COUNTY	NAME OF MOTHER	YEAR	COUNTY
1 Millard Fillmore	Dead	Choc Roll	Lottie Fillmore	Dead	Choc. resid'g in Chick Dist.

(NOTES)

No. 1 on Chickasaw Roll as Silas Filmore
No. 1 Husband of Mary Ann Fillmore, Chickasaw Roll Card #888
No. 1 Originally enrolled on Choctaw Card #323, and
    transferred to this card Oct. 13, 1902.

Sept. 30, 1898.

RESIDENCE: Chickasaw Nation   ~~COUNTY~~   CARD NO.
POST OFFICE: Wiley, I.T.   FIELD NO.

NAME	RELATION-SHIP TO PERSON FIRST NAMED	AGE	SEX	BLOOD	TRIBAL ENROLLMENT		
					YEAR	COUNTY	PAGE
1 Fillmore, Elias	NAMED	40	M	1/2	1896	Pontotoc	59

TRIBAL ENROLLMENT OF PARENTS

NAME OF FATHER	YEAR	COUNTY	NAME OF MOTHER	YEAR	COUNTY
1 Millard Fillmore	Dead	Chick Roll	Maria Fillmore	Dead	Choc Roll

(NOTES)

No. 1 on Chickasaw Roll as Elias Filmore
No. 1 Husband of Epsie Fillmore, Chickasaw Roll Card #893
No. 1 Originally enrolled on Choctaw Card No. 324 and
    transferred to this card Oct. 13, 1902.

Sept. 30/98.

RESIDENCE: Chickasaw Nation   ~~COUNTY~~   CARD NO.
POST OFFICE: Norton, I.T.   FIELD NO.

	NAME	RELATION-SHIP TO PERSON FIRST NAMED	AGE	SEX	BLOOD	TRIBAL ENROLLMENT		
						YEAR	COUNTY	PAGE
1	Brandy, Johnson	NAMED	27	M	1/4	1896	Tishomingo	33
2	" Ada	Wife	18	F	I.W.	1896	"	33
3	" Dave	Son	5MO	M	1/8			

113

Chickasaw Enrollment Cards 1898-1914
Chickasaw by Blood   Volume V

TRIBAL ENROLLMENT OF PARENTS						
NAME OF FATHER	YEAR	COUNTY	NAME OF MOTHER	YEAR	COUNTY
1 John Brandy	Dead	Non Citizen	Sealy Brandy now Norton		Choc resid'g in Chick Dist.
2 Frank Caldwell		" "	Ada Caldwell	Dead	Non Citizen
3 No. 1			No. 2		

(NOTES)

No. 1 on Chickasaw Roll as Johnson Brandy
No. 2 name of, is Ada Catherine Brandy; See letter from her filed Oct. 1, 1901.
No. 2 Enrolled Aug. 12, 1899.
No. 3 Enrolled Oct. 1, 1901.
No's 1,2 & 3 Originally enrolled on Choctaw Card #329 and
    transferred to this card October 13, 1902.

Oct. 1, 1898

RESIDENCE: Chickasaw Nation   ~~COUNTY~~   CARD No.
POST OFFICE: Chickasha, I.T.   FIELD No.

NAME	RELATIONSHIP TO PERSON FIRST NAMED	AGE	SEX	BLOOD	TRIBAL ENROLLMENT		
					YEAR	COUNTY	PAGE
1 Perry, Charley	NAMED	23	M	1/2	1896	Panola	7

TRIBAL ENROLLMENT OF PARENTS						
NAME OF FATHER	YEAR	COUNTY	NAME OF MOTHER	YEAR	COUNTY
1 Levi Perry	Dead	Choc resid'g in Chick Dist.	Ellen Willis Pery	Dead	Choc resid'g in Chick Dist.

(NOTES)

No. 1 originally enrolled on Choctaw Card No. 331 and
    transferred to this card Oct. 13, 1902.

Oct. 1, 1898

RESIDENCE: Chickasaw Nation   ~~COUNTY~~   CARD No.
POST OFFICE: Tishomingo, I.T.   FIELD No.

NAME	RELATIONSHIP TO PERSON FIRST NAMED	AGE	SEX	BLOOD	TRIBAL ENROLLMENT		
					YEAR	COUNTY	PAGE
1 Chapman, Thomas Jefferson	NAMED	48	M	I.W.	1896	Pickens	79
2 " Susan	Wife	46	F	3/4	1896	Tishomingo	35
3 " Edward	Son	18	M	3/8	1896	"	35
4 " Ellen	Dau	15	F	3/8	1896	"	35
5 " James Thomas	Son	12	M	3/8	1896	"	34

6	"	John Napoleon		"	9	"	3/8	1896		"		34

TRIBAL ENROLLMENT OF PARENTS

	NAME OF FATHER	YEAR	COUNTY	NAME OF MOTHER	YEAR	COUNTY
1	G.W. Chapman	1897	Non citizen	Liza Chapman	Dead	Non Citizen
2	John E. Anderson	Dead	Tishomingo	Jincy Hayes	"	Tishomingo
3	No. 1			No. 2		
4	No. 1			No. 2		
5	No. 1			No. 2		
6	No. 1			No. 2		

(NOTES)

No. 1 See decision of June 13, '04.
No. 1 affidavit of Judge Brown as to License, to be supplied, Rec'd Oct. 21, '98.
No. 1 on Chickasaw Rolls as T.I. Chapman
No. 3 "   "   "   " Edmon "
No. 5 "   "   "   " James "
No. 6 "   "   "   " John   "
No's 1 to 6 inclusive originally enrolled on Choctaw Card #332 and
    transferred to this card Oct. 13, 1902.
Certified copy of divorce proceedings between Susan and Henry Norman filed April 8, 1903.

Oct. 1, 1898.

RESIDENCE: Chickasaw Nation	~~COUNTY~~				CARD NO.		
POST OFFICE: Buckchillo, I.T.					FIELD NO.		

NAME	RELATION-SHIP TO PERSON FIRST NAMED	AGE	SEX	BLOOD	TRIBAL ENROLLMENT		
					YEAR	COUNTY	PAGE
1 Thompson, Selena Isabella		8	F	1/2	1896	Tishomingo	35

TRIBAL ENROLLMENT OF PARENTS

	NAME OF FATHER	YEAR	COUNTY	NAME OF MOTHER	YEAR	COUNTY
1	Thos. B. Thompson	1897	Tishomingo Chick. Roll	Isabella Thompson	1897	Blue

(NOTES)

No. 1 On Chickasaw Roll "Selena Thompson" See Choc. Card #3807
No. 1 Originally enrolled on Choctaw Card No. 334 and
    transferred to this card Oct. 13, 1902.

Oct. 1, 1898.

Chickasaw Enrollment Cards 1898-1914
Chickasaw by Blood   Volume V

RESIDENCE: Chickasaw Nation   ~~COUNTY~~   CARD NO.

POST OFFICE: Marietta, I.T.   FIELD NO.

NAME	RELATION-SHIP TO PERSON FIRST NAMED	AGE	SEX	BLOOD	TRIBAL ENROLLMENT		
					YEAR	COUNTY	PAGE
1 East, Frances	NAMED	67	F	1/2	1896	Pickens	26
2 Green, Daniel	Son	24	M	1/4	1896	"	26
3 Adams, Charles	"	18	"	1/4	1896	"	26
4 East, Theophilus H.	Hus.	50	M	I.W.			

TRIBAL ENROLLMENT OF PARENTS

NAME OF FATHER	YEAR	COUNTY	NAME OF MOTHER	YEAR	COUNTY
1 Dave? Colbert	Dead	Chick Roll	Mamie Colbert	Dead	Choc Roll
2 Daniel Green	"	Non Citizen	No. 1		
3 Charles Adams	" "		No. 1		
4 Alvis H. East	Dead	"	Jane East	Dead	non citz.

(NOTES)

No. 1 on Chickasaw Roll as Francis East

No's 2 and 3 Originally enrolled on Choctaw Card #336 (and)
   transferred to this card Oct. 13, 1902.

No. 4 Enrolled by Department Chickasaw *(illegible)* - 1897 Transferred from
   Chickasaw Card No. C.209.

Oct. 3, 1898.

RESIDENCE: Chickasaw Nation   ~~COUNTY~~   CARD NO.

POST OFFICE: Johnson, I.T.   FIELD NO.

NAME	RELATION-SHIP TO PERSON FIRST NAMED	AGE	SEX	BLOOD	TRIBAL ENROLLMENT		
					YEAR	COUNTY	PAGE
1 Thompson, Minnie Lee	NAMED	24	F	1/4	1896	Pontotoc	61
2 " Mamie Francis	Dau	7	"	1/8	1896	"	61
3 " Robert Lee	Son	5	M	1/8	1896	"	61
4 " Charles William	"	3	"	1/8	1896	"	61
5 " Emma Augusta	Dau	1	F	1/8	1896	"	86
6 " Jessie May	"	5mo	"	1/8			

TRIBAL ENROLLMENT OF PARENTS

NAME OF FATHER	YEAR	COUNTY	NAME OF MOTHER	YEAR	COUNTY
1 Daniel Green	Dead	Non Citizen	Frances East		Choc. resid'g in Chic. Dist.
2 J.W. Thompson		White man	No. 1		
3 "		" "	No. 1		

4	"		" "		No. 1		
5	"		" "		No. 1		
6	"				No. 1		

(NOTES)

Granted May 23, 1905
No. 4 Dismissed Sep. 23, 1904
No. 1 on Chickasaw Roll as Minnie L. Thompson
No. 2 "   "   "   " Francis   "
No. 3 "   "   "   " R.L.   "
No. 4 "   "   "   " C.W.   " - was also admitted as a
    Chickasaw by blood by U.S. Court, Sou. Dist, Ind. Ter. March 12, 1898, in Court Case No. 54.
No. 5 Certificate of birth received and filed Aug. 24, 1900.
No. 6 Enrolled Nov. 1, 1899
No's 1 to 6 inclusive Originally enrolled on Choc. Card #338.
    Transferred to this Card Oct. 14, 1902.
Action of Commission of Sept. 23, 1904, rescinded May 23, 1905.
  See Chickasaw C. #9.   On Chickasaw Card Sept. 16, '98.
P.O. Okra, I.T. 1/28-04   "   Choctaw   "   Oct. 3, '98.

RESIDENCE: Chickasaw Nation   ~~COUNTY~~   **CARD NO.**

POST OFFICE: Marietta, I.T.   **FIELD NO.**

NAME	RELATIONSHIP TO PERSON FIRST NAMED	AGE	SEX	BLOOD	TRIBAL ENROLLMENT		
					YEAR	COUNTY	PAGE
1 Cochran, William Hunter	NAMED	30	M	1/4	1896	Pickens	26
2 " Willie	Dau	3	F	1/8	1896	"	26
3 " Vertis	"	8mo	"	1/8			
4 " Samuel F.	Son	9mo	M	1/8			
5 " Carrie	Wife	25	F	I.W.			

TRIBAL ENROLLMENT OF PARENTS

	NAME OF FATHER	YEAR	COUNTY	NAME OF MOTHER	YEAR	COUNTY
1	Samuel Hunter	Dead	Non Citizen	Frances East		Choc. resid'g in Chic. District
2	No. 1			Carrie Cochran		White woman
3	No. 1			" "		" "
4	No. 1			" "		" "
5	I.W. Hill		non citizen	Julie Hill		non citizen

(NOTES)

No. 1 on Chickasaw Roll as Hunter Cochran
    Evidence of marriage between No. 1 and Carrie E. Hill, a non Citizen filed 7/25/1901
No. 3 Evidence of birth received and filed Feb'y. 13, 1902.
No. 4 Enrolled July 2, 1901; See letter D.G. Bartlett as to given name of No. 4 filed July 16, 1901.

No's 1 to 4 inclusive Originally enrolled on Choctaw Card #341 (and)
   transferred to this card Oct. 14, 1902.
No. 1 is the Husband of Carrie Cochran on Choctaw Card #D.62
No. 5 transferred from Chickasaw card #D.62 Oct. 31, 1904. See decision of Oct. 15, 1904.

Oct. 3, 1898.

RESIDENCE: Chickasaw Nation   ~~COUNTY~~   CARD NO.

POST OFFICE: Lebanon, I.T. (Orphan Home)   FIELD NO.

NAME	RELATION-SHIP TO PERSON FIRST NAMED	AGE	SEX	BLOOD	TRIBAL ENROLLMENT		
					YEAR	COUNTY	PAGE
1 Kay, Minnie	NAMED	12	F	1/2	1896	Tishomingo	30

TRIBAL ENROLLMENT OF PARENTS

NAME OF FATHER	YEAR	COUNTY	NAME OF MOTHER	YEAR	COUNTY
1 Charles Kay	Dead	Non Citizen	Minnie Kay	Dead	Choc. Roll

(NOTES)

No. 1 on Chickasaw Roll as "Minnie Key"
No. 1 Originally enrolled on Choctaw Card No. 348
   Transferred to this card October 14, 1902.

Oct. 5, 1898.

RESIDENCE: Chickasaw Nation   ~~COUNTY~~   CARD NO.

POST OFFICE: Buckhorn, I.T.   FIELD NO.

NAME	RELATION-SHIP TO PERSON FIRST NAMED	AGE	SEX	BLOOD	TRIBAL ENROLLMENT		
					YEAR	COUNTY	PAGE
1 Kay, Charley	NAMED	6	M	1/2	1896	Tishomingo	27

TRIBAL ENROLLMENT OF PARENTS

NAME OF FATHER	YEAR	COUNTY	NAME OF MOTHER	YEAR	COUNTY
1 Charley Kay	Dead	Non Citizen	Minnie Kay	Dead	Choc. Roll

(NOTES)

No. 1 on Chickasaw Roll as Charley Key
 "   lives with W.C. Garrett, U.S. Citizen
No. 1 Originally enrolled on Choctaw Card No. 349;
   Transferred to this card Oct. 14, 1902.

Oct. 5, 1898.

118

RESIDENCE: Chickasaw Nation   ~~COUNTY~~   CARD NO.

POST OFFICE: Yarnaby, I.T.   FIELD NO.

NAME	RELATION-SHIP TO PERSON FIRST NAMED	AGE	SEX	BLOOD	TRIBAL ENROLLMENT		
					YEAR	COUNTY	PAGE
1 Perry, Eli	NAMED	41	M	1/2	1896	Panola	3
2 " Lillie Marie	Dau	3 1/2 mo	F	1/4			
3 " Hattie Lee	"	2mo	"	1/4			
4 " Carlos Troy	Son	4	M	1/4			

TRIBAL ENROLLMENT OF PARENTS

	NAME OF FATHER	YEAR	COUNTY	NAME OF MOTHER	YEAR	COUNTY
1	Morgan Perry	Dead	Panola Co. Chick Roll	Elizabeth Perry	Dead	Choc. resid'g in Chick Dist.
2	No. 1			Emma Perry		White woman
3	No. 1			" '		" "
4	No. 1			Amy Goldsberry		" "

(NOTES)

Evidence of marriage of No. 1 and Emma Byrd filed Jan. 2, 1901.

No. 2 Enrolled Jan. 2, 1901

No. 3 Born March 13, 1902; Enrolled May 1, 1902.

No's 1,2 and 3 Originally enrolled on Choctaw Card #352, (and)
    transferred to this card Oct. 14, 1902.

No. 4 Born Dec. 4, 1898; enrolled Dec. 24, 1902

No. 1 Evidence of marriage to mother of No. 4 filed Dec. 24, 1902.
    See affidavit of Eli Perry a to birth of No. 4 Jany. 26, 1903.

Oct. 10, 1898.

RESIDENCE: Chickasaw Nation   ~~COUNTY~~   CARD NO.

POST OFFICE: Silo, I.T.   FIELD NO.

NAME	RELATION-SHIP TO PERSON FIRST NAMED	AGE	SEX	BLOOD	TRIBAL ENROLLMENT		
					YEAR	COUNTY	PAGE
1 Kemp, Roberson	NAMED	59	M	Full	1896	Tishomingo	31

TRIBAL ENROLLMENT OF PARENTS

	NAME OF FATHER	YEAR	COUNTY	NAME OF MOTHER	YEAR	COUNTY
1	Reuben Kemp	Dead	Chick Roll	Becky Turnbull Kemp	Dead	Choc Roll.

(NOTES)

No. 1 Husband of Julia Kemp, Chickasaw Roll Card #1073

No. 1 Originally enrolled on Choctaw Card No. 354 and transferred to this card Oct. 13, 1902.

(Notation illegible)

119

Chickasaw Enrollment Cards 1898-1914
Chickasaw by Blood   Volume V

RESIDENCE: Blue   COUNTY   CARD NO.
POST OFFICE: Caddo, I.T.   FIELD NO.

NAME	RELATION-SHIP TO PERSON FIRST NAMED	AGE	SEX	BLOOD	TRIBAL ENROLLMENT		
					YEAR	COUNTY	PAGE
1 Maytubby, Samuel W.	NAMED	36	M	1/4	1896	Chick Roll Choc. Dist	74
2 " Lula A	Wife	33	F	I.W.			
3 " Samuel W., Jr.	Son	6	M	1/8	1896	Chick. Roll Choc. Dist.	74
4 " Floyd E.	"	4	"	1/8	1896	"	74
5 " Dudley	"	2	"	1/8	1896	"	74
6 " Inez Mabel	Dau	7mo	F	1/8			
7 " Kaliteo	"	3wks	"	1/8			

TRIBAL ENROLLMENT OF PARENTS

NAME OF FATHER	YEAR	COUNTY	NAME OF MOTHER	YEAR	COUNTY
1 Peter Maytubby		Chick resid'g in Blue Co	Melvina Maytubby	Dead	Blue
2 Jim Mebane	Dead	Non Citizen	Susan Mebane		Non Citizen
3 No. 1			No. 2		
4 No. 1			No. 2		
5 No. 1			No. 2		
6 No. 1			No. 2		
7 No. 1			No. 2		

(NOTES)

No. 1 on Chickasaw Roll as "S.W. Maytubby"   *(No. 2 Dawes' Roll No. 295)*
No. 6 For information as to death of, see letter of S.W. Maytubby dated Jan. 7, 1900.
No. 7 Born Dec. 30, 1899; On Choctaw Card #0.557. Transferred to Choctaw Card #355, May 24, 1902.
No's. 1 to 7 inclusive Originally enrolled on Choctaw Card #355 and
        transferre to this card Oct. 14, 1902.
See affidavit of LeRoy Long, M.D., as to physical inability of No. 2 to appear before Commission to give evidence as
        to status as intermarried Citizen Sept. 25, 1902, filed herein Nov. 19, 1902.

                                                            Oct. 10, 1898

RESIDENCE: Blue   COUNTY   CARD NO.
POST OFFICE: Caddo, I.T.   FIELD NO.

NAME	RELATION-SHIP TO PERSON FIRST NAMED	AGE	SEX	BLOOD	TRIBAL ENROLLMENT		
					YEAR	COUNTY	PAGE
1 Goforth, William H.	NAMED	37	M	1/2	1896	Choc. Dist.	72

2	" Mary	Dau	16	F	3/4	1896	"	"	72
3	" Alba	Wife	21	"	I.W.				
4	" Ora Emly	Dau	4mo	"	1/4				
5	" Lena May	"	5mo	"	1/4				

TRIBAL ENROLLMENT OF PARENTS

	NAME OF FATHER	YEAR	COUNTY	NAME OF MOTHER	YEAR	COUNTY
1	Solomon Goforth	1897	Chick resid'g in Choc. N. 3rd Dist.	Caroline Goforth	Dead	Blue
2	No. 1			Susie Goforth	"	"
3	Tom Wilfong		Non Citizen	Mary Wilfong		Non Citizen
4	No. 1			No. 3		
5	No. 1			No. 3		

(NOTES)

No. 1 on Chickasaw Roll as W.H. Goforth
No. 1 Father of children on Chickasaw Card #1098
No. 4 Enrolled June 7, 1900.
No. 5 Born Nov. 22, 1901; Enrolled April 22, 1902
No. 3 Enrolled Aug. 31, 1899
No's 1 to 5 inclusive originally enrolled on Choctaw Card No. 356
    Transferred to this card Oct. 14, 1902
No. 4 died Nov. 5, 1900; Proof filed Nov. 22, 1902.

Oct. 10, 1898

RESIDENCE:	Chickasaw Nation	COUNTY			CARD NO.			
POST OFFICE:	Kemp, I.T.				FIELD NO.			

NAME	RELATION-SHIP TO PERSON FIRST NAMED	AGE	SEX	BLOOD	TRIBAL ENROLLMENT		
					YEAR	COUNTY	PAGE
1 Rains, Catherine	NAMED	50	F	1/4	1896	Panola	6
2 " Bessie	Dau	9	"	1/8	1896	"	7

TRIBAL ENROLLMENT OF PARENTS

	NAME OF FATHER	YEAR	COUNTY	NAME OF MOTHER	YEAR	COUNTY
1	Morgan Perry	Dead	Choc Roll	Isabella Perry	Dead	Choc Roll
2	William Rains		Non citizen	No. 1		

(NOTES)

No's 1 and 2 Originally enrolled on Choctaw Card No. 358;
    Transferred to this card Oct. 14, 1902.

Oct. 10, 1898.

Chickasaw Enrollment Cards 1898-1914
Chickasaw by Blood   Volume V

RESIDENCE: Chickasaw Nation   ~~COUNTY~~   CARD NO.

POST OFFICE: Yarnaby, I.T.   FIELD NO.

NAME	RELATION-SHIP TO PERSON FIRST	AGE	SEX	BLOOD	TRIBAL ENROLLMENT		
					YEAR	COUNTY	PAGE
1 Perry, Henry Clay	NAMED	35	M	1/2	1896	Panola	1
2 " Emma Frank	Wife	34	F	I.W.	1896	"	76
3 " Willie Clay	Son	12	M	1/4	1896	"	1
4 " Minnie May	Dau	8	F	1/4	1896	"	1
5 " Frank Calvin	Son	3	M	1/4	1896	"	1
6 " Ray Morgan	"	16mo	"	1/4	1896	"	85
7 " John Henry	"	6mo	"	1/4			

TRIBAL ENROLLMENT OF PARENTS

	NAME OF FATHER	YEAR	COUNTY	NAME OF MOTHER	YEAR	COUNTY
1	Morgan Perry	Dead	Panola Co. Chick Roll	Elizabeth Perry	Dead	Choc resid'g in Chick. District
2	Frank Webb	"	Non Citizen	Polly Webb		Non Citizen
3	No. 1			No. 2		
4	No. 1			No. 2		
5	No. 1			No. 2		
6	No. 1			No. 2		
7	No. 1			No. 2		

(NOTES)

No. 1 on Chickasaw Roll as "H.C. Perry" Died Mch. 19, 1899; Proof of death filed Aug. 29, 1902.
No. 2 "   "   " " "E.F.   " "
No. 3 "   "   " " "W.C.   " "
No. 4 "   "   " " "Minnie " "
No. 5 "   "   " " "Frank " "
No. 7 Enrolled Nov. 1, 1899.
No's 1 to 7 inclusive Originally enrolled on Choctaw Card #360; Transferred to
    this card Oct. 14, 1902.
No. 6 Died March 9, 1899; Proof of death filed Nov. 6, 1902.

11/6 '02 PO Sterrett I.T.   Oct. 11, 1898.

RESIDENCE: Chickasaw Nation   ~~COUNTY~~   CARD NO.

POST OFFICE: Yarnaby, I.T.   FIELD NO.

NAME	RELATION-SHIP TO PERSON FIRST	AGE	SEX	BLOOD	TRIBAL ENROLLMENT		
					YEAR	COUNTY	PAGE
1 Connelly, John William	NAMED	37	M	1/2	1896	Panola	3

Chickasaw Enrollment Cards 1898-1914
Chickasaw by Blood   Volume V

2	"	Hannah	Wife	36	F	I.W.	1896	"	76
3	"	Elizabeth	Dau	14	"	1/4	1896	"	3
4	"	Alfred	Son	12	M	1/4	1896	"	3
5	"	William	"	11	"	1/4	1896	"	3
6	"	Henry N	"	9	"	1/4	1896	"	3
7	"	Jennie	Dau	6	F	1/4	1896	"	3
8	"	Emma May	"	5	"	1/4	1896	"	3
9	"	John W.	Son	3	M	1/4	1896	"	3
10	"	Irene	Dau	10mo	F	1/4			
11	"	James B.	Son	1mo	M	1/4			
12	"	Douglas H.	"	2mo	"	1/4			

TRIBAL ENROLLMENT OF PARENTS

	NAME OF FATHER	YEAR	COUNTY	NAME OF MOTHER	YEAR	COUNTY
1	Ish-kah-nah	Dead	Chick Roll	Elizabeth Hunter	Dead	Blue
2	Ambrose Powell	"	Non Citizen	Margaret Powell		Non Citizen
3	No. 1			No. 2		
4	No. 1			No. 2		
5	No. 1			No. 2		
6	No. 1			No. 2		
7	No. 1			No. 2		
8	No. 1			No. 2		
9	No. 1			No. 2		
10	No. 1			No. 2		
11	No. 1			No. 2		
12	No. 1			No. 2		

(NOTES)

No. 1 on Chick Roll as J.W. Connelly
No. 2 "   "   "   " Hannah Connely
No. 3 "   "   "   " Lizzie Connelly
No. 5 "   "   "   " Billie   "
No. 8 "   "   "   " Ema   "
No. 9 Evidence of birth received and filed Feby 21, 1902.
No. 11 Enrolled Nov. 1, 1899
No. 12 Born Nov. 30, 1901. Enrolled Feb'y 7, 1902.
No. 12 died Mch 14, 1902; Proof of death filed Nov. 8. 1902
No. 11 died Jan 19, 1902; Proof of death filed Nov. 8, 1902
Decision of Commission of Nov. 29, 1904 refusing No. 2
        affirmed by Secretary of Interior Jan. 9, 1905 (I.T.D. 13044-1904) (DC 2546-1905)
No's 1 to 12 inclusive Originally enrolled on Choctaw Card #364.
        Transferred to this card Oct. 14, 1902.

Oct. 11, 1898.

Chickasaw Enrollment Cards 1898-1914
Chickasaw by Blood   Volume V

RESIDENCE: Blue   COUNTY   CARD NO.
POST OFFICE: Cale, I.T.   FIELD NO.

NAME	RELATION-SHIP TO PERSON FIRST NAMED	AGE	SEX	BLOOD	TRIBAL ENROLLMENT		
					YEAR	COUNTY	PAGE
1 Moore, Mary Ellen	NAMED	25	F	1/2	1896	Choc. Dist.	75
2 " Harold	Son	11mo	M	1/4			
3 " Claude M	"	1mo	"	1/4			
4 " Floy	Dau	1mo	F	1/4			

TRIBAL ENROLLMENT OF PARENTS

	NAME OF FATHER	YEAR	COUNTY	NAME OF MOTHER	YEAR	COUNTY
1	Peter Maytubby	1897	Chick resid'g in Choc N. 3rd Dist.	Refina Maytubby	Dead	(Illegible)
2	John C. Moore		Non Citizen	No. 1		
3	" " "		" "	No. 1		
4	" " "		" "	No. 1		

(NOTES)

No. 1 on Chickasaw Roll as Mary Moore; Wife of John C. Moore on Chickasaw Card #1511,
No. 3 Enrolled Oct. 11, 1899.
No. 4 Born Dec. 13, 1901; Enrolled January 17, 1902.
No's 1,2,3 and 4 Originally enrolled on Choctaw Card No. 372; transferred to this card Oct. 14, 1902.

Oct. 12, 1898.

RESIDENCE: Chickasaw Nation   ~~COUNTY~~   CARD NO.
POST OFFICE: Yarnaby, I.T.   FIELD NO.

NAME	RELATION-SHIP TO PERSON FIRST NAMED	AGE	SEX	BLOOD	TRIBAL ENROLLMENT		
					YEAR	COUNTY	PAGE
1 Hamblin, Albert H.	NAMED	21	M	1/4	1896	Panola	5

TRIBAL ENROLLMENT OF PARENTS

	NAME OF FATHER	YEAR	COUNTY	NAME OF MOTHER	YEAR	COUNTY
1	Henry Hamblin (I.W.)		Blue	Mollie Hamblin	Dead	Choc resid'g in Chick. Dist.

(NOTES)

No. 1 was originally enrolled on Choctaw Card No. 276 and
    transferred to this card Oct. 14, 1902.

Oct. 12, 1898.

RESIDENCE: Blue   COUNTY   CARD No.

POST OFFICE: Durant, I.T.   FIELD No.

NAME	RELATION-SHIP TO PERSON FIRST NAMED	AGE	SEX	BLOOD	TRIBAL ENROLLMENT		
					YEAR	COUNTY	PAGE
1 Marshall, J. Horace	NAMED	23	M	I.W.			
2 " Lillie	Wife	20	F	1/8	1896	Panola	4
3 " Hazel	Dau	1	"	1/16			
4 " Colbert	Son	4mo	M	1/16			

TRIBAL ENROLLMENT OF PARENTS

	NAME OF FATHER	YEAR	COUNTY	NAME OF MOTHER	YEAR	COUNTY
1	Wm H. Marshall		Non Citizen	Martha Marshall		Non Citizen
2	Dan Colbert	Dead	Choc resid'g in Chick. District	Rebecca Colbert	I.W.	Choc resid'g in Chick District
3	No. 1			No. 2		
4	No. 1			No. 2		

(NOTES)

No. 2 on Chickasaw Roll as "Lillie Colbert"

No. 2 Correct way of spelling given name "Lyllie" See letter of No. 1 filed May 7, 1901.

No. 3 Enrolled Oct. 6, 1899

No. 4 Enrolled April 20, 1901

No's 1 to 4 inclusive originally enrolled on Choctaw Card#379.

    Transferred to this card Oct. 14, 1902.

11/10/02 PO Colbert, I.T.   Oct. 12, 1898.

RESIDENCE: Chickasaw Nation   ~~COUNTY~~   CARD No.

POST OFFICE: Kemp, I.T.   FIELD No.

NAME	RELATION-SHIP TO PERSON FIRST NAMED	AGE	SEX	BLOOD	TRIBAL ENROLLMENT		
					YEAR	COUNTY	PAGE
1 Shico, Martin	NAMED	27	M	1/4	1896	Panola	7

TRIBAL ENROLLMENT OF PARENTS

	NAME OF FATHER	YEAR	COUNTY	NAME OF MOTHER	YEAR	COUNTY
1	Charley Shico	Dead	Chick Roll	Catherine Rains		Choc resid'g in Chick District.

(NOTES)

No. 1 on Chickasaw Roll as "Bud Shico"

No. 1 Originally enrolled on Choctaw Card #383

    Transferred to this card Oct. 14, 1902.

Oct. 13, 1898.

RESIDENCE: Chickasaw Nation   ~~COUNTY~~   CARD NO.

POST OFFICE: Yarnaby, I.T.   FIELD NO.

	NAME	RELATION-SHIP TO PERSON FIRST NAMED	AGE	SEX	BLOOD	TRIBAL ENROLLMENT		
						YEAR	COUNTY	PAGE
1	Powell, Thomas Parter		37	M	I.W.	1896	Panola	83
2	" Ellen Jane	Wife	30	F	1/4	1896	"	1
3	" Annie Viola	Dau	13	"	1/8	1896	"	1
4	" Charles Ambrose	Son	11	M	1/8	1896	"	1
5	" Ray	Son	9	"	1/8	1896	"	1
6	" Rutha	Dau	5	F	1/8	1896	"	1
7	" Preston	Son	3	M	1/8	1896	"	1
8	" Mary	Dau	3mo	F	1/8			
9	" Thomas Clifford	Son	6mo	M	1/8			

TRIBAL ENROLLMENT OF PARENTS

	NAME OF FATHER	YEAR	COUNTY	NAME OF MOTHER	YEAR	COUNTY
1	Ambrose Powell	Dead	Non Citizen	Easter Powell	Dead	Non Citizen
2	Charley Shico	"	Chick Roll	Catherine Raines		Choc resid'g in Chick District.
3	No. 1			No. 2		
4	No. 1			No. 2		
5	No. 1			No. 2		
6	No. 1			No. 2		
7	No. 1			No. 2		
8	No. 1			No. 2		
9	No. 1			No. 2		

(NOTES)

No. 1 on Chickasaw Roll as T.B. Powell   *(No. 1 Dawes' Roll No. 179)*
No. 2 "   "   " " E.J. "
No. 3 "   "   " " Ola "
No. 4 "   "   " " Charles "
No. 9 Enrolled July 8, 1901
No's 1 to 9 inclusive originally enrolled on Choctaw Card No. 389.
    Transferred to this card Oct. 14, 1902.

12/10/02 PO Kemp I.T.   Oct. 13, 1898.

RESIDENCE: Blue   **COUNTY**   **CARD NO.**

POST OFFICE: Durant, I.T.   **FIELD NO.**

NAME	RELATION-SHIP TO PERSON FIRST NAMED	AGE	SEX	BLOOD	TRIBAL ENROLLMENT		
					YEAR	COUNTY	PAGE
1 Colbert, Charley	NAMED	35	M	1/4	1896	Panola	5
2 " Abbie	Wife	23	F	I.W.			

TRIBAL ENROLLMENT OF PARENTS

	NAME OF FATHER	YEAR	COUNTY	NAME OF MOTHER	YEAR	COUNTY
1	Jim Colbert	Dead	Chick Roll	?henius Colbert		Choc resid'g in Chick Dist.
2	John P. Davis		non citizen	Mary P. Davis		non citizen

(NOTES)

No. 1 Husband of Abbie Colbert on ~~Chickasaw~~ Choctw Card #D.762, July 22, 1902.

No. 1 Originally enrolled on Choctaw Card No. 394; Transferred to this card October 14, 1902.

No. 2 transferred from Choctaw card #D.762 Oct. 31, 1904; See decision of Oct. 15, 1904.

Oct. 13, '98.

RESIDENCE: Chickasaw Nation   ~~COUNTY~~   **CARD NO.**

POST OFFICE: Kemp, I.T.   **FIELD NO.**

NAME	RELATION-SHIP TO PERSON FIRST NAMED	AGE	SEX	BLOOD	TRIBAL ENROLLMENT		
					YEAR	COUNTY	PAGE
1 Shico, Robert	NAMED	25	M	1/4	1896	Panola	7

TRIBAL ENROLLMENT OF PARENTS

	NAME OF FATHER	YEAR	COUNTY	NAME OF MOTHER	YEAR	COUNTY
1	Charley Shico	Dead	Chick Roll	Catherine Raines		Choc resid'g in Chick District.

(NOTES)

No. 1 on Chickasaw Roll as "Rob Shico"

No. 1 originally enrolled on Choctaw Card #397;
    transferred to this card Oct. 14, 1902

No. 1 died Feb'y 1, 1899; Proof of death filed Nov. 6, 1902

Oct. 13, 1898.

CANCELLED Stamped across card
Died prior to Sept. 25, *(remainder illegible)*

RESIDENCE: Blue   COUNTY   CARD NO.

POST OFFICE: Caddo, I.T.   FIELD NO.

NAME	RELATION-SHIP TO PERSON FIRST	AGE	SEX	BLOOD	TRIBAL ENROLLMENT		
					YEAR	COUNTY	PAGE
1 Maytubby, Peter J.	NAMED	25	M	1/4	1896	Pontotoc	57

TRIBAL ENROLLMENT OF PARENTS

NAME OF FATHER	YEAR	COUNTY	NAME OF MOTHER	YEAR	COUNTY
1 Peter Maytubby	1897	Chick resid'g in Choc N. 3rd Dist.	Rafina Maytubby	Dead	Blue

(NOTES)

No. 1 Originally enrolled on Choctaw Card No. 398.
    Transferred to this card Oct. 14, 1902.

Oct. 14, 1898.

RESIDENCE: Chickasaw Nation   ~~COUNTY~~   CARD NO.

POST OFFICE: Colbert, I.T.   FIELD NO.

NAME	RELATION-SHIP TO PERSON FIRST	AGE	SEX	BLOOD	TRIBAL ENROLLMENT		
					YEAR	COUNTY	PAGE
1 Colbert, Cornie	NAMED	18	M	1/4	1896	Panola	4
2 " Lela	Sister	16	F	1/4	1896	"	4
3 Collins, Nancy	"	14	"	1/4	1896	"	4
4 Colbert, Rebecca	Mother	43	F	I.W.	1896	"	71

TRIBAL ENROLLMENT OF PARENTS

NAME OF FATHER	YEAR	COUNTY	NAME OF MOTHER	YEAR	COUNTY
1 David Colbert	Dead	Choc resid'g in Chick District	Rebecca Colbert		White woman
2 " "	"	"	" "		" "
3 " "	"	"	" "		" "
4 Charles Harris	"	non citizen	Rebecca Harris	dead	non citizen

(NOTES)

No. 1 on Chickasaw Roll as "Connie Colbert"

No's 1,2 and 3 Originally enrolled on Choctaw Card #401.
    Transferred to this card Oct. 14, 1902.

No. 3 is wife of Dan. Collins Chickasaw Roll Card No. 1122
    Evidence of marriage filed Dec. 24, 1902.

On Dec. 24, 1875, No. 4 was married to Dave Colbert, a recognized and enrolled citizen by blood of the Chick.
Nation; identified on the 1878 Chick Annuity Roll, Panola Co. #92 as David Colbert. Dave Colbert died in 1890.
No. 4 is identified on 1878 Chick Annuity Roll, Panola Co. #92 as the wife of David Colbert,
No. 4 "   "   " 1893 "   Pay Roll #2, page 8 as Mrs. Beckey Colbert.
No. 4 originally listed for enrollment on Choctqaw card D77; transferred to Chickasaw Card D.452 Feb. 7, 1903;

128

Chickasaw Enrollment Cards 1898-1914
Chickasaw by Blood   Volume V

transferred to this card Jan. 23, 1905. See decision of Jan. 7, 1905.

Oct. 14, '98.

RESIDENCE:	Chickasaw Nation	COUNTY				CARD NO.		
POST OFFICE:	Petersburg, I.T.					FIELD NO.		

	NAME	RELATION-SHIP TO PERSON FIRST NAMED	AGE	SEX	BLOOD	TRIBAL ENROLLMENT		
						YEAR	COUNTY	PAGE
1	Bourland, William Franklin		25	M	1/4	1896	Pickens	21
2	" James Patrick	Bro	21	M	1/4	1896	"	21
3	" Lulu Catherine	Sis	16	F	1/4	1896	"	21
4	" Lorinda Melvina	"	12	"	1/4	1896	"	21
5	" Robert Love	Bro	8	M	1/4	1896	"	21
6	" Michael Frazier	"	5	"	1/4	1896	"	21

TRIBAL ENROLLMENT OF PARENTS

	NAME OF FATHER	YEAR	COUNTY	NAME OF MOTHER	YEAR	COUNTY
1	William Howard Bourland	Dead	Chick Roll	Lorinda Melvina Bourland	Dead	Choc resid'g in Chock[sic] District
2	"			"		
3	"			"		
4	"			"		
5	"			"		
6	"			"		

(NOTES)

No. 1 on Chickasaw Roll as "W.F. Bourland"
No. 2 "   "   "   " "J.D.   "   "
No. 3 "   "   "   " "L.C.   "   "
No. 4 "   "   "   " "L.M.   "   "
No. 5 "   "   "   " "R.L   "   "
No. 6 "   "   "   " "M.F.   "   "
William Howard Bourland, father of 1,2,3,4,5,6 on Chickasaw Roll Card #1290.
Lorinda Melvina   "   mother " 1,2,3,4,5,6 "   Choctaw   "   " #417
No. 1 is now the Husband of Lulu Bynum on Chickasaw Card #919, Nov. 12, 1902.
No's 1 to 6 inclusive originally enrolled on Choctaw Card #417.
    Transferred to this card Oct. 14, 1902.

129

Chickasaw Enrollment Cards 1898-1914
Chickasaw by Blood   Volume V

RESIDENCE: Chickasaw Nation ~~COUNTY~~					CARD NO.		
POST OFFICE: Ryan, I.T.					FIELD NO.		

	NAME	RELATION-SHIP TO PERSON FIRST NAMED	AGE	SEX	BLOOD	TRIBAL ENROLLMENT		
						YEAR	COUNTY	PAGE
1	Ryan, Thomas Walker	NAMED	18	M	1/8	1896	Pickens	20
2	Campbell, Ada Pearl	Sister	16	F	1/8	1896	"	20
3	Ryan, Gussie Van Buren	"	14	F	1/8	1896	"	20
4	" Elbert Lewellyn	Bro	9	M	1/8	1896	"	20
5	Campbell, William G.	Son of No. 2	5mo	"	1/16			

TRIBAL ENROLLMENT OF PARENTS

	NAME OF FATHER	YEAR	COUNTY	NAME OF MOTHER	YEAR	COUNTY
1	Stephen Walker Ryan		White man	Carrie Cheadle Ryan	Dead	Choc Roll
2	" " "		"	"	"	" "
3	" " "		"	"	"	" "
4	" " "		"	"	"	" "
5	John E. Campbell		"	No. 2		

(NOTES)

No. 1 on Chickasaw Roll as "Tom Ryan"
No. 2 "   "   " " "Ada   " " Now the wife of John E. Campbell a Non Cit.
    Evidence of marriage filed Sept. 24, 1901
No. 3 On Chickasaw Roll as "Gussie Ryan"
No. 4 "   "   " " "Elbert   " "
No. 5 Enrolled Sept. 24, 1901
No's 1 to 5 inclusive originally enrolled on Choctaw Card No. 438 (and)
    transferred to this card Oct. 14, 1902.

Oct. 20, 1898

RESIDENCE: Blue COUNTY					CARD NO.		
POST OFFICE: Caddo, I.T.					FIELD NO.		

	NAME	RELATION-SHIP TO PERSON FIRST NAMED	AGE	SEX	BLOOD	TRIBAL ENROLLMENT		
						YEAR	COUNTY	PAGE
1	Goforth, Levi P.	NAMED	27	M	1/4	1896	Choc Dist.	74

TRIBAL ENROLLMENT OF PARENTS

	NAME OF FATHER	YEAR	COUNTY	NAME OF MOTHER	YEAR	COUNTY
1	Solomon Goforth		Chick resid'g in Choc N. 3rd Dist.	Caroline Goforth	Dead	Choc Roll

(NOTES)

130

No. 1 on Chickasaw Roll as "L.P. Goforth"
No. 1 Originally enrolled on Choctaw Card #449;
   Transferred to this Card Oct. 14, 1902.
No. 1 died May, 1899; Proof of death filed Nov. 1, 1902.

Nov. 24, 1898.

CANCELLED Stamped across card
Died prior to Sept. *(remainder illegible)*

RESIDENCE: Blue   COUNTY   CARD NO.
POST OFFICE: Caddo, I.T.   FIELD NO.

NAME	RELATION-SHIP TO PERSON FIRST NAMED	AGE	SEX	BLOOD	TRIBAL ENROLLMENT		
					YEAR	COUNTY	PAGE
1 Goforth, Joe H.	NAMED	25	M	1/4	1896	Choc Dist	74
2 " Jessie	Dau	1	F	1/8			

TRIBAL ENROLLMENT OF PARENTS

	NAME OF FATHER	YEAR	COUNTY	NAME OF MOTHER	YEAR	COUNTY
1	Solomon Goforth		Chick resid'g in Choc N. 3rd Dist.	Caroline Goforth	Dead	Choc Roll
2	No. 1			Cordelia Goforth		Non Citizen

(NOTES)
No. 1 Originally enrolled on Choctaw Card No. 450;
   transferred to this card Oct. 14, 1901.
No. 2 Born Sept. 15, 1901; enrolled Nov. 24, 1902.
No. 1 Now Husband of Cordelia Goforth, non Citizen;
   Evidence of marriage requested Nov. 24, 1902. Received and filed Dec. 5, 1902.
Cordelia Goforth, wife of No. 1 is on Choctaw Card R.#214 as Cordelia Nelson.

Nov. 24, '98.

RESIDENCE: Chickasaw Nation   ~~COUNTY~~   CARD NO.
POST OFFICE: Wayne, I.T.   FIELD NO.

NAME	RELATION-SHIP TO PERSON FIRST NAMED	AGE	SEX	BLOOD	TRIBAL ENROLLMENT		
					YEAR	COUNTY	PAGE
1 Seifried, William	NAMED	24	M	1/4	1896	Pontotoc	62
2 " Eula Beatrice	Dau	1wk	F	1/8			

TRIBAL ENROLLMENT OF PARENTS

	NAME OF FATHER	YEAR	COUNTY	NAME OF MOTHER	YEAR	COUNTY
1	Wm F. Seifried	Dead	Non citizen	Julia Seifried	Dead	Choc Roll
2	No. 1			Mary F. Seifried		

Chickasaw Enrollment Cards 1898-1914
Chickasaw by Blood   Volume V

(NOTES)

No. 1 on Chickasaw Roll as Willie Seifried; wife, Mary L. Seifried, on Card #D.519.   *(No. 2 Dawes' Roll No. 710)*

No. 1 was admitted by Dawes Commission in 1896 as a Chickasaw by blood, Chickasaw Case #270. No appeal.

No. 1 on Chickasaw Card Sept. 14. 1898; On Choctaw Card #4933, Nov. 18, 1899.

No. 1 Correct name is William T. Seifried; See letter of April 24, 1901; filed 5/2, '01

No. 2 Enrolled April 20, 1901

No. 1 & 2 Originally enrolled on Choctaw Card No. 4933 (and)
         transferred to this card Oct. 14, 1902.

Certified copy of marriage license and certificate of No. 1 and mother[sic] received and filed March 27, 1903.

P.O. Purcell, I.T.

RESIDENCE: Chickasaw Nation	~~COUNTY~~				CARD NO.		
POST OFFICE: Wayne, I.T.					FIELD NO.		

	NAME	RELATION-SHIP TO PERSON FIRST NAMED	AGE	SEX	BLOOD	TRIBAL ENROLLMENT		
						YEAR	COUNTY	PAGE
1	Seifried, Minnie	NAMED	23	F	1/4	1896	Pontotoc	62
2	" Henry	Bro	19	M	1/4	1896	"	62
3	" Charley	"	17	"	1/4	1896	"	62
4	" Mattie	Sister	14	F	1/4	1896	"	62
5	" Mary	"	12	"	1/4	1896	"	62
6	" Lucy	"	10	"	1/4	1896	"	62

TRIBAL ENROLLMENT OF PARENTS

	NAME OF FATHER	YEAR	COUNTY	NAME OF MOTHER	YEAR	COUNTY
1	William F. Seifried	Dead	Non Citizen	Julia Seifried	Dead	Choc Roll
2	"	"	" "	" "	"	" "
3	"	"	" "	" "	"	" "
4	"	"	" "	" "	"	" "
5	"	"	" "	" "	"	" "
6	"	"	" "	" "	"	" "

(NOTES)

No's 1,2,4,5 and 6 admitted by Dawes Commission in 1896 as Chickasaws by blood; Chickasaw Card 270; No appeal.

No. 6 on Chickasaw Roll as "Lula Seifried:

All on Chickasaw Card Sept. 1, 1899; On Choctaw Card #4934; Nov. 18, 1899.

No. 1 to 6 inclusive originally enrolled on Choctaw Card No. 4934 (and)
         transferred to this card Oct. 14, 1902.

No. 2 is now the Husband of Emma Seifried on Choc. Card #D.816. Oct. 21, '02

RESIDENCE: Pontotoc COUNTY   CARD NO.
POST OFFICE: Stonewall, I.T.   FIELD NO.

NAME	RELATION-SHIP TO PERSON FIRST NAMED	AGE	SEX	BLOOD	TRIBAL ENROLLMENT		
					YEAR	COUNTY	PAGE
1 Rowe, Letitia	NAMED	21	F	3/8	1896	Pontotoc	49
2 " Rena	Dau	3mo	"	3/16			
3 " Alaric	Son	11/2 mo	M	3/16			

TRIBAL ENROLLMENT OF PARENTS

	NAME OF FATHER	YEAR	COUNTY	NAME OF MOTHER	YEAR	COUNTY
1	Wood Smith I.W.	1896	Pontotoc	Rena Smith	1896	Pontotoc
2	Clyde Rowe		White man	No. 1		
3	" "		" "	No. 1		

(NOTES)

No. 1 on Chickasaw Roll as Leticia Smith
No. 1 For Citizenship of mother see Choctaw Card #307.
No. 1 Correct way of spelling given name is "Letitia" See letter of her parents on file - 4/27, '01.
No. 3 enrolled April 27, 1901.
No's 1,2 and 3 originally enrolled on Choctaw Card #4935;
    Transferred to this card Oct. 14, 1902.

RESIDENCE: Chickasaw Nation COUNTY   CARD NO.
POST OFFICE: Pontotoc, I.T.   FIELD NO.

NAME	RELATION-SHIP TO PERSON FIRST NAMED	AGE	SEX	BLOOD	TRIBAL ENROLLMENT		
					YEAR	COUNTY	PAGE
1 Lewis, Serena	NAMED	45	F	Full	1896	Pontotoc	56

TRIBAL ENROLLMENT OF PARENTS

	NAME OF FATHER	YEAR	COUNTY	NAME OF MOTHER	YEAR	COUNTY
1	Chafatubby	Dead	Chickasaw	Iney	Dead	Chickasaw

(NOTES)

This woman appears to be a delinquent and says she drew money in 1893 under name of Serena Colbert.

Nov. 11, 1902.

Chickasaw Enrollment Cards 1898-1914
Chickasaw by Blood   Volume V

RESIDENCE: Chickasaw Nation   ~~COUNTY~~   CARD NO.

POST OFFICE: Berwyn, I.T.   FIELD NO.

	NAME	RELATION-SHIP TO PERSON FIRST NAMED	AGE	SEX	BLOOD	TRIBAL ENROLLMENT		
						YEAR	COUNTY	PAGE
1	Morris, Wharton H	NAMED	55	M	I.W.	1896	Pickens	77
2	" Elizabeth	Wife	50	F	1/8	1896	"	20
3	" Joseph Daniel	Son	24	M	1/16	1896	"	20
4	" Catherine	Dau	12	F	1/16	1896	"	20
5	" Lilla	"	9	"	1/16	1896	"	20
6	" Lena	"	5	"	1/16	1896	"	20
7	" Lena	Dau of No. 3	1	"	1/32			

TRIBAL ENROLLMENT OF PARENTS

	NAME OF FATHER	YEAR	COUNTY	NAME OF MOTHER	YEAR	COUNTY
1	Jonathan Morris	Dead	Non Citizen	Mary Morris	Dead	Non Citizen
2	Joseph D. Harris	"	Chic Roll	Catherine Nail Harris	"	Choc Roll
3	No. 1			No. 2		
4	No. 1			No. 2		
5	No. 1			No. 2		
6	No. 1			No. 2		
7	No. 3			Maggie Morris		non citizen

(NOTES)

No. 1 married in 1864 to Choctaw woman   *(No. 1 Dawes' Roll No. 556)*
No. 2 on 1896 Roll as "Lizzie"   *(No. 7 Dawes' Roll No. 4966)*
No. 3 "   "   "   " "Joseph"
No. 4 "   "   "   " "Kittie"
No's 1 to 6 inclusive originally enrolled on Choctaw Card #255;
       Transferred to this card November 11, 1902.
See affidavit of Minerva Waldran, former wife of No. 1, as to her divorce from No. 1; filed April 13, 1903
No. 7 Born Sept. 23, 1902; application received April 10, 1905, under Act of Congress, approved March 3, 1905.
       Evidence of marriage of parents filed May 22, 1905, 9 N.B. 231.

P.O. Roff, I.T.

Chickasaw Enrollment Cards 1898-1914
Chickasaw by Blood   Volume V

RESIDENCE: Chickasaw Nation   ~~COUNTY~~   CARD NO.

POST OFFICE: FIELD NO.

NAME	RELATION-SHIP TO PERSON FIRST NAMED	AGE	SEX	BLOOD	TRIBAL ENROLLMENT		
					YEAR	COUNTY	PAGE
1 Anderson, Martha	NAMED	24	F	Full	1897	Pontotoc	54
2 Perry, Isaac	Son	4	M	1/2	1897	"	54

TRIBAL ENROLLMENT OF PARENTS

NAME OF FATHER	YEAR	COUNTY	NAME OF MOTHER	YEAR	COUNTY
1 McKee King	Dead	Blue		Dead	Choctaw
2 Houston Perry	"	Chickasaw	No. 1		

(NOTES)

No. 1 wife of Rogers Anderson - Chickasaw - Transferred to Choctaw Roll by Dawes Commission
No's 1 and 2 originally enrolled on Choctaw Card No. 4951 (and)
    transferred to this card Nov. 20, 1902.
No. 2 died June 29, 1901; Proof of death filed December 5, 1902.

P.O. Connerville   Dec. 8, 1899.

RESIDENCE: COUNTY   CARD NO.

POST OFFICE: Guertie, I.T   FIELD NO.

NAME	RELATION-SHIP TO PERSON FIRST NAMED	AGE	SEX	BLOOD	TRIBAL ENROLLMENT		
					YEAR	COUNTY	PAGE
1 Lewis, Hullicher	NAMED	40	F	1/2	1896	Choc District	70

TRIBAL ENROLLMENT OF PARENTS

NAME OF FATHER	YEAR	COUNTY	NAME OF MOTHER	YEAR	COUNTY
1 John Docker	Dead	Creek	Onati	Dead	Chickasaw

(NOTES)

No. 1 is wife of John Lewis on Choctaw Card #4941.
No. 1 is mother of Thompson and Dickson Lewis on Choctaw Card #5385
Also of Ellen Lewis on Choctaw Card #5502, and Martha Colbert on Chickasaw Card No. 28?

RESIDENCE: Cedar   COUNTY   CARD NO.

POST OFFICE: Antlers, I.T.   FIELD NO.

NAME	RELATION-SHIP TO PERSON FIRST NAMED	AGE	SEX	BLOOD	TRIBAL ENROLLMENT		
					YEAR	COUNTY	PAGE
1 Cheadle, Margaret	NAMED	56	F	I.W.	1897	Tishomingo	92

TRIBAL ENROLLMENT OF PARENTS					
NAME OF FATHER	YEAR	COUNTY	NAME OF MOTHER	YEAR	COUNTY
1 Andy Jones		non-citizen	Mary Jones		non citizen

(NOTES)

As to marriage see affidavit of John Ward and Mrs. Sarah York

Also see testimony of herself

No. 1 originally enrolled on Choctaw card #4601; transferred to this card Dec. 11, 1902.

No. 1 formerly wife of Thomas Cheadle, a recognized Chickasaw by blood who died about 1872.

Sept. 6/99.

RESIDENCE: Choctaw Nation   **COUNTY**   **CARD NO.**

POST OFFICE: Bower, I.T.   **FIELD NO.**

NAME	RELATION-SHIP TO PERSON FIRST NAMED	AGE	SEX	BLOOD	TRIBAL ENROLLMENT		
					YEAR	COUNTY	PAGE
1 Kanawa, Louana	FIRST NAMED	18	F	1/2	1893	Chick in Choc Nation Ieshatubby Roll	3
2 " Albert	Bro	16	M	1/2	1893	" "	3

TRIBAL ENROLLMENT OF PARENTS					
NAME OF FATHER	YEAR	COUNTY	NAME OF MOTHER	YEAR	COUNTY
1 Conawah Harjo	dead	Chickasaw	Unknown	dead	Creek
2 " "	"	"	"	"	"

(NOTES)

No's 1 and 2 are wards of Richard P. Jennings on Choctaw card #4760.

Dec. 5, 1902.

RESIDENCE: Pontotoc **COUNTY**   **CARD NO.**

POST OFFICE: Mill Creek, I.T.   **FIELD NO.**

NAME	RELATION-SHIP TO PERSON FIRST NAMED	AGE	SEX	BLOOD	TRIBAL ENROLLMENT		
					YEAR	COUNTY	PAGE
1 Finley, Mary C.	NAMED	31	F	12	1897	Pontotoc	48
2 Ragland, Wm Nathan	Son	13	M	1/4	1897	"	48
3 " Walter D.	Son	12	M	1/4	1897	"	48
4 " Roy Nelson	Son	6	M	1/4	1897	"	48
5 Finley, Rosa Lorina	Dau	3	F	1/4			
6 " Emma Elzada	Dau	1	F	1/4			

Chickasaw Enrollment Cards 1898-1914
Chickasaw by Blood   Volume V

	TRIBAL ENROLLMENT OF PARENTS						
	NAME OF FATHER	YEAR	COUNTY	NAME OF MOTHER	YEAR	COUNTY
1	Tisheotomey Brown	Dead	Chickasaw roll	Lottie Wilson	Dead	Cherokee Indian
2	J.W. Ragland		non citizen	No. I		
3	" "		" "	No. I		
4	" "		" "	No. I		
5	J.B. Finley		" "	No. I		
6	" "		" "	No. I		

(NOTES)

No's I-4 inclusive children of J.W. Ragland on Chickasaw Roll
No. I now wife of J.B. Finley, a non-citizen
No. I on Chickasaw roll as M.C. Ragland
No. 2 "   "   " " William "

Dec. 5, 1902

RESIDENCE: U.S. Penitentiary   COUNTY   CARD NO.
POST OFFICE: Columbus, Ohio   FIELD NO.

NAME	RELATION-SHIP TO PERSON FIRST NAMED	AGE	SEX	BLOOD	TRIBAL ENROLLMENT		
					YEAR	COUNTY	PAGE
1 James, Felsie		65	F	Full	1897	Pontotoc	94

	TRIBAL ENROLLMENT OF PARENTS						
	NAME OF FATHER	YEAR	COUNTY	NAME OF MOTHER	YEAR	COUNTY
1	(This line blank microfilm)					

(NOTES)

No. I on 1893 Leased District payment roll No. 2, page 123 as Filsey James.
No. I also on 1897 Chickasaw roll page 94, as Filsie James in a list of names of citizens of the Chickasaw Nation
    found on roll of 1893 but not on the 1896 roll.
No. 2 is serving life sentence for murder, in Penitentiary at Columbus, Ohio.
    See testimony of William M. Cravens taken May 20, 1902.

December 17, 1902.

RESIDENCE: Cherokee Nation   COUNTY   CARD NO.
POST OFFICE: Fairland, I.T.   FIELD NO.

	NAME	RELATION-SHIP TO PERSON FIRST NAMED	AGE	SEX	BLOOD	TRIBAL ENROLLMENT		
						YEAR	COUNTY	PAGE
1	Ford, Mollie Willis		34	F	1/16	1896	Pickens	22
2	" Mollie Willis, Jr.	Dau	9	F	1/32	1896	"	22
3	" Hugh W.	Son	5	M	1/32	1896	"	22

137

| 4 | "   John J. | | Son | 1 1/2 | M | 1/32 | | | |

TRIBAL ENROLLMENT OF PARENTS

	NAME OF FATHER	YEAR	COUNTY	NAME OF MOTHER	YEAR	COUNTY
1	John Willis	Dead	Chickasaw	Elizabeth Willis	Dead	Cherokee
2	W.H. Ford		non-citizen	No. 1		
3	" "		" "	No. 1		
4	" "		" "	No. 1		

(NOTES)

No. 1 on 1896 Chickasaw roll as Mollie Willis Ford
No. 2 "   "   "   "   " Mollie Willis Ford, jr.
No. 3 "   "   "   "   " Wm H. Ford, jr.
No. 1 on Chickasaw pay roll 1893, Pickens County page 81 as M.W. Ford
No. 2 "   "   "   "   "   "   "   "   " M.W. Ford, jr
No. 3 "   "   "   "   "   "   "   "   " H.W. Ford

P.O. Sulphur Springs   December 17, 1902.

| RESIDENCE: Pontotoc   COUNTY | | CARD NO. | |
| POST OFFICE: Center, Ind. Ter. | | FIELD NO. | |

NAME	RELATION- SHIP TO PERSON FIRST NAMED	AGE	SEX	BLOOD	TRIBAL ENROLLMENT		
					YEAR	COUNTY	PAGE
1 Moif, Emily H	NAMED	47	F	1/2	1893	Pontotoc	P.R.#2 102

TRIBAL ENROLLMENT OF PARENTS

	NAME OF FATHER	YEAR	COUNTY	NAME OF MOTHER	YEAR	COUNTY
1	Elijah Green	Dead	non citizen	Siney Coob	Dead	Chickasaw roll

(NOTES)

On Chickasaw roll as Emily A. Hudson.

December, 1902.

| RESIDENCE: Cherokee Nation   ~~COUNTY~~ | | CARD NO. | |
| POST OFFICE: Webber Falls, I.T. | | FIELD NO. | |

NAME	RELATION- SHIP TO PERSON FIRST	AGE	SEX	BLOOD	TRIBAL ENROLLMENT		
					YEAR	COUNTY	PAGE
1 Watson, Noah	NAMED	39	M	Full	1896	Choc Dist.	72
2 " Jigj O	Son	0	M	12	1896	" "	72

Chickasaw Enrollment Cards 1898-1914
Chickasaw by Blood   Volume V

TRIBAL ENROLLMENT OF PARENTS

	NAME OF FATHER	YEAR	COUNTY	NAME OF MOTHER	YEAR	COUNTY
1	Bob Watson	Dead	Chickasaw roll	Ah-lah-ree	Dead	Chickasaw roll
2	No. 1			Emily Watson		white *(illegible)* Cherokee

(NOTES)

No. 1 on 1896 Chickasaw roll page 72 as Noah Waters
No. 2 "   "   "   "   "   "   " Hughie Waters
No. 1 has lived in Cherokee Nation fifteen years
No. 1 also on Chickasaw 1897 roll page 92 as Noll Watson
No. 1 on Chickasaw pay roll of 1893 as Noel Watson.

December 17, 1902.

RESIDENCE: Tobucksy   COUNTY   CARD NO.
POST OFFICE: Calvin I.T.   FIELD NO.

NAME	RELATION-SHIP TO PERSON	AGE	SEX	BLOOD	TRIBAL ENROLLMENT		
					YEAR	COUNTY	PAGE
1 Leader, Edward	FIRST NAMED	58	M	Full	1896	Choctaw Nation First District	71

TRIBAL ENROLLMENT OF PARENTS

	NAME OF FATHER	YEAR	COUNTY	NAME OF MOTHER	YEAR	COUNTY
1	Jim Leader	Dead	Gaines	Nancy Leader	Dead	Tobucksy

(NOTES)

No. 1 is father of Hepsie Leader on Creek card field No. 2486.
No. 1 "   "   " Nancy Leader "   "   "   "   " 2300.
No. 1 "   "   " Emma Leader "   "   "   "   " 2299
No. 1 "   "   " Barney Leader "   "   "   "   " 2236
No. 1 originally on Choctaw card #3275;
        transferred to this card December 31, 1902

RESIDENCE: Choctaw Nation   COUNTY   CARD NO.
POST OFFICE: Tushkahomma I.T.   FIELD NO.

NAME	RELATION-SHIP TO PERSON	AGE	SEX	BLOOD	TRIBAL ENROLLMENT		
					YEAR	COUNTY	PAGE
1 Anderson, Osborne	FIRST NAMED	14	M	Full	1896	Chickasaw residing in Choctaw Nation 3rd Dist.	73

Chickasaw Enrollment Cards 1898-1914
Chickasaw by Blood   Volume V

TRIBAL ENROLLMENT OF PARENTS						
NAME OF FATHER	YEAR	COUNTY	NAME OF MOTHER	YEAR	COUNTY
1 Cranford Anderson		Choctaw	Lottie Tupper		Chickasaw residing in Choc Nation

(NOTES)

Mother of No. 1 is Lottie Hiheha, Chickasaw card #?
   See her testimony Dec. 11, 1902.

Dec. 11, 1902.

RESIDENCE:	COUNTY					CARD NO.		
POST OFFICE: Wapanucka						FIELD NO.		

NAME	RELATION-SHIP TO PERSON FIRST	AGE	SEX	BLOOD	TRIBAL ENROLLMENT		
					YEAR	COUNTY	PAGE
1 Taylor, Stephen Lee	NAMED	28	M	I.W.			
2 " Mary Ann	Wife	22	F	3/4	1896	Pontotoc	51

TRIBAL ENROLLMENT OF PARENTS						
NAME OF FATHER	YEAR	COUNTY	NAME OF MOTHER	YEAR	COUNTY
1 W.A. Taylor		non citizen	Eliz. Taylor	Dead	non citizen
2 McKee James		Chick Dist	Rhoena James		Chick Dist.

(NOTES)

No. 2 on 1896 Chickasaw roll as Mary James   *(No. 1 Dawes' Roll No. 492)*
Nos. 1-2 originally enrolled on Choctaw card #4451;
   Transferred to this caard January 13, 1903.

Jan. 13, 1903.

RESIDENCE: Chickasaw Nation	~~COUNTY~~					CARD NO.		
POST OFFICE: Ardmore, Ind. Ter.						FIELD NO.		

NAME	RELATION-SHIP TO PERSON FIRST	AGE	SEX	BLOOD	TRIBAL ENROLLMENT		
					YEAR	COUNTY	PAGE
1 Brown, Charles A	NAMED	41	M	1/4	1896	Pickens	25
2 " ~~Josephine~~	~~Wife~~	~~39~~	~~F~~	~~I.W.~~	~~1896~~	~~"~~	~~74~~
3 " Nathaniel	Son	18	M	1/8	1896	"	25
4 ~~Lindsey, Ethel~~	~~Dau~~	~~16~~	~~F~~	~~1/8~~	~~1896~~	~~"~~	~~25~~
5 Elmore, Sorena	"	14	F	1/8	1896	"	25
6 Brown, Martin E.	Son	10	M	1/8	1896	"	25
7 " Martha J	Dau	5	F	1/8	1896	"	25
8 " Joe E.	Son	5mo	M	1/8			
9 Elmore, Floyd Lee	G.Son	1mo	M	1/16			

Chickasaw Enrollment Cards 1898-1914
Chickasaw by Blood   Volume V

10	Lindsey, Gracie	G.Dau	4mo	F	1/16			
11	Brown, Bessie A.	Dau ~~Son~~	8mo	F ~~M~~	1/8			

TRIBAL ENROLLMENT OF PARENTS

	NAME OF FATHER	YEAR	COUNTY	NAME OF MOTHER	YEAR	COUNTY
1	Joshua Brown	Dead	Chickasaw roll	Nancy Curtis Brown	Dead	Choctaw roll
2	~~Jim Kemp Refused~~	"	~~non-citizen~~		"	~~non-citizen~~
3	No. 1			No. 2		
4	~~No. 1~~			~~No. 2~~		
5	No. 1			No. 2		
6	No. 1			No. 2		
7	No. 1			No. 2		
8	No. 1			No. 2		
9	Geo. M. Elmore		non-citizen	No. 5		
10	B.H. Lindsey			No. 4		
11	No. 1			No. 2		

(NOTES)

No's 1 to 11 inclusive originally enrolled on Choctaw Card 259;
transferred to this card Jan. 29, 1903.

No. 4 on Chickasaw roll as Etta Brown; Is now the wife of B.H. Lindsey, a non-citizen. Evidence of marriage filed Sept. 27, 1901.

No. 5 on Chickasaw roll as Rena Brown; Is now the wife of Geo. M. Elmore, a non-citizen. Evidence of marriage filed Sept. 27, 1901.

No. 9 Enrolled Sept. 21, 1901.

No. 10 Born Dec. 2, 1901. Enrolled Dec. 27, 1901.

No. 11 Born Dec. 23, 1901. Enrolled July 31, 1902.

Nos. 1 & 2 marriage certificate destroyed; affidavit of some outside party as to their having lived together and been recognized as a man and wife to be supplied. Received Sept. 23/98.
Sept. 23/98.

(No. 1 Dawes' Roll No. 4774)
(No. 3 Dawes' Roll No. 4775)
(No. 4 Dawes' Roll No. 4776)
(No. 5 Dawes' Roll No. 4777)
(No. 6 Dawes' Roll No. 4778)
(No. 7 Dawes' Roll No. 4779)
(No. 8 Dawes' Roll No. 4780)
(No. 9 Dawes' Roll No. 4781)
(No. 10 Dawes' Roll No. 4782)
(No. 11 Dawes' Roll No. 4783)

RESIDENCE: Chickasaw Nation   ~~COUNTY~~   **CARD NO.**

POST OFFICE: Tishomingo Ind. Ter.   **FIELD NO.**

	NAME	RELATIONSHIP TO PERSON FIRST NAMED	AGE	SEX	BLOOD	TRIBAL ENROLLMENT		
						YEAR	COUNTY	PAGE
1	Kemp, Elizabeth Minerva	NAMED	35	F	1/4	1896	Tishomingo	34
2	" Theodocia Abagail	Dau	19	"	1/8	1896	"	34
3	" Eli Clem	Son	12	M	1/8	1896	"	34
4	" James Earl	"	10	"	1/8	1896	"	34
5	" Frances Elizabeth	Dau	8	F	1/8	1896	"	33
6	" Mary Montressa	"	5	"	1/8	1896	"	33

| 7 | " | Raymond Herrel | Son | 2 | M | 1/8 | 1896 | | " | | 33 |
| 8 | " | Joe L. | " | 9mo | " | 1/8 | | | | | |

TRIBAL ENROLLMENT OF PARENTS

	NAME OF FATHER	YEAR	COUNTY	NAME OF MOTHER	YEAR	COUNTY
1	Morgan Perry	Dead	Chickasaw roll	Isabel Perry	Dead	Choctaw roll
2	Joel Carr Kemp		Chick residing in Tishomingo Co.	No. 1		
3	" " "		"	No. 1		
4	" " "		"	No. 1		
5	" " "		"	No. 1		
6	" " "		"	No. 1		
7	" " "		"	No. 1		
8	" " "		"	No. 1		

(NOTES)

No. 1 on Chickasaw roll as E.M. Kemp   *(No. 1 Dawes' Roll No. 4054)*
No. 2 on Chickasaw roll as Theo Docien "   *(No. 2 Dawes' Roll No. 4055)*
No. 3 on Chickasaw roll as Eli C. "   *(No. 3 Dawes' Roll No. 4056)*
No. 4 on Chickasaw roll as James E. "   *(No. 4 Dawes' Roll No. 4057)*
No. 5 on Chickasaw roll as Frances E "   *(No. 5 Dawes' Roll No. 4058)*
No. 6 on Chickasaw roll as Mary M "   *(No. 6 Dawes' Roll No. 4059)*
No. 7 on Chickasaw roll as Raymond H "   *(No. 7 Dawes' Roll No. 4060)*
No. 8 Enrolled Dec. 14, 1899.   *(No. 8 Dawes' Roll No. 4061)*
Nos. 1 to 8 inclusive originally enrolled on Choctaw card #286;
    transferred to this card Jan. 30, 1903.

Sept. 26, 1898.

RESIDENCE: Chickasaw Nation	~~COUNTY~~		CARD NO.			
POST OFFICE: Earl, Ind. Ter.			FIELD NO.			

	NAME	RELATIONSHIP TO PERSON FIRST NAMED	AGE	SEX	BLOOD	TRIBAL ENROLLMENT		
						YEAR	COUNTY	PAGE
1	Norton, Yancey M	NAMED	42	M	I.W.	1896	Tishomingo	79
2	" Sealy	Wife	45	F	1/2	1896	"	33
3	" Thomas Owen	Son	10	M	1/4	1896	"	33
4	" Henry Taylor	"	8	"	1/4	1896	"	33
5	" Lewis Bird	"	6	"	1/4	1896	"	33
6	" Jesse Melton	"	2	"	1/4	1896	"	33

TRIBAL ENROLLMENT OF PARENTS

	NAME OF FATHER	YEAR	COUNTY	NAME OF MOTHER	YEAR	COUNTY
1	John F. Norton	dead	Non-citizen	Lucy C. Norton	dead	non-citizen
2	J.E. Anderson	"	Chickasaw roll	Jincy Anderson	"	Choctaw roll

Chickasaw Enrollment Cards 1898-1914
Chickasaw by Blood   Volume V

3	No. 1			No. 2		
4	No. 1			No. 2		
5	No. 1			No. 2		
6	No. 1			No. 2		

(NOTES)

No. 1 on Chickasaw roll as Yancey N. Norton
No. 2 "   "   "   "   Sealy Morton
No. 3 "   "   "   "   Thomas Oin "
No. 4 "   "   "   "   Henry J.   "
No. 5 "   "   "   "   Lewis B.   "
No. 6 "   "   "   "   Jessie M.   "
Nos. 1 to 6 inclusive originally enrolled on Choctaw card 305; transferred to this card Jan. 30, 1903.

Sept. 29, 98.

RESIGNE: Chickasaw Nation   ~~COUNTY~~   CARD NO.
POST OFFICE: Bob, Ind. Ter,   FIELD NO.

	NAME	RELATION-SHIP TO PERSON FIRST NAMED	AGE	SEX	BLOOD	TRIBAL ENROLLMENT		
						YEAR	COUNTY	PAGE
1	Green, Redie Jackson		28	M	1/4	1893	Pontotoc	No. 2 90
2	" William Elvie	Son	8	"	1/8	1893	"	90
3	" Myrtle Emma	Dau	6	F	1/8	1893	"	90
4	" Etta	Wife	32	F	I.W.			

TRIBAL ENROLLMENT OF PARENTS

	NAME OF FATHER	YEAR	COUNTY	NAME OF MOTHER	YEAR	COUNTY
1	Daniel Green	dead	Non citizen	Frances East		Choctaw residing in Chick Dist.
2	No. 1			Etta Green		white woman
3	No. 1			" "		" "
4	Carroll Bowen	Dead	non citizen	Callie Bowen		non citizen

(NOTES)

No. 1 married under name of Dutch Green   (No. 1 Dawes' Roll No. 4062)
No. 1 is the husband of Etta Green on Choctaw card #D.61   (No. 2 Dawes' Roll No. 4063)
No. 2 on Chickasaw roll as Wm E. Green   (No. 3 Dawes' Roll No. 4064)
No. 3 "   "   " " Myrtle E. "   (No. 4 Dawes' Roll No. 345)
Nos 1,2, & 3 originally enrolled on Choctaw Card #337; transferred to this card Jan. 30, 1903.
No. 4 transferred from Choctaw card D.61, April 7, 1904.
    See decision of March 15, 1904.

Oct. 3, 98

143

Chickasaw Enrollment Cards 1898-1914
Chickasaw by Blood   Volume V

	RESIDENCE: Choctaw Nation COUNTY			CARD NO.			
	POST OFFICE: So. McAlester, Ind. Ter.			FIELD NO.			

NAME	RELATION-SHIP TO PERSON FIRST NAMED	AGE	SEX	BLOOD	TRIBAL ENROLLMENT		
					YEAR	COUNTY	PAGE
1 Cartlidge, Benj F.	NAMED	11	M	1/2	1897	Choctaw Dist.	70
2 " Nadea S.	Sister	7	F	1/2	1896	"	70

TRIBAL ENROLLMENT OF PARENTS						
NAME OF FATHER	YEAR	COUNTY	NAME OF MOTHER	YEAR	COUNTY	
1 Elestra Cartlidge		Non Citizen	Frances Cartledge	Dead	Chickasaw	
2 " "		" "	" "	"	"	

(NOTES)

(Notation illegible)
No. 2 also enrolled with mother on 1893 Ieshatubby roll Page 2.   *(No. 1 Dawes' Roll No. 4148)*
Nos. 1 & 2 originally enrolled on Chickasaw card #359.   *(No. 2 Dawes' Roll No. 4149)*
    Transferred to this card Feb. 7, 1903.

So. McAlester, Mar. 22/99.

	RESIDENCE: Chickasaw Nation COUNTY			CARD NO.			
	POST OFFICE: Tishomingo, I.T.			FIELD NO.			

NAME	RELATION-SHIP TO PERSON FIRST NAMED	AGE	SEX	BLOOD	TRIBAL ENROLLMENT		
					YEAR	COUNTY	PAGE
1 Thompson, Jacob Loren	NAMED	24	M	1/16	1896	Tishomingo	32

TRIBAL ENROLLMENT OF PARENTS						
NAME OF FATHER	YEAR	COUNTY	NAME OF MOTHER	YEAR	COUNTY	
1 T.J. Thompson	Dead	Tishomingo	Lee J. Thompson	1896	Choc. residing in Tishomingo Co.	

(NOTES)

No. 1 also on 1896 Choctaw census roll, page 328 #12560 as ? Thompson
No. 1 is husband of Mollie Thompson and father of Inez and Frankie M. Thompson on Chickasaw card #910.
No. 1 originally enrolled on Choctaw card #327; transferred to this card Feby. 24, 1903.

P.O. Beebe, I.T.   9-30-98.

	RESIDENCE: Chickasaw Nation COUNTY			CARD NO.			
	POST OFFICE: Stonewall, Ind. Ter.			FIELD NO.			

NAME	RELATION-SHIP TO PERSON FIRST NAMED	AGE	SEX	BLOOD	TRIBAL ENROLLMENT		
					YEAR	COUNTY	PAGE
1 Byrd, Susan F.	NAMED	54	F	1/2	1896	Pontotoc	80

144

TRIBAL ENROLLMENT OF PARENTS						
NAME OF FATHER	YEAR	COUNTY	NAME OF MOTHER	YEAR	COUNTY	
1 David Folsom	Dead	Choctaw roll	Jane Folsom	Dead	Choctaw roll	

(NOTES)

Wife of William L. Byrd Chickasaw card No. 323.

Also on 1896 Choctaw census roll page 49 *(illegible)* as Susan Byrd, Chick district Dec. 5, 1899.

Originally enrolled on Choctaw card #65; transferred to this card Feby. 25, 1903.

See copy of letter from No. 1 Feby. 7, 1903, filed Feby. 25, 1903.

Sept. 7/98.

RESIDENCE: Choctaw Nation ~~COUNTY~~   CARD NO.

POST OFFICE: Red oak, I.T.   FIELD NO.

NAME	RELATION-SHIP TO PERSON FIRST NAMED	AGE	SEX	BLOOD	TRIBAL ENROLLMENT		
					YEAR	COUNTY	PAGE
1 Welch, Robert C.	FIRST NAMED	31	M	1/8	1893	Ieshatubby P.R. Chickasaw	
2 " Minnie L.	Wife	30	F	I.!.	1893	"	
3 " Alice	Dau	9	"	1/16	1893	"	
4 " Joe	Son	7	M	1/16	1893	"	
5 " Frank	"	4	"	1/16			
6 " John H.	"	2	"	1/16			
7 " Mildred B.	Dau	6mo	F	1/16			
8 " Nellie A.	wife	28	F	I.W.			

TRIBAL ENROLLMENT OF PARENTS						
NAME OF FATHER	YEAR	COUNTY	NAME OF MOTHER	YEAR	COUNTY	
1 Wm A. Welch, I.W.		Chick. residing in Choc. N. 3rd Dist.	Alice Welch	Dead	Chick residing in Choctaw N. 3rd Dist.	
2 James Carter	Dead	Non citizen	Rebecca Carter		Non citizen	
3 No. 1			No. 2			
4 No. 1			No. 2			
5 No. 1			No. 2			
6 No. 1			No. 2			
7 No. 1			No. 2			
8 Foster S. Mason		non-citizen	Sarah ? Mason		non citizen	

(NOTES)

No. 3 on Chickasaw roll as E. Belvin

No. 4 "   "   " " A. "

No. 5 "   "   " " Rosa "

Nos 1 to 7 inclusive transferred from Chickasaw D.#91

    See decision of February 25, 1903.

Chickasaw Enrollment Cards 1898-1914
Chickasaw by Blood   Volume V

RESIDENCE:	COUNTY			CARD NO.			
POST OFFICE:	Vireton I T			FIELD NO.			

	NAME	RELATION-SHIP TO PERSON FIRST	AGE	SEX	BLOOD	TRIBAL ENROLLMENT		
						YEAR	COUNTY	PAGE
1	Jennings, Mary J.	NAMED	21	F	1/32	1896	Choctaw District	7
2	" James A.	Son	4	M	1/64			
3	Baldwin, Lee P.	Bro	19	M	1/32	1896	Choctaw District	7
4	Powell, Gabriel	1/2 Bro	11	M	1/32	1896	"	7
5	Surber, Mannie	1/2 Sis	17	F	1/32	1896	"	7
6	Jennings, Charles ?	Son	2	M	1/64			

TRIBAL ENROLLMENT OF PARENTS

	NAME OF FATHER	YEAR	COUNTY	NAME OF MOTHER	YEAR	COUNTY
1	John Baldwin	Dead	non citizen	Nancy Baldwin	Dead	Gaines
2	Wm Jennings			No. 1		
3	John Baldwin			Nancy Baldwin	Dead	Gaines
4	Saml Powell			" "	"	"
5	Will Surber			" "	"	"
7	William Jennings			No. 1		

(NOTES)

No. 1 on 1896 Chickasaw roll as Mary Powell
No. 3 " " " " " Lee "
No. 4 " " " " " Samuel "
No. 5 " " " " " Maude "
No. 1 to 6 inclusive transferred from Chickasaw D.#274.
   See decision of February 25, 1903

RESIDENCE:	COUNTY			CARD NO.			
POST OFFICE:	(Illegible) I.T.			FIELD NO.			

	NAME	RELATION-SHIP TO PERSON FIRST	AGE	SEX	BLOOD	TRIBAL ENROLLMENT		
						YEAR	COUNTY	PAGE
1	Neighbors, William	NAMED	30	M	1/2			
2	" Lillian Ethel	Wife	25	F	I.W.			
3	" Bulah G.	Dau	5	F	1/4			
4	" Winnie L.	Dau	2	F	1/4			
5	" Conrad	Father	69	M	I.W.			

Chickasaw Enrollment Cards 1898-1914
Chickasaw by Blood   Volume V

TRIBAL ENROLLMENT OF PARENTS

	NAME OF FATHER	YEAR	COUNTY	NAME OF MOTHER	YEAR	COUNTY
1	Conrad Neighbors		non citizen	Mary Neighbors	1893	Ieshatubby Pay Roll
2	Wm Evans		"	Catherine Evans		non citizen
3	No. 1			No. 2		
4	No. 1			No. 2		
5	*(This line left blank on microfilm)*					

(NOTES)

No. 1 on Ieshatubby roll of 1893, page 4, Chickasaw residing in Choctaw Nation,   *(No. 2 Dawes' Roll No. 68)*
First District.
Nos. 1-3 and 4 transferred from Chickasaw D.#223.
No. 1 transferred from Chickasaw card D#363
    See decision of February 28, 1903.
No. 5 placed hereon under order of the Commissioner to the Five Civilized Tribes of Dec. 18, 1906 holding that
    application was made for her enrollment with the time provided by the Act of Congress, approved
    April 26, 1906.
No. 5 was formerly husband of Mary neighbors 1893 Ieshatubby pay roll, now deceased.

P.O. Sulphur 11/4/04.

RESIDENCE: Cherokee Nation   **COUNTY**   **CARD NO.**
POST OFFICE: Webbers Falls, I.T.   **FIELD NO.**

	NAME	RELATION-SHIP TO PERSON FIRST NAMED	AGE	SEX	BLOOD	TRIBAL ENROLLMENT		
						YEAR	COUNTY	PAGE
1	Vann, Lottie	NAMED	100	F	1/8	1896	Pickens	15
2	" Jim	Son	30	M	1/16	1896	"	15
3	" Lolo	Dau	23	F	1/16	1896	"	15
4	" William	Son	17	M	1/16	1896	"	15

TRIBAL ENROLLMENT OF PARENTS

	NAME OF FATHER	YEAR	COUNTY	NAME OF MOTHER	YEAR	COUNTY
1	Hamp Willis	Dead	non citizen	Amanda *(Illegible)* Willis	Dead	Chickasaw roll
2	William Vann		Cherokee citizen	No. 1		
3	"		"	No. 1		
4	"		"	No. 1		

(NOTES)

No. 3 on Chickasaw roll as Lula Van
No. 4 "   "   " " Billie "
Surname "   "   " " Van
Nos. 1 to 4 inclusive transferred to this card from Chickasaw card D.#115
    See decision of February 25, 1903.

Chickasaw Enrollment Cards 1898-1914
Chickasaw by Blood   Volume V

RESIDENCE: Cherokee Nation   COUNTY   CARD No.

POST OFFICE: Webbers Falls, I.T.   FIELD No.

NAME	RELATION-SHIP TO PERSON FIRST NAMED	AGE	SEX	BLOOD	TRIBAL ENROLLMENT		
					YEAR	COUNTY	PAGE
1 Vann, David	NAMED	34	M	1/16	1896	Pickens	15
2 " Arthur	Son	5	M	1/32			
3 " Jennie	Dau	1	F	1/32			

TRIBAL ENROLLMENT OF PARENTS

	NAME OF FATHER	YEAR	COUNTY	NAME OF MOTHER	YEAR	COUNTY
1	William Vann		Cherokee citizen	Lottie Vann	1896	Pickens
2	No. 1			Fannie Vann		non citizen
3	No. 1			" "		"

(NOTES)

Surname of No. 1 on Chickasaw roll Van.
Nos. 1-3 inclusive transferred from Chickasaw card D.#123
    See decision of February 25, 1903.

RESIDENCE: Cherokee Nation   COUNTY   CARD No.

POST OFFICE: Webbers Falls, I.T.   FIELD No.

NAME	RELATION-SHIP TO PERSON FIRST NAMED	AGE	SEX	BLOOD	TRIBAL ENROLLMENT		
					YEAR	COUNTY	PAGE
1 Lynch, Georgia Vann	NAMED	16	F	1/16	1896	Pickens	15

TRIBAL ENROLLMENT OF PARENTS

	NAME OF FATHER	YEAR	COUNTY	NAME OF MOTHER	YEAR	COUNTY
1	William Vann		Cherokee citizen	Lottie Vann	1896	Pickens

(NOTES)

No. 1 on Chickasaw roll as Georgia Vann.
No. 1 transferred Chickasaw card D.#125
    See decision of February 25, 1903.

RESIDENCE: COUNTY   CARD No.

POST OFFICE: Tishomingo, I.T.   FIELD No.

NAME	RELATION-SHIP TO PERSON FIRST NAMED	AGE	SEX	BLOOD	TRIBAL ENROLLMENT		
					YEAR	COUNTY	PAGE
1 McKinney, Oyd	NAMED	24	M		1893 PR#1	Pickens	140
2 " Georgie	Dau	1	F				

148

TRIBAL ENROLLMENT OF PARENTS						
NAME OF FATHER	YEAR	COUNTY	NAME OF MOTHER	YEAR	COUNTY	
1			Mary McKinney			
2	No. 1			Fannie McKinney		non citizen

(NOTES)

No. 1 transferred from Chickasaw card D.#334
    See decision of February 26, 1903
No. 2 born May 2, 1902. Application received April 6, 1905, under Act of Congress   *(No. 2 Dawes' Roll No. 4980)*
    approved March 3, 1905.

March 9, 1903.

RESIDENCE: Cherokee Nation   *COUNTY*   *CARD NO.*
POST OFFICE: Webbers Falls, I.T.   *FIELD NO.*

NAME	RELATION-SHIP TO PERSON FIRST NAMED	AGE	SEX	BLOOD	TRIBAL ENROLLMENT		
					YEAR	COUNTY	PAGE
1 Graves, Ellen		78	F	1/16	1896	Pickens	15

TRIBAL ENROLLMENT OF PARENTS						
NAME OF FATHER	YEAR	COUNTY	NAME OF MOTHER	YEAR	COUNTY	
1 William Vann		Cherokee citizen	Lottie Vann	1896	Pickens	

(NOTES)

No. 1 on 1896 Chickasaw roll as Ellen Vann.
No. 1 transferred from Chickasaw card D.#26?
    See decision of Feby. 25m 1893.

RESIDENCE: Panola   *COUNTY*   *CARD NO.*
POST OFFICE: Platter, I.T.   *FIELD NO.*

NAME	RELATION-SHIP TO PERSON FIRST NAMED	AGE	SEX	BLOOD	TRIBAL ENROLLMENT		
					YEAR	COUNTY	PAGE
1 McKinney, Harris		37	M	*(1/4)*	1893	Panola	PR#2 8
2 " Laura Etta	Dau	5	F	*(1/8)*			
3 " Cecial Berthal	Dau	2	F	*(1/8)*			
4 " Maude Lee	Dau	9	F	*(1/8)*			

TRIBAL ENROLLMENT OF PARENTS						
NAME OF FATHER	YEAR	COUNTY	NAME OF MOTHER	YEAR	COUNTY	
1 Wm McKinney	Dead		Sarah McKinney	Dead	non citizen	
2 No. 1			Mollie McKinney		"	
3 No. 1			Mary E. McKinney		"	

4	No. 1			" " "		"

(NOTES)

Nos. 1-4 inclusive transferred from Chickasaw card D.#116
 See decision of February 2?, 1903.
As to Chickasaw blood of Nos. 1 to 4 inclusive, see affidavit of No. 1 of June 12, 1906. 6/20/06
No. 1 is 1/4 Chickasaw blood and No. 2 to 4 inclusive are 1/8 Chickasaw blood

March 9, 1903.

RESIDENCE: Choctaw Nation   COUNTY   CARD NO.
POST OFFICE: Stringtown, I.T.   FIELD NO.

	NAME	RELATION-SHIP TO PERSON FIRST NAMED	AGE	SEX	BLOOD	TRIBAL ENROLLMENT		
						YEAR	COUNTY	PAGE
1	Garsides, Joseph	NAMED	48	M	I.W.	1893	Maytubby payment roll #2	
2	" Fannie	Dau	18	F		"		
3	" Ben	Son	17	M		"		
4	" Alix	Son	16	M		"		
5	" Jim	Son	15	M		"		
6	" Nellie	Dau	14	F		"		
7	" Mattie	Dau	12	F		"		
8	" Joe, jr.	Son	10	M		"		
9	Self, James	Husband of No. 2	20	M	I.W.			

TRIBAL ENROLLMENT OF PARENTS

	NAME OF FATHER	YEAR	COUNTY	NAME OF MOTHER	YEAR	COUNTY
1	Benj. Garsides	Dead	non-citizen	Fannie Garsides		non-citizen
2	No. 1			Mary Louisa McKinney	Dead	Chickasaw
3	No. 1			" "		"
4	No. 1			" "		"
5	No. 1			" "		"
6	No. 1			" "		"
7	No. 1			" "		"
8	No. 1			" "		"
9	W.A. Self		non-citizen	Arinda Self		non-citizen

(NOTES)

Nos. 1-8 inclusive transferred from Chickasaw Card#592
 See decision of February 26, 1903.
No. 9 transferred from Chickasaw card D.448 April 7, 1904.   *(No. 9 Dawes' Roll No. 346)*
 See decision of March 15, 1904.

March 9, 1903.

RESIDENCE:	COUNTY					CARD NO.		
POST OFFICE: Belton, I.T.						FIELD NO.		

NAME	RELATION-SHIP TO PERSON FIRST NAMED	AGE	SEX	BLOOD	TRIBAL ENROLLMENT		
					YEAR	COUNTY	PAGE
1 Woody, Charles H.		40	M	I.W.			

	TRIBAL ENROLLMENT OF PARENTS						
NAME OF FATHER	YEAR	COUNTY	NAME OF MOTHER	YEAR	COUNTY		
1 James Woody		non citizen	Eliz. Woody		non citizen.		

(NOTES)

No. 1 transferred from Chickasaw card #D290 March 29, 1903   *(No. 1 Dawes' Roll No. 69)*
See decision of March 13, 1903.

RESIDENCE: Tishomingo	COUNTY					CARD NO.		
POST OFFICE: Tishomingo						FIELD NO.		

NAME	RELATION-SHIP TO PERSON FIRST NAMED	AGE	SEX	BLOOD	TRIBAL ENROLLMENT		
					YEAR	COUNTY	PAGE
1 Colbert, Benjamin		26	M	1/8	1896	Atoka	2916

	TRIBAL ENROLLMENT OF PARENTS						
NAME OF FATHER	YEAR	COUNTY	NAME OF MOTHER	YEAR	COUNTY		
1 Jason Colbert	Dead	Chick Roll	Athenius Colbert		Atoka		

(NOTES)

No. 1 on 1896 Choctaw Census roll Atoka County #2916.
Also on 1897 Chickasaw roll, page 7, Panola County.
No. 1 originally enrolled on Choctaw card #3366, transferred to this card May 16, 1903.
See decision of April 29, 1903.

May 16, 1903.

RESIDENCE: Chickasaw Nation	~~COUNTY~~					CARD NO.		
POST OFFICE: Comanche, I.T.						FIELD NO.		

NAME	RELATION-SHIP TO PERSON FIRST NAMED	AGE	SEX	BLOOD	TRIBAL ENROLLMENT		
					YEAR	COUNTY	PAGE
1 Duncan, John *(Illegible)*		30	M	3/4	1893	*(Illegible)*Co. Pay roll No. 1	136

	TRIBAL ENROLLMENT OF PARENTS						
NAME OF FATHER	YEAR	COUNTY	NAME OF MOTHER	YEAR	COUNTY		
1 Howard Duncan	Dead	Chickasaw		Dead	Cherokee		

151

Chickasaw Enrollment Cards 1898-1914
Chickasaw by Blood   Volume V

(NOTES)

No. 1 transferred from Chickasaw card #K.337   *(No. 1 Dawes' Roll No. 4759)*
See testimony of April 25, 1903.

April 25, 1903.

RESIDENCE: Pontotoc COUNTY					CARD NO.		
POST OFFICE: Wiley, I.T.					FIELD NO.		

NAME	RELATION-SHIP TO PERSON FIRST	AGE	SEX	BLOOD	TRIBAL ENROLLMENT		
					YEAR	COUNTY	PAGE
1 Underwood, Lewis	NAMED	25	M	1/2	1897	Pontotoc	57

TRIBAL ENROLLMENT OF PARENTS

	NAME OF FATHER	YEAR	COUNTY	NAME OF MOTHER	YEAR	COUNTY
1	Simpson Underwood		Chickasaw	*(Illegible)* Underwood	dead	*(Illegible)*

(NOTES)

(All notations illegible)   *(No. 1 Dawes' Roll No. 4760)*
May 20, 1903.

RESIDENCE: Chickasaw Nation COUNTY					CARD NO.		
POST OFFICE: Purcell, I.T.					FIELD NO.		

NAME	RELATION-SHIP TO PERSON FIRST	AGE	SEX	BLOOD	TRIBAL ENROLLMENT		
					YEAR	COUNTY	PAGE
1 Turner, Hiram G.	NAMED	40	M	I.W.			
2 " Daisy	Wife	21	F	1/8	1897	Pontotoc	97
3 " Ludie May	S.Dau	8mo	F	1/16			
4 " Mary	Dau	6mo	F	1/16			

TRIBAL ENROLLMENT OF PARENTS

	NAME OF FATHER	YEAR	COUNTY	NAME OF MOTHER	YEAR	COUNTY
1	Richard Turner		Non Citz	Josephine Turner		Non Citz
2	Hamp Willis	Dead	Chick Roll	Delilah Davis		Towson
3	T.E. Sanborn		Towson	No. 2		
4	No. 1			No. 2		

(NOTES)

No. 2 1896 Towson 13194.   *(No. 1 Dawes' Roll No. 536)*
No. 2 on 97 Chick Roll as Daisy Willis; Transferred to Choctaw Roll by Dawes Com;   *(No. 2 Dawes' Roll No. 4815)*
No. 2 also on 1896 Roll page 340 #12953, as Daisie Willsi, Gaines Co.   *(No. 3 Dawes' Roll No. 4816)*
No. 4 Enrolled Aug. 2, 1901.   *(No. 4 Dawes' Roll No. 4817)*
No. 3 has been legally adopted by Nos. 1 & 2, and her name indexed as Ludie Turner, June 10, 1902.
Nos. 2 & 3 Enrolled Oct. 20 - 1898.

152

Chickasaw Enrollment Cards 1898-1914
Chickasaw by Blood   Volume V

No. 1[sic] Enrolled at Calvin, I.T. 8/8/99 as Daisy Willis, This notation should read No. 2
Testimony of No. 1 as to his status, as an intermarried Citizen, Sept. 25, '02, taken at Pauls Valley, I.T. Oct. 21, '02.
Nos. 1 to 4 originally enrolled on Choctaw card #430.
    Transferred to this card July 2, 1903.

July 2, 1903.

		RELATION-				TRIBAL ENROLLMENT		
NAME		SHIP TO PERSON FIRST NAMED	**AGE**	**SEX**	**BLOOD**	**YEAR**	**COUNTY**	**PAGE**

RESIDENCE: Chickasaw Nation **COUNTY**   **CARD NO.**
POST OFFICE: Yarnaby, I.T.   **FIELD NO.**

	NAME	RELATIONSHIP TO PERSON FIRST NAMED	AGE	SEX	BLOOD	YEAR	COUNTY	PAGE
1	Potts, Fannie E.	NAMED	23	F	1/8	1893	Pay Roll No. 2	P.11
2	" Nina June	Dau	3	"	1/16			
3	" Maud	Dau	9M	"	1/16			
4	" Lela	Dau	1M	"	1/16			
5	" Joel Cecil	Son	2	M	1/16			
6	" Edward Forrest	Hus	38	M	T.W.			

TRIBAL ENROLLMENT OF PARENTS

	NAME OF FATHER	YEAR	COUNTY	NAME OF MOTHER	YEAR	COUNTY
1	Charley Shico	Dead	Chickasaw Roll	Catherine Raines	1896	Panola
2	Edward Forrest Potts		White man	No. 1		
3	" "		" "	No. 1		
4	" "		" "	No. 1		
5	" "		" "	No. 1		
6	Joel Potts	Dead	Non Citizen	Frances Potts		non citizen

(NOTES)

No. 1 on Page 11, original of Panola County No. 21,   *(No. 1 Dawes' Roll No. 4912)*
    (this notation refers to 1893 Chick Pay Roll No. 2)
No. 2 on Chickasaw Roll as *(Illegible)* Potts.   *(No. 2 Dawes' Roll No. 4913)*
No. 4 Enrolled May 24, 1902; Born April 8, 1900.   *(No. 3 Dawes' Roll No. 4914)*
No. 5 Born July 19, 1902; enrolled July 31, 1902.   *(No. 4 Dawes' Roll No. 4915)*
Nos. 1 to 5 inclusive transferred from Choctaw card #388 Nov. 20, 1903. *(No. 5 Dawes' Roll No. 4916)*
No. 3 Born Nov. 22, 1897; affidavits to birth on file *(remainder illegible)*
Nos. 2 and 3 Affidavits of birth filed Nov. 22, 1904.
No. 6 transferred from Chickasaw Card D.#13 Oct. 21, 1905.
    See Decision of October 5, 1905.

Oct. 13/98.

153

Chickasaw Enrollment Cards 1898-1914
Chickasaw by Blood Volume V

RESIDENCE: Chickasaw Nation	~~COUNTY~~				CARD NO.			
POST OFFICE: Pauls Valley, I.T.					FIELD NO.			

NAME	RELATION- SHIP TO PERSON FIRST NAMED	AGE	SEX	BLOOD	TRIBAL ENROLLMENT		
					YEAR	COUNTY	PAGE
1 McClure, Jemison Gordon	NAMED	15mo	M	3/8			

TRIBAL ENROLLMENT OF PARENTS

NAME OF FATHER	YEAR	COUNTY	NAME OF MOTHER	YEAR	COUNTY
1 Jemison McClure	Dead	Pickens	Minnie McClure		White Woman

(NOTES)

Father of No. 1, Jemison McClure, 1893 Pickens Co. Pay Roll #2, Page *(blank)*. who died in 1899
No. 1 Born June 10, 1897.
Mother of No. 1 is Minnie McClure now Hoggars - on Chickasaw card D-19.
Evidence of marriage of parents of No. 1 on file with the record in Chickasaw D-19
No. 1 transferred from Chickasaw Card D-19.

Sept. 13, 1898.

RESIDENCE:	COUNTY				CARD NO.			
POST OFFICE: Springer, I.T.					FIELD NO.			

NAME	RELATION- SHIP TO PERSON FIRST NAMED	AGE	SEX	BLOOD	TRIBAL ENROLLMENT		
					YEAR	COUNTY	PAGE
1 Brown, Susan Frances	NAMED	44	F	1/2	1896	Panola	6
2 " Eben Foster	Son	24	M	1/4	1896	"	6
3 " Natha	Dau	18	F	1/4	1896	"	6
4 " Amos	Son	12	M	1/4	1896	"	6

TRIBAL ENROLLMENT OF PARENTS

NAME OF FATHER	YEAR	COUNTY	NAME OF MOTHER	YEAR	COUNTY
1 Van Colbert	Dead	Chick Roll	Sedalia Colbert	Dead	Chick Roll
2 John B. Brown		Cherokee	No. 1		
3 " "		"	No. 1		
4 " "		"	No. 1		

(NOTES)

No. 1 on Chickasaw roll as Fannie Brown.   *(No. 1 Dawes' Roll No. 4884)*
No. 2 " " " " Ebin Brown.   *(No. 2 Dawes' Roll No. 4885)*
No. 3 " " " " Martha Brown.   *(No. 3 Dawes' Roll No. 4886)*
Nos. 1-4 inclusive transferred from Chickasaw D.202   *(No. 4 Dawes' Roll No. 4887)*
     See decision December 5, 1903.

Dec. 21, 1903.

RESIDENCE: Pontotoc COUNTY					CARD NO.			
POST OFFICE: Wayne I.T.					FIELD NO.			

	NAME	RELATION-SHIP TO PERSON FIRST NAMED	AGE	SEX	BLOOD	TRIBAL ENROLLMENT		
						YEAR	COUNTY	PAGE
1	~~Goldsby, John E.~~	NAMED	40	M	1/32	1893	~~Chick Pay Roll No. 2~~	91
2	" ~~Sadie~~	~~Wife~~	33	F	I.W.	1893	" " " " " "	91
3	" ~~Linniet E.~~	~~Son~~	12	M	1/64	1893	" " " " "	91
4	" ~~Bessie~~	~~Dau~~	9	F	1/64	1893	" " " " "	91
5	" ~~Murray Milton~~	~~Son~~	3wks	M	1/64			

	TRIBAL ENROLLMENT OF PARENTS						
	NAME OF FATHER	YEAR	COUNTY	NAME OF MOTHER	YEAR	COUNTY
1	~~P.R. Goldsby~~	~~Dead~~	~~Chickasaw~~	~~Nancy A. Goldsby~~	~~Dead~~	~~Chickasaw~~
2	~~J.A. Bonine~~	"	~~Non-Citz~~	~~Lois Bonine~~	"	~~non-citz~~
3	~~No. 1~~			~~No. 2~~		
4	~~No. 1~~			~~No. 2~~		
5	~~No. 1~~			~~No. 2~~		

(NOTES)

Nos. 1 to 4 inclusive were admitted by the Dawes Commission Nov. 23, 1896 and   *(No. 1 Dawes' Roll No. 4984)*
U.S. Court for the Southern District of the Indian Territory March 19, 1898.   *(No. 3 Dawes' Roll No. 4985)*
Court Case No. 58 Dawes Commission Case No. 25?   *(No. 4 Dawes' Roll No. 4986)*
No. 3 Linniet E. Goldsby as Lemmiet E. Goldsby and Sadie Goldsby   *(No. 5 Dawes' Roll No. 4987)*
    as Sally Goldsby and as an intermarried citizen
No. 5 Enrolled January 3, 1903.
Nos. 1 to 5 inclusive transferred from Chickasaw card #C4 Oct. 6, 1905.
    All Dismissed,
No. 2 Refused May 23, 1905.
Nos. 1,3,4 & 5 Granted May 23, 1905.
    Record forwarded Department May 23, 1905.
Action
Notice of Departmental Action forwarded attorneys for Choctaw and Chickasaw Nations, Oct. 14, 1905.
Notice of Departmental Action forwarded attorney for applicant Oct. 14, 1905.
Notice of Departmental Action forwarded applicant. Oct. 14, 1905.

P.O. Purcell, I.T. 6/11/03   9-14-98.

Chickasaw Enrollment Cards 1898-1914
Chickasaw by Blood   Volume V

RESIDENCE: Pickens   COUNTY   CARD NO.
POST OFFICE: Duncan, I.T.   FIELD NO.

NAME	RELATION-SHIP TO PERSON FIRST NAMED	AGE	SEX	BLOOD	TRIBAL ENROLLMENT		
					YEAR	COUNTY	PAGE
1 ~~Keyes. W.S.~~	NAMED	54	M	I.W.			
2 " ~~Ella~~	~~Dau~~	11	F	1/2			

TRIBAL ENROLLMENT OF PARENTS

	NAME OF FATHER	YEAR	COUNTY	NAME OF MOTHER	YEAR	COUNTY
1	~~Wm keyes~~	~~Dead~~	~~Non-Citz~~	~~Jane Keyes~~	~~Dead~~	~~Non-Citz~~
2	No. 1			Mollie Keyes		Chickasaw

(NOTES)
Nos. 1 and 2 admitted by Dawes Commission in 1896 Chickasaw Case #67.
Admitted by the U.S. Court, Ardmore, I.T. Dec. 21, 1897 Court Case No. 41.
No. 1 was married to a Chickasaw Indian from whom he has been divorced
The child Ella, No. 2, is by the marriage
Nos. 1 & 2 transferred from Chickasaw Card C.109.

9/23/98.

RESIDENCE: Pickens   COUNTY   CARD NO.
POST OFFICE: Madill, I.T.   FIELD NO.

NAME	RELATION-SHIP TO PERSON FIRST NAMED	AGE	SEX	BLOOD	TRIBAL ENROLLMENT		
					YEAR	COUNTY	PAGE
1 Lewis, Mary L.	NAMED	27	F	I.W.	1897	Pickens	13

TRIBAL ENROLLMENT OF PARENTS

	NAME OF FATHER	YEAR	COUNTY	NAME OF MOTHER	YEAR	COUNTY
1	C.C. Yeargam		non citizen	Sally Yeargam		non citizen

(NOTES)
No. 1 is wife of Isaay Overton Lewis, Chickasaw card #698.   (No. 1 Dawes' Roll No. 297)
   Transferred from Chickasaw card #D.84. See decision of March 5, 1904. Mar. 23, 1904.

Mar. 23, 1904.

RESIDENCE: Chickasaw Nation   ~~COUNTY~~   CARD NO.
POST OFFICE: Orr, Ind. Ter.   FIELD NO.

NAME	RELATION-SHIP TO PERSON FIRST NAMED	AGE	SEX	BLOOD	TRIBAL ENROLLMENT		
					YEAR	COUNTY	PAGE
1 Hare, Frances M.	NAMED	55	M	I.W.	1897	Pickens	77

TRIBAL ENROLLMENT OF PARENTS						
NAME OF FATHER	YEAR	COUNTY	NAME OF MOTHER	YEAR	COUNTY	
1 Jeff Hare	Dead	Cherokee citz.	Eliz. T. Hare	Dead	Cherokee citiz.	

(NOTES)

No. 1 is husband of Sarah Hare on Chickasaw card #948,

No. 1 transferred from Chickasaw card #109. See decision of March 5, 1904. Mar. 23, 1904.

Mar. 23, 1904.

RESIDENCE: Cherokee Nation   COUNTY   CARD NO.

POST OFFICE: Chelsea, I.T.   FIELD NO.

NAME	RELATIONSHIP TO PERSON FIRST NAMED	AGE	SEX	BLOOD	TRIBAL ENROLLMENT		
					YEAR	COUNTY	PAGE
1 Moreland, Fannie	NAMED	31	F	1/4	1896	Panola	6
2 Keys, Thomas	Son	12	M	1/8	1896	"	6
3 " Willie	Son	8	M	1/8	1896	"	6
4 " Charlie	Son	5	M	1/8			

TRIBAL ENROLLMENT OF PARENTS						
NAME OF FATHER	YEAR	COUNTY	NAME OF MOTHER	YEAR	COUNTY	
1 Tuck Rider	dead	Cherokee	Aggie Rider	dead	Chickasaw	
2 John Keys		Non Citizen	No. 1			
3 " "		" "	No. 1			
4 " "		" "	No. 1			

(NOTES)

No. 1 on 1896 Chickasaw roll as Fannie Keys   *(No. 1 Dawes' Roll No. 4818)*

No. 2 " 1896   "   " " Tommie Keys, Jr.   *(No. 2 Dawes' Roll No. 4819)*

No. 3 " 1896   "   " " Jimmie Keys.   *(No. 3 Dawes' Roll No. 4820)*

No. 4 Evidence of birth received and filed August 9, 1902.   *(No. 4 Dawes' Roll No. 4821)*

Nos. 1 - 4 inclusive transferred from Chickasaw card #D.204.

See decision of March 15, 1904.

April 7, 1904.

RESIDENCE: Choctaw Nation   COUNTY   CARD NO.

POST OFFICE: Durant, I.T.   FIELD NO.

NAME	RELATIONSHIP TO PERSON FIRST NAMED	AGE	SEX	BLOOD	TRIBAL ENROLLMENT		
					YEAR	COUNTY	PAGE
1 Baker, William M.	NAMED	31	M	I.W.			
2 " Fannie	Wife	29	F	1/4	1896	Panola	2
3 " Louise C.	Dau		F	1/8			

| 4 | "   Colbert La?mer | | Son | 1 | M | 1/8 | | | |

TRIBAL ENROLLMENT OF PARENTS

	NAME OF FATHER	YEAR	COUNTY	NAME OF MOTHER	YEAR	COUNTY
1	Geo. P. Baker		Non Citizen	Hattie C. Baker		Non Citizen
2	Frank Colbert	dead	Panola	Lou Colbert	1896	Panola
3	No. 1			No. 2		
4	No. 1			No. 2		

(NOTES)

No. 2 on Chickasaw roll as Fannie Colbert.   *(No. 1 Dawes' Roll No. 416)*

No. 3 born June 12, 1899. Evidence of birth filed August 9. 1899.   *(No. 2 Dawes' Roll No. 4823)*

No. 4 born March 25, 1902; evidence of birth filed April 16, 1902.   *(No. 3 Dawes' Roll No. 4824)*

No. 1 transferred from Chickasaw card D.245.   *(No. 4 Dawes' Roll No. 4825)*

Nos. 2-4 inclusive tansferred from Chickasaw card D.181.

     See decision of March 15, 1904.

April 7, 1904.

RESIDENCE: Choctaw Nation   **COUNTY**   **CARD NO.**

POST OFFICE: **FIELD NO.**

NAME	RELATION-SHIP TO PERSON FIRST NAMED	AGE	SEX	BLOOD	TRIBAL ENROLLMENT		
					YEAR	COUNTY	PAGE
1 Winter, Anna Louise	NAMED	50	F	1/32	1893	Panola	PR#2 6
2 " George Alexander	husband	51	M	I.W.			

TRIBAL ENROLLMENT OF PARENTS

	NAME OF FATHER	YEAR	COUNTY	NAME OF MOTHER	YEAR	COUNTY
1	P.R. Goldsby	dead	Non Citizen	Nancy Ann Goldsby	dead	Chickasaw
2	Charles A. Winter		" "	Amanda L. Winter		Non citizen

(NOTES)

No. 1 on Chickasaw roll as Mrs. A.L. Colbert.   *(No. 1 Dawes' Roll No. 4822)*

No. 1 transferred from Chickasaw card D.175. See decision of March 13, 1904.   *(No. 2 Dawes' Roll No. 557)*

No. 2 originally listed for enrollment on Chickasaw card #D.175. Oct. 14/98;

     transferred to this card Nov. 26, 1904. See decision of Nov. 5, 1904.

Apr. 7, 1904.

RESIDENCE: Chickasaw Nation   **COUNTY**   **CARD NO.**

POST OFFICE: Conway, I.W.   **FIELD NO.**

NAME	RELATION-SHIP TO PERSON FIRST	AGE	SEX	BLOOD	TRIBAL ENROLLMENT		
					YEAR	COUNTY	PAGE
1 Nelson, Chilley	NAMED	46	M	Full	1896	Pontotoc	47

TRIBAL ENROLLMENT OF PARENTS						
NAME OF FATHER	YEAR	COUNTY	NAME OF MOTHER	YEAR	COUNTY	
1 Nelson	Dead	Choctaw	La-po-te-na	Dead	Choctaw	

(NOTES)

No. 1 transferred from Choctaw card #22   *(No. 1 Dawes' Roll No. 4826)*
See decision of March 15, 1904.

Apr. 7, 1904.

RESIDENCE:	COUNTY				CARD NO.		
POST OFFICE: Franks, I.T.					FIELD NO.		

NAME	RELATION-SHIP TO PERSON FIRST	AGE	SEX	BLOOD	TRIBAL ENROLLMENT		
					YEAR	COUNTY	PAGE
1 Owens, Neely A.	NAMED	27	M	I.W.			

TRIBAL ENROLLMENT OF PARENTS						
NAME OF FATHER	YEAR	COUNTY	NAME OF MOTHER	YEAR	COUNTY	
1 W.C. Owens		non citizen	Adeline Owens		non citizen	

(NOTES)

Husband of Mattie Underwood, '96 Pickens *(remainder illegible)*   *(No. 1 Dawes' Roll No. 347)*
No. 1 transferred from Chickasaw card #D.220.
See decision of March 15, 1904.

Apr. 7, 1904.

RESIDENCE:	COUNTY				CARD NO.		
POST OFFICE: Tishomingo. I.T.					FIELD NO.		

NAME	RELATION-SHIP TO PERSON FIRST	AGE	SEX	BLOOD	TRIBAL ENROLLMENT		
					YEAR	COUNTY	PAGE
1 Shelton, William J.	NAMED	24	M	I.W.			

TRIBAL ENROLLMENT OF PARENTS						
NAME OF FATHER	YEAR	COUNTY	NAME OF MOTHER	YEAR	COUNTY	
1 J.M. Shelton		non citizen	Missie Shelton		non citizen	

(NOTES)

Husband of Clemmie Shelton, field card No. 9-980, #2945 on final roll.   *(No. 1 Dawes' Roll No. 348)*
No. 1 transferred from Chickasaw card #D.276
See decision of March 15, 1904.

Apr. 7, 1904.

RESIDENCE: Choctaw Nation   ~~COUNTY~~   CARD NO.

POST OFFICE: Tushhohomma, I.T.   FIELD NO.

NAME	RELATION-SHIP TO PERSON	AGE	SEX	BLOOD	TRIBAL ENROLLMENT		
					YEAR	COUNTY	PAGE
1 Colbert, James	FIRST NAMED	40	M	Full	1896	Chick residing in Choc. Dist.	73

TRIBAL ENROLLMENT OF PARENTS

NAME OF FATHER	YEAR	COUNTY	NAME OF MOTHER	YEAR	COUNTY
1 James Colbert	Dead	Chick Roll	Maria A. Colbert	Dead	

(NOTES)

No. 1 on 1896 Chickasaw roll as Dennis Colbert.   *(No. 1 Dawes' Roll No. 4941)*

Also on 1893 Maytubbee roll #2 as *(Illegible)*

Wife on Choctaw card #D.174.

Transferred from Chickasaw card #D.233. April 15, 1904.

No. 1 on 1885 Choctaw Census Roll *(remainder illegible)*

RESIDENCE: Pontotoc   COUNTY   CARD NO.

POST OFFICE: Johnson, I.T.   FIELD NO.

NAME	RELATION-SHIP TO PERSON	AGE	SEX	BLOOD	TRIBAL ENROLLMENT		
					YEAR	COUNTY	PAGE
1 Thompson, J.W.	FIRST NAMED	32	M	I.W.			

TRIBAL ENROLLMENT OF PARENTS

NAME OF FATHER	YEAR	COUNTY	NAME OF MOTHER	YEAR	COUNTY
1 Jno. M. Thompson	Dead	Non Citz	Eliza J. Thompson	Dead	Non Citz.

(NOTES)

No. 1 was admitted by Commission in '96 - Chickasaw Case #162.   *(No. 1 Dawes' Roll No. 353)*

No. 1 admitted by U.S. Court for Southern District, Ind. Ter., Ardmore. I.T. March 12, 1898, in
    Court case No. 54 as an intermarried citizen.

Judgement of U.S. Court admitting No. 1 *(remainder illegible)*

Transferred from Chickasaw Card #C.9.

9-16-93.
6/26/'00.

Chickasaw Enrollment Cards 1898-1914
Chickasaw by Blood   Volume V

RESIDENCE: Pickens COUNTY					CARD NO.			
POST OFFICE: Deerwood, Ind. Ter.					FIELD NO.			

	NAME	RELATION-SHIP TO PERSON FIRST NAMED	AGE	SEX	BLOOD	TRIBAL ENROLLMENT		
						YEAR	COUNTY	PAGE
1	Adams, Ella	NAMED	24	F	1/2			
2	McSwain, Harry	Son	6	M	1/4			
3	" Minnie	Dau	4	F	1/4			
4	" Bessie	"	3	"	1/4			
5	" Romey	"	8mo	"	1/4			

TRIBAL ENROLLMENT OF PARENTS

	NAME OF FATHER	YEAR	COUNTY	NAME OF MOTHER	YEAR	COUNTY
1	Houston (Illegible)	Dead	Chick Citz.	Esther (Illegible)		Non Citz
2	J.L. McSwain		Non citz	No. 1		
3	" "		" "	No. 1		
4	" "		" "	No. 1		
5	" "		" "	No. 1		

(NOTES)

Nos. 1, 2 and 3 admitted by Com. in '96 Chick Case #??
Mother of No. 1 is Esther McLish, Chickasaw Card #D.381.
Nos 1 to 4 inclusive admitted by U.S. Court, Ardmore I.T. March 12, 1898. Court case No. 31,
Judgement of U.S. Court admitting Nos. 1 to 4 *(remainder illegible)*
Nos. 1 to 4 inclusive admitted *(remainder illegible)*
Transferred from Chickasaw card #C-10.

9-20-98.

RESIDENCE: Tishomingo COUNTY					CARD NO.			
POST OFFICE: Tishomingo, I.T.					FIELD NO.			

	NAME	RELATION-SHIP TO PERSON FIRST NAMED	AGE	SEX	BLOOD	TRIBAL ENROLLMENT		
						YEAR	COUNTY	PAGE
1	McSwain, Belle	NAMED	22	F	1/2			
2	" Maud	Dau	4	"	1/4			
3	" Willie	"	2	"	1/4			
4	" Charles H.	Son	1	M	1/4			
5	" Joel D.	"	8mo	"	1/4			
6	" Luella	Dau	5mo	F	1/4			

TRIBAL ENROLLMENT OF PARENTS

	NAME OF FATHER	YEAR	COUNTY	NAME OF MOTHER	YEAR	COUNTY
1	Houston Brown	Dead	Chick. Citz.	Esther Brown		Non Citz.

2	Chas. McSwain		" "	No. 1		
3	" "		" "	No. 1		
4	" "		" "	No. 1		
5	" "		" "	No. 1		
6	" "		" "			

(NOTES)

Nos. 1,2 and 3 admitted by Com. in '96 Chick Case # *(illegible)*
Mother of No. 1 is Esther McLish, Chickasaw Card *(remainder illegible)*
No. 1 is wife of Charles McSwain, Chickasaw Card # *(illegible)*
Nos. 1,2 an 3 admitted by U.S. Court, Ardmore, I.T. March 12, 1898. Court Case 763.
No. 4 born Sept. 13, 1897; proof of birth requested June 11, 1904. Received and filed June 28, 1904.
No. 5 born March 13, 1899; enrolled Nov. 4, 1899.
No. 6 born April 23, 1901; enrolled Sept. 11, 1901.
Judgement of U.S. Court admitting 1,2 and 3 vacated and set aside by deree of C.C.C.C. Dec. 17, ????
Nos. 1-2 and 3 admitted by C.C.C.C. May 11, 1904.
Transferred from Chickasaw Card #G.188.

9-29-98.

RESIDENCE: Choctaw Nation ~~*COUNTY*~~ *CARD NO.*
POST OFFICE: Peggy Depot, I.T. *FIELD NO.*

	NAME	RELATIONSHIP TO PERSON FIRST NAMED	AGE	SEX	BLOOD	TRIBAL ENROLLMENT		
						YEAR	COUNTY	PAGE
1	Pittman, W.R.		39	M	I.W.			

TRIBAL ENROLLMENT OF PARENTS

	NAME OF FATHER	YEAR	COUNTY	NAME OF MOTHER	YEAR	COUNTY
1	Tim Pittman	Dead	Non Citizen	Martha Pittman	Dead	Non Citizen

(NOTES)

No. 1 Denied by Dawes Commission in 1896, case #206, *(No. 1 Dawes' Roll No. 354)*
No. 1 Admitted by U.S. Court, Southern Dist. Ardmore, I.T. Dec. 21, 1898. Court case #105,
as an intermarried citizen.
Admitted as an intermarried citizen by *(remainder illegible)*
Transferred from Chickasaw Card #C-55.

9/22/98.
JUN 20 1904

Chickasaw Enrollment Cards 1898-1914
Chickasaw by Blood   Volume V

RESIDENCE: Pickens   COUNTY

POST OFFICE: Ardmore, I.T.

CARD NO.

FIELD NO.

NAME	RELATION-SHIP TO PERSON FIRST NAMED	AGE	SEX	BLOOD	TRIBAL ENROLLMENT		
					YEAR	COUNTY	PAGE
1 Underwood, Mary	NAMED	28	F	I.W.			

TRIBAL ENROLLMENT OF PARENTS

NAME OF FATHER	YEAR	COUNTY	NAME OF MOTHER	YEAR	COUNTY
1 Geo. W. Pate	Dead	non citizen	Nancy C. Pate		non citizen

(NOTES)

No. 1 admitted as an intermarried citizen by Dawes Commission in 1896 Case #252. *(No. 1 Dawes' Roll No. 355)*
Admitted by U.S. Court, Ardmore, I.T. Dec. 22, 1897, Court Case #60.

No. 1 was formerly wife of Henry Greenwood, Chickasaw Card #941, by whom she became an intermarried
citizen of the Chickasaw Nation. She was divorced from him and married William Underwood,
Chickasaw Card #??. Evidence of marriage to W.R. Underwood filed Nov. 10, 1902.

(Notation illegible)
Transferred from Chickasaw Card C-99.

9/22/98
JUN 20 1904

RESIDENCE: Chickasaw Nation   ~~COUNTY~~

POST OFFICE: Nebo, Ind. Ter.

CARD NO.

FIELD NO.

NAME	RELATION-SHIP TO PERSON FIRST NAMED	AGE	SEX	BLOOD	TRIBAL ENROLLMENT		
					YEAR	COUNTY	PAGE
1 James, Liddy Ann	NAMED	30	F	I.W.			
2 " George Newton	Son	4	M	1/2			
3 " Sallie Ann	Dau	2	F	1/2			
4 " Malsey	"	5mo	"	1/2			
5 Thomas, Fannie	"	13	"	1/2			

TRIBAL ENROLLMENT OF PARENTS

NAME OF FATHER	YEAR	COUNTY	NAME OF MOTHER	YEAR	COUNTY
1 Eugemus Moore	Dead	Non Citizen	Sally Greene Moore		Non Citizen
2 Eastman James	"		No. 1		
3 " "	"		No. 1		
4 " "	"		No. 1		
5 Folsom Thomas	"	Tishomingo	No. 1		

(NOTES)

No. 1 transferred from Choctaw card #D-52 June 29 '04 See decision of June 13, 1904.
Nos. 2,3 and 4 "   "   "   " #298
No. 5   "   " Chickasaw " #D-10 "   "   "   "   "   " 13, 1904.

163

Nos. 1 and 5 admitted by Commission as Chickasaws 1896 Case #51.

6/29/04.

		RESIDENCE: Choctaw Nation	COUNTY				CARD NO.			
		POST OFFICE: Lehigh, Ind. Ter.					FIELD NO.			
	NAME	RELATION-SHIP TO PERSON FIRST NAMED	AGE	SEX	BLOOD	TRIBAL ENROLLMENT			
						YEAR	COUNTY	PAGE		
1	Downing, Mose	NAMED	21	M	1/4	1896	Tishomingo	38
2	" Mattie	Wife	22	F	I.W.			
3	" Mary Mozelle	Dau	1mo	"	1/8			

	TRIBAL ENROLLMENT OF PARENTS						
	NAME OF FATHER	YEAR	COUNTY	NAME OF MOTHER	YEAR	COUNTY
1	George Downing	Dead	Non Citizen	Malissa Downing	Dead	Chick Roll
2	Henry Hall		Non Citizen	America Hall		Non Citizen
3	No. 1			No. 2		

(NOTES)

Nos. 1 and 3 transferred from Choctaw Card #5562.
No. 2   "   "   Chickasaw "   #D-361. See decision of June 13, '04.
No. 3 Born June 5, 1902; Enrolled July 17, 1902.

6/29/04.

		RESIDENCE: Pickens COUNTY					CARD NO.			
		POST OFFICE: Ardmore, IT.					FIELD NO.			
	NAME	RELATION-SHIP TO PERSON FIRST NAMED	AGE	SEX	BLOOD	TRIBAL ENROLLMENT			
						YEAR	COUNTY	PAGE		
1	Law, N.N.	NAMED	53	M	I.W.			
2	Spencer, Margaret	Dau	16	F	1/8	1897	Pickens	

	TRIBAL ENROLLMENT OF PARENTS						
	NAME OF FATHER	YEAR	COUNTY	NAME OF MOTHER	YEAR	COUNTY
1	Harvey Law	Dead	non citizen	Elizabeth L. Law		non citizen
2	No. 1			Margaret ? ? Law		Chick

(NOTES)

Nos. 1 and 2 admitted by Com in 1896 Chick Case #??
Nos. 1 and 2 admitted by U.S. Court, Ardmore, I.T. Dec. 29, 1897, Court Case #25; No. 1 as an intermarried citizen;
No. 2 as a citizen by blood.
(Four notations illegible)
Nos. 1 and 2 transferred from Chickasaw cad C-144, July 15, 1904.

JUL 15 1904

Chickasaw Enrollment Cards 1898-1914
Chickasaw by Blood   Volume V

RESIDENCE: Pickens   COUNTY   CARD NO.
POST OFFICE: Marietta, I.T.   FIELD NO.

NAME	RELATION-SHIP TO PERSON FIRST NAMED	AGE	SEX	BLOOD	TRIBAL ENROLLMENT		
					YEAR	COUNTY	PAGE
1 Washington, Jeremiah C.	NAMED	41	M	I.W.			
2 " Jeremiah C, Jr.	Son	13	"				
3 " Russell L.	"	11	"				

TRIBAL ENROLLMENT OF PARENTS

NAME OF FATHER	YEAR	COUNTY	NAME OF MOTHER	YEAR	COUNTY
1 James R. Washington		non citizen	Sallie Washington	Dead	Non citizen
2 No. 1			Mabelle Washington	"	Chick. Ind.
3 No. 1			" "	"	" "

(NOTES)

Nos. 1,2 and 3 admitted by Com in '96 Chick Case #??   *(No. 1 Dawes' Roll No. 357)*
Admitted by U.S. Court, Ardmore, I.T. Dec. 22, 1898. Court Case ??
(Other notations illegible)

JUL 15, 1904.

RESIDENCE: Pickens   COUNTY   CARD NO.
POST OFFICE: Lynn, I.T.   FIELD NO.

NAME	RELATION-SHIP TO PERSON FIRST NAMED	AGE	SEX	BLOOD	TRIBAL ENROLLMENT		
					YEAR	COUNTY	PAGE
1 Love, Joe N.	NAMED	19	M				

TRIBAL ENROLLMENT OF PARENTS

NAME OF FATHER	YEAR	COUNTY	NAME OF MOTHER	YEAR	COUNTY
1 Robt. N. Love	Dead	Non Citizen	Anna E. *(Illegible)*		

(NOTES)

No. 1 denied by Com. in 1896 Chick. Case #20.
Admitted by U.S. Court, Ardmore, I.T. March 7, 1898. Court Case #??
No. 1 an illegitimate child.
Judgement of U.S. Court admitting No. 1 *(remainder illegible)*
(Notation illegible)
Transferred from Chickasaw Card #C.185 July 15, 1904.

JUL 15, 1904

RESIDENCE: Pickens **COUNTY**		**CARD NO.**					
POST OFFICE: Marietta, I.T.		**FIELD NO.**					
	NAME	**RELATIONSHIP TO PERSON FIRST NAMED**	**AGE**	**SEX**	**BLOOD**	**TRIBAL ENROLLMENT**		
						YEAR	**COUNTY**	**PAGE**
1	King, Robert O.		19	M	1/8	1897	Pickens	11
2	" Lou M	Sis	16	F	1/8	1897	"	11

TRIBAL ENROLLMENT OF PARENTS

	NAME OF FATHER	**YEAR**	**COUNTY**	**NAME OF MOTHER**	**YEAR**	**COUNTY**
1	Oliver L. King		Non Citizen	Maude W. King	Dead	Chick Ind.
2	" " "		" "	" " "	"	" "

(NOTES)

Nos. 1 and 2 admitted in '96 Chic. Cit. *(remainder illegible)*
(Notation illegible)
Admitted by U.S. Court, Ardmore, I.T. Dec. 22, 1898 Case *(illegible)*
(Notation illegible)
Father of Nos. 1 & 2 on Chickasaw *(remainder illegible)*
Nos. 1 and 2 transferred to this card from Chickasaw 691, page ??

9/22/98.

RESIDENCE: Pickens **COUNTY**		**CARD NO.**					
POST OFFICE: Duncan, I.T.		**FIELD NO.**					
	NAME	**RELATIONSHIP TO PERSON FIRST NAMED**	**AGE**	**SEX**	**BLOOD**	**TRIBAL ENROLLMENT**		
						YEAR	**COUNTY**	**PAGE**
1	Doak, James		40	M	I.W.	1897	Pickens	83
2	" Lula E.	Dau	15	F	1/2	1897	"	25

TRIBAL ENROLLMENT OF PARENTS

	NAME OF FATHER	**YEAR**	**COUNTY**	**NAME OF MOTHER**	**YEAR**	**COUNTY**
1	J.L. Doak	Dead	Non Citz	Lizzie Doak	Dead	Non Citz
2	No. 1			Lena Doak		Chick Citz.

(NOTES)

Nos. 1 and 2 admitted by Comm. 96 Chick Case ?? *(No. 1 Dawes' Roll No. 358)*
No. 1 admitted as a citizen by intermarriage *(remainder illegible)*
Admitted by the U.S. Court, Ardmore, I.T. Dec. 22, '98 Court Case No. 2
No. 2 on Chickasaw Roll as Lula Doak
Judgement of U.S. Court admitting Nos. 1 and 2 *(remainder illegible)*
Nos. 1 and 2 transferred to this card from C.106 July 20/04

9/23/98.

RESIDENCE: Chickasaw Nation	*COUNTY*				*CARD NO.*		
POST OFFICE: Pauls Valley, I.T.					*FIELD NO.*		

NAME	RELATION-SHIP TO PERSON FIRST NAMED	AGE	SEX	BLOOD	TRIBAL ENROLLMENT		
					YEAR	COUNTY	PAGE
1 Paul, Sammie	NAMED	7	M				

TRIBAL ENROLLMENT OF PARENTS

NAME OF FATHER	YEAR	COUNTY	NAME OF MOTHER	YEAR	COUNTY
1 Sam Paul	Dead	Chickasaw	Altha Paul		non citz

(NOTES)

No. I admitted as a *(remainder illegible)*
Admitted by U.S. Ct. Southern District, March 12, 1898, Court Case #86, Althia Paul
(Notation illegible)
No. I denied by Com. in '96 Chick Case #205
No. I transferred to this card July 20, '04.

RESIDENCE:	*COUNTY*				*CARD NO.*		
POST OFFICE:					*FIELD NO.*		

NAME	RELATION-SHIP TO PERSON FIRST NAMED	AGE	SEX	BLOOD	TRIBAL ENROLLMENT		
					YEAR	COUNTY	PAGE
1 Reynolds, Sarah Jane	NAMED		F	I.W.			
2 Potts, Robert	Son		M				

TRIBAL ENROLLMENT OF PARENTS

NAME OF FATHER	YEAR	COUNTY	NAME OF MOTHER	YEAR	COUNTY
1					
2 John Taylor Potts			No. I		

(NOTES)

Nos. I and 2 admitted by Com. in '96 Chickasaw Case #275   *(No. I Dawes' Roll No. 359)*
Nos. I and 2 denied by U.S. Ct. at Ardmore *(remainder illegible)*

July 20, '04.

RESIDENCE: Pickens	*COUNTY*				*CARD NO.*		
POST OFFICE: Oakland, I.T.					*FIELD NO.*		

NAME	RELATION-SHIP TO PERSON FIRST NAMED	AGE	SEX	BLOOD	TRIBAL ENROLLMENT		
					YEAR	COUNTY	PAGE
1 Wiggs, Richard C.	NAMED	60	M	I.W.			

TRIBAL ENROLLMENT OF PARENTS

	NAME OF FATHER	YEAR	COUNTY	NAME OF MOTHER	YEAR	COUNTY
1	Richard Wiggs	Dead	Non Citz	Elizabeth Wiggs	Dead	Non Citz

(NOTES)

No. 1 admitted as an intermarried citizen by C.C.C.C. *(remainder illegible)* *(No. 1 Dawes' Roll No. 360)*
No. 1 married a Chickasaw Indian, who died, *(Illegible)* married a white woman by whom he has one child, Mary E.
Admitted by U.S. Court, Ardmore, I.T. Dec. 22, 1897. Court Case 27.
Judgement of U.S. Court admitting No. 1 *(remainder illegible)*
No. 1 admitted by Com. in 1896 Chick Case #170.
No. 1 transferred to this card July 20, '04.

9/23/98

RESIDENCE: Pontotoc ***COUNTY*** ***CARD NO.***
POST OFFICE: Chickasha, I.T. ***FIELD NO.***

	NAME	RELATIONSHIP TO PERSON FIRST NAMED	AGE	SEX	BLOOD	TRIBAL ENROLLMENT YEAR	COUNTY	PAGE
1	Bradshaw, John C.		38	M	I.W.	1897	Pontotoc	84

TRIBAL ENROLLMENT OF PARENTS

	NAME OF FATHER	YEAR	COUNTY	NAME OF MOTHER	YEAR	COUNTY
1	John Bradshaw		Non Citz.	Lizzie Bradshaw	Dead	Non Citz.

(NOTES)

On 1896 roll as John Bradshaw *(No. 1 Dawes' Roll No. 361)*
No. 1 admitted by Dawes Com. in 1896, Chickasaw Docket Case ?
Admitted by U.S. Court, Ardmore, I.T. Feby 1, 1898 Court Case No. ?
(Other notations illegible)

9/23/98.

RESIDENCE: Pontotoc ***COUNTY*** ***CARD NO.***
POST OFFICE: Purcell, I.T. ***FIELD NO.***

	NAME	RELATIONSHIP TO PERSON FIRST NAMED	AGE	SEX	BLOOD	TRIBAL ENROLLMENT YEAR	COUNTY	PAGE
1	Story, Zula		35	F	I.W.			

TRIBAL ENROLLMENT OF PARENTS

	NAME OF FATHER	YEAR	COUNTY	NAME OF MOTHER	YEAR	COUNTY
1	James Howard	Dead	Non Citizen	Martha Howard		Non Citizen

(NOTES)

No. 1 admitted as an intermarried citizen in 1896 Chick Case ?? *(No. 1 Dawes' Roll No. 362)*
No. 1 admitted by U.S. Ct. Ardmore I.T. March 12, 1898, Case #38
Judgement of U.S. Ct. admitting No. 1 vacated and set aside by decree of C.C.C.C.

(Notation illegible)
Husband and children on Chickasaw Card ??
No. 1 transferred from C.1 July 20 -'04.

9/14/98.

RESIDENCE: Pickens **COUNTY** **CARD NO.**
POST OFFICE: Kingston, I.T. **FIELD NO.**

	NAME	RELATIONSHIP TO PERSON FIRST NAMED	AGE	SEX	BLOOD	TRIBAL ENROLLMENT		
						YEAR	COUNTY	PAGE
1	Bounds, E.H.		41	M	I.W.			

TRIBAL ENROLLMENT OF PARENTS

	NAME OF FATHER	YEAR	COUNTY	NAME OF MOTHER	YEAR	COUNTY
1	Obediah Bounds		Non Citz	Parthenia Bounds		Non Citz.

(NOTES)

No. 1 admitted by Com in 1896 Chick Case #? *(No. 1 Dawes' Roll No. 363)*
No. 1 admitted by U.S. Court, Ardmore, I.T. Dec. 22, 1899, Court Case #??
Judgement of U.S. Ct. admitting No. 1 *(remainder illegible)*
White wife and children on Chickasaw Card 623.
No. 1 transferred from 623 to this card July 20, '04.

9/22/98.

RESIDENCE: Chickasaw Nation **COUNTY** **CARD NO.**
POST OFFICE: Pauls Valley, I.T. **FIELD NO.**

	NAME	RELATIONSHIP TO PERSON FIRST NAMED	AGE	SEX	BLOOD	TRIBAL ENROLLMENT		
						YEAR	COUNTY	PAGE
1	Murray, Annie		25	F	I.W.			

TRIBAL ENROLLMENT OF PARENTS

	NAME OF FATHER	YEAR	COUNTY	NAME OF MOTHER	YEAR	COUNTY
1	Sam Langden	D'd	Non Citz.	Amanda Langden		Non Citz.

(NOTES)

Admitted by U.S. Court at Ardmore, March 12th 1898. Case 154 on appeal from citizenship committee Chickasaw Nation *(No. 1 Dawes' Roll No. 364)*
(Other notations illegible)
Transferred to this card from Chickasaw Card C.212.

RESIDENCE: Panola   COUNTY

POST OFFICE: Colbert, I.T.

CARD NO.

FIELD NO.

NAME	RELATION-SHIP TO PERSON FIRST NAMED	AGE	SEX	BLOOD	TRIBAL ENROLLMENT		
					YEAR	COUNTY	PAGE
1 Standifer, Frank	NAMED	40	M	I.W.			

TRIBAL ENROLLMENT OF PARENTS

NAME OF FATHER	YEAR	COUNTY	NAME OF MOTHER	YEAR	COUNTY
1 J.F. Standifer	D'd	Non Citz.	Sarah E. Standifer		Non Citz.

(NOTES)

Admitted by Com in 1896 Chickasaw Case #153   *(No. I Dawes' Roll No. 365)*

"   "   U.S. Court, Ardmore I.T. Jan. 20, 1898, Court Case #32.

(Other notations Illegible)

No. I transferred from 9 C 192

10/12/98.

RESIDENCE: Pickens   COUNTY

POST OFFICE: Oakland, I.T.

CARD NO.

FIELD NO.

NAME	RELATION-SHIP TO PERSON FIRST NAMED	AGE	SEX	BLOOD	TRIBAL ENROLLMENT		
					YEAR	COUNTY	PAGE
1 Woody, John L.	NAMED	34	M	I.W.			

TRIBAL ENROLLMENT OF PARENTS

NAME OF FATHER	YEAR	COUNTY	NAME OF MOTHER	YEAR	COUNTY
1 J.W. Woody		Non Citizen	Elizabeth Woody		Non Citz.

(NOTES)

(Other notations illegible)   *(No. I Dawes' Roll No. 366)*

White wife and child on Chickasaw card 6146.

No. I transferred from 6146 to this card July 20, '04.

9-23-98.

RESIDENCE: Chickasaw Nation   COUNTY

POST OFFICE: Oscar, I.T.

CARD NO.

FIELD NO.

NAME	RELATION-SHIP TO PERSON FIRST NAMED	AGE	SEX	BLOOD	TRIBAL ENROLLMENT		
					YEAR	COUNTY	PAGE
1 Seay, O.W.	NAMED	31	M	I.W.			

TRIBAL ENROLLMENT OF PARENTS

NAME OF FATHER	YEAR	COUNTY	NAME OF MOTHER	YEAR	COUNTY
1 *(Name Illegible)*			*(Name Illegible)*		

(NOTES)

No. 1 admitted by Com. in 1896 in Chickasaw Case #156   *(No. 1 Dawes' Roll No. 367)*

No. 1   "   " U.S. Court, Ardmore, I.T. Dec. 22, 1897 Court Case No. 26

(Other notations illegible)

Transferred from 9-C44.

9/22/98.

	RESIDENCE: Pickens COUNTY				CARD NO.			
	POST OFFICE: Weaverton, I.T.				FIELD NO.			
NAME	RELATION-SHIP TO PERSON FIRST NAMED	AGE	SEX	BLOOD	TRIBAL ENROLLMENT			
					YEAR	COUNTY	PAGE	
1 Jones, Charles L.	NAMED	40	M	I.W.				

	TRIBAL ENROLLMENT OF PARENTS						
NAME OF FATHER	YEAR	COUNTY	NAME OF MOTHER	YEAR	COUNTY		
1 David A. Jones	Dead	Non Citizen	Melvina Jones		Non Citizen		

(NOTES)

No. 1 Admitted by Comm in 1896 Chickasaw Cit. Case #223   *(No. 1 Dawes' Roll No. 368)*

  (Claimed thru Eliza Love)

No. 1 Admitted by U.S. Ct. at Ardmore Dec. 22, 1897, Case No. 10.

(Other notations illegible)

White wife and children on Chickasaw Card 668.

No. 1 transferred from C-68 to this card July 20, '04.

9/22/98.

	RESIDENCE: Pickens COUNTY				CARD NO.			
	POST OFFICE: Overbrook, I.T.				FIELD NO.			
NAME	RELATION-SHIP TO PERSON FIRST NAMED	AGE	SEX	BLOOD	TRIBAL ENROLLMENT			
					YEAR	COUNTY	PAGE	
1 Craig, Amanda J.	NAMED	50	F	I.W.				

	TRIBAL ENROLLMENT OF PARENTS						
NAME OF FATHER	YEAR	COUNTY	NAME OF MOTHER	YEAR	COUNTY		
1 W.C. Brown	Dead	Non Citizen	Ann Brown		Non Citizen		

(NOTES)

No. 1 admitted by Com. in 96 Chickasaw Case #71 (Claimed thro' Overton Love)   *(No. 1 Dawes' Roll No. 369)*

  Admitted as Mrs. A.J. Love

No. 1 admitted by U.S. Ct, Ardmore, I.T. Dec. 21, 1897, Court Case #22

(Other notations illegible)

Wife of Charles E. Craig on Chickasaw Card C-114.

No. 1 transferred from C-114 to this card July 20, '04.   9-23-98.

Chickasaw Enrollment Cards 1898-1914
Chickasaw by Blood   Volume V

RESIDENCE: Tishomingo COUNTY					CARD NO.			
POST OFFICE: Tishomingo, I.T.					FIELD NO.			
NAME	RELATION-SHIP TO PERSON FIRST	AGE	SEX	BLOOD	TRIBAL ENROLLMENT			
					YEAR	COUNTY		PAGE
1 Scoby, Arthur E.	NAMED	29	M	I.W.	1897	Tishomingo		83

TRIBAL ENROLLMENT OF PARENTS							
NAME OF FATHER	YEAR	COUNTY	NAME OF MOTHER	YEAR	COUNTY		
1 D.M. Scoby		Non Citz	Margaret Scoby	Dead	Non Citz		

(NOTES)

Admitted by Chickasaw Case #79 in '96 by Com.   *(No. 1 Dawes' Roll No. 370)*
"   " U.S. Court, Ardmore, I.T. March 15, 1898. Court Case #60.
Supposed to be on Chickasaw Roll as an intermarried citizen.
(Other notations illegible)
Transferred from 9-6189.

9/29/98.

RESIDENCE: Pickens COUNTY					CARD NO.			
POST OFFICE: Pauls Valley, I.T.					FIELD NO.			
NAME	RELATION-SHIP TO PERSON FIRST	AGE	SEX	BLOOD	TRIBAL ENROLLMENT			
					YEAR	COUNTY		PAGE
1 Dorchester, John M	NAMED	33	M	I.W.				

TRIBAL ENROLLMENT OF PARENTS							
NAME OF FATHER	YEAR	COUNTY	NAME OF MOTHER	YEAR	COUNTY		
1 John Dorchester	Dead	Non Citizen	Fanny Dorchester	Dead	Non Citizen		

(NOTES)

No. 1 Admitted by Com in 1896 Chickasaw Case #49. Claimed thro' Rhoda Lee.   *(No. 1 Dawes' Roll No. 371)*
No. 1 Admitted by U.S. Ct, Ardmore, I.T. March 12, 1898, Court Case #45.
(Other notations illegible)
His children (white) are enrolled on C-7
No. 1 transferred from C-7 to this card July 20 '04

9-15-98.

RESIDENCE: Pickens COUNTY					CARD NO.			
POST OFFICE: Ardmore, I.T.					FIELD NO.			
NAME	RELATION-SHIP TO PERSON FIRST	AGE	SEX	BLOOD	TRIBAL ENROLLMENT			
					YEAR	COUNTY		PAGE
1 Phillips, Dora	NAMED	34	F	I.W.	1893	Pay Roll #2		181

172

TRIBAL ENROLLMENT OF PARENTS						
NAME OF FATHER	YEAR	COUNTY	NAME OF MOTHER	YEAR	COUNTY	
1 Calvin Smith	D'd	Non Citz	Martha Smith	D'd	Non Citz	

(NOTES)

No. 1 admitted by Com in 1896 Chickasaw Case #120 (Claimed as widow of Jim Goins) *(No. 1 Dawes' Roll No. 372)*
Admitted by the U.S. Court, Ardmore, I.T. Mar. 17, 1898 Court case #55
(Other notations illegible)
Transferred from 9-C143
White husband and children on 9-C143.

9/24/98.

RESIDENCE: Pickens   *COUNTY*   *CARD NO.*
POST OFFICE: Hennepin, I.T.   *FIELD NO.*

NAME	RELATION-SHIP TO PERSON FIRST NAMED	AGE	SEX	BLOOD	TRIBAL ENROLLMENT		
					YEAR	COUNTY	PAGE
1 Poe, George M.		43	M	I.W.			

TRIBAL ENROLLMENT OF PARENTS						
NAME OF FATHER	YEAR	COUNTY	NAME OF MOTHER	YEAR	COUNTY	
1 John Poe	D'd	Non Citz	Margaret B. Poe		Non Citz	

(NOTES)

No. 1 admitted by the U.S. Court, Ardmore, I.T. Nov. 15, 1898 Court Case #39   *(No. 1 Dawes' Roll No. 373)*
(Other notations illegible)
No. 1 transferred from 9-C 8

9/15/98.

RESIDENCE: Pickens   *COUNTY*   *CARD NO.*
POST OFFICE: Duncan, I.T.   *FIELD NO.*

NAME	RELATION-SHIP TO PERSON FIRST NAMED	AGE	SEX	BLOOD	TRIBAL ENROLLMENT		
					YEAR	COUNTY	PAGE
1 Duncan, Sallie		53	F	I.W.			

TRIBAL ENROLLMENT OF PARENTS						
NAME OF FATHER	YEAR	COUNTY	NAME OF MOTHER	YEAR	COUNTY	
1 Wm Thornhill	Dead	Non Citizen	Tabitha Thornhill	Dead	Non Citizen	

(NOTES)

No. 1 Admitted by Comm in 1896 Chickasaw Case #248   *(No. 1 Dawes' Roll No. 374)*
    Claimed thro' Bradford Johnson
No. 1 Admitted by U.S. Court at Ardmore, I.T. Dec. 22, 1897 Case #48
(Other notations illegible)
Now wife of William Duncan on 9-6193

No. I transferred from 9-C193 to this card July 21, '04

10-17-98.

RESIDENCE: Pickens COUNTY					CARD NO.		
POST OFFICE: Lebanon, I.T.					FIELD NO.		
NAME	RELATION-SHIP TO PERSON FIRST	AGE	SEX	BLOOD	TRIBAL ENROLLMENT		
					YEAR	COUNTY	PAGE
1 Wolford, George M.D.	NAMED	34	M	I.W.			

TRIBAL ENROLLMENT OF PARENTS							
NAME OF FATHER	YEAR	COUNTY		NAME OF MOTHER	YEAR	COUNTY	
1 Walter A. Wolford		Non Citz		Amanda Wolford		Non Citz.	

(NOTES)

No. I admitted by Com. in 96 Cjoclasaw Case #63 (Claimed thro' Agnes James)   *(No. I Dawes' Roll No. 375)*
No. I admitted by U.S. Court, Ardmore, I.T. Dec. 22, 1897 Court Case #??
(Other notations illegible)
No. I transferred from 9-C92.
Children by white wife on 9-C-92

9-22-98

RESIDENCE: Pickens COUNTY					CARD NO.		
POST OFFICE: Woolsey, I.T.					FIELD NO.		
NAME	RELATION-SHIP TO PERSON FIRST	AGE	SEX	BLOOD	TRIBAL ENROLLMENT		
					YEAR	COUNTY	PAGE
1 Woolsey, N.B.	NAMED	49	M	I.W.			

TRIBAL ENROLLMENT OF PARENTS							
NAME OF FATHER	YEAR	COUNTY		NAME OF MOTHER	YEAR	COUNTY	
1 Thos. Woolsey	D'd	Non Citz.		Eliza Woolsey	D'd	Non Citz.	

(NOTES)

No. I admitted in 96 Chickasaw Case #135 (Claimed thro' Mrs. Jane Tussy deceased) *(No. I Dawes' Roll No. 376)*
No. I admitted by U.S. Court, Ardmore, I.T. Dec. 21, 1897 Court Cae No. 8
(Other notations illegible)
No. I transferred from 9-C194
Children by white wife on 9-C194

10/17/98.

Chickasaw Enrollment Cards 1898-1914
Chickasaw by Blood   Volume V

RESIDENCE: Pickens COUNTY					CARD NO.		
POST OFFICE: Cornish, I.T.					FIELD NO.		

NAME	RELATION- SHIP TO PERSON FIRST NAMED	AGE	SEX	BLOOD	TRIBAL ENROLLMENT		
					YEAR	COUNTY	PAGE
1 Cornish, John H.	NAMED	41	M	I.W.			

TRIBAL ENROLLMENT OF PARENTS							
NAME OF FATHER	YEAR	COUNTY	NAME OF MOTHER		YEAR	COUNTY	
1 John Cornish	Dead	Non Citizen	Helen Cornish		Dead	Non Citizen	

(NOTES)

(Notation illegible)   *(No. I Dawes' Roll No. 377)*

No. I admitted by Com in 96 Chickasaw Case #30 (Claimed thro' Mollie Gar???)

No. I admitted by U.S. Ct. at Ardmore, I.T. Dec. 22, '97 Court Case #29.

(Notation illegible)

Children by white wife on 9693

No. I transferred from 9C93 to this card July 20, '04

9/22/98.

RESIDENCE: Pickens COUNTY					CARD NO.		
POST OFFICE: Alex, I.T.					FIELD NO.		

NAME	RELATION- SHIP TO PERSON FIRST NAMED	AGE	SEX	BLOOD	TRIBAL ENROLLMENT		
					YEAR	COUNTY	PAGE
1 Alexander, W. V.	NAMED	65	M	I.W.			

TRIBAL ENROLLMENT OF PARENTS							
NAME OF FATHER	YEAR	COUNTY	NAME OF MOTHER		YEAR	COUNTY	
1 Arthur Alexander	D'd	Non Citz.	Nancy Alexander		D'd	Non Citz.	

(NOTES)

No. I Admitted by Comm in 1896 Chickasaw Case #47   *(No. I Dawes' Roll No. 378)*

(Claimed thro' Rebekah Colbert, Deceased)

Admitted by the U.S. Court, Ardmore, I.T. Dec. 22, 1897 Court Case #??

(Other notations illegible)

No. I transferred from 9-C-186

White wife and children on 618.

9/28/98.

RESIDENCE: Pickens **COUNTY** **CARD NO.**
POST OFFICE: Ardmore, I.T. **FIELD NO.**

	NAME	RELATIONSHIP TO PERSON FIRST NAMED	AGE	SEX	BLOOD	TRIBAL ENROLLMENT		
						YEAR	COUNTY	PAGE
1	Allbright, J.E.C.		52	M	I.W.	1897	Pickens	83

TRIBAL ENROLLMENT OF PARENTS

	NAME OF FATHER	YEAR	COUNTY	NAME OF MOTHER	YEAR	COUNTY
1	Solomon Allbright	D'd	Non Citz	Penime Allbright	D'd	Non Citz.

(NOTES)

(All notations illegible) *(No. 1 Dawes' Roll No. 379)*

RESIDENCE: Choctaw Nation **COUNTY** **CARD NO.**
POST OFFICE: Sterrett, I.T. **FIELD NO.**

	NAME	RELATIONSHIP TO PERSON FIRST NAMED	AGE	SEX	BLOOD	TRIBAL ENROLLMENT		
						YEAR	COUNTY	PAGE
1	Waitman, Ludia		14	M	adopted white	1892	Maytubby Roll	2
2	" Henry J.	Bro	8	M	"			
3	" General J.	Father	40	M	I.W.	1893	Maytubby Roll	2

TRIBAL ENROLLMENT OF PARENTS

	NAME OF FATHER	YEAR	COUNTY	NAME OF MOTHER	YEAR	COUNTY
1	General J. Waitman			Dora A. Waitman	Dead	Chickasaw roll
2	" "			" "	"	" "
3	Henry Waitman	dead	non citizen	E.J. Waitman		non citizen

(NOTES)

The name of Dora A. Waitman (Bacon) wife of No. 3 appears on 1896 Cherokee census Roll, Delaware District, and *(remainder illegible)*
Nos. 1-2 transferred from Chickasaw Card D-171
See decision of July 19, 1904
Nos. 1 and 2 are children of General J. Waitman, Chickasaw Card D-171
No. 1 is Male. Change made under Departmental instructions of Feb. 21, 1905 (FTD #1746) DC # *(illegible)*
No. 3 was formerly husband of Dora A. Waitman (Bacon) citizen by adoption of Chickasaw Nation whose name appears on 1893 Leased District Roll Choctaw District
Said Dora A. Waitman (Bacon) died July 7, 1899.
No. 3 transferred from Chickasaw card D.171 November 29, 1905;
See decision of November 13-1905

Aug. 3-1904.

Chickasaw Enrollment Cards 1898-1914
Chickasaw by Blood   Volume V

RESIDENCE: Pontotoc COUNTY					CARD NO.			
POST OFFICE: Norman, O.T.					FIELD NO.			
NAME	RELATIONSHIP TO PERSON FIRST NAMED	AGE	SEX	BLOOD	TRIBAL ENROLLMENT			
					YEAR	COUNTY	PAGE	
1 Brittain, Marcus L.	NAMED	47	M	I.W.	1897	Pontotoc	84	

TRIBAL ENROLLMENT OF PARENTS

NAME OF FATHER	YEAR	COUNTY	NAME OF MOTHER	YEAR	COUNTY
1 R.N. Brittain	Dead	Non citizen	Elizabeth Brittain	Dead	Non Citizen

(NOTES)

Chilcren on Chickasaw Card #424   *(No. I Dawes' Roll No. 444)*
Transferred from Chickasaw Card #D.21. See decision of August 17, 1904.

Sept. 1, 1904

RESIDENCE: Pontotoc COUNTY					CARD NO.			
POST OFFICE: Noble, O.T.					FIELD NO.			
NAME	RELATIONSHIP TO PERSON FIRST NAMED	AGE	SEX	BLOOD	TRIBAL ENROLLMENT			
					YEAR	COUNTY	PAGE	
1 Gardner, Janie May	NAMED	21	F	I.W.				

TRIBAL ENROLLMENT OF PARENTS

NAME OF FATHER	YEAR	COUNTY	NAME OF MOTHER	YEAR	COUNTY
1 R.M. Davis		non citizen	Martha Davis		non citizen

(NOTES)

Wife of Simpson Dulin, Chickasaw Card #738   *(No. I Dawes' Roll No. 445)*
First married under U.S. Law, then under Chickasaw Law.
Transferred from Chickasaw Card #D.26. See Decision of August 17, 1904.

SEP. 1, 1904

RESIDENCE: Pontotoc COUNTY					CARD NO.			
POST OFFICE: Franks, I.T.					FIELD NO.			
NAME	RELATIONSHIP TO PERSON FIRST NAMED	AGE	SEX	BLOOD	TRIBAL ENROLLMENT			
					YEAR	COUNTY	PAGE	
1 Harden, Andrew	NAMED	48	M	I.W.	1893	Pontotoc	PR#2 103	
2 " Elizabeth	Wife	36	F	1/2	1893	"	103	
3 " Sarah E.	Dau	21	F	1/4	1893	"	103	
4 " Andrew J. Jr.	Son	17	M	1/4	1893	"	103	
5 " Frank Byrd	Son	15	M	1/4	1893	"	103	

6	"	Maude	Dau	13	F	1/4	1893	"		103
7	"	Josiah	Son	11	M	1/4	1893	"		103
8	"	Wood M	Son	9	M	1/4	1893	"		103
9	"	Bland V	Son	6	M	1/4	1893	"		103
10	"	Dewey	Son	4	M	1/4				
11	"	Daws	Son	2	M	1/4				

TRIBAL ENROLLMENT OF PARENTS

	NAME OF FATHER	YEAR	COUNTY	NAME OF MOTHER	YEAR	COUNTY
1	J.R. Hardin		non citizen	Elizabeth Harden		Non Citizen
2	Conrad Neighbors		"	Mary Neighbors	1893	Ishatubby Pay Roll
3	No. 1			No. 2		
4	No. 1			No. 2		
5	No. 1			No. 2		
6	No. 1			No. 2		
7	No. 1			No. 2		
8	No. 1			No. 2		
9	No. 1			No. 2		
10	No. 1			No. 2		
11	No. 1			No. 2		

(NOTES)

No. 4 on Chickasaw 1893 roll as A.J. Hardin, Jr.
No. 6 on Chickasaw 1893 roll as Maudy Hardin
No. 11 Enrolled December 22, 1900
Nos. 1 to 11 inclusive transferred from Chickasaw card D224. See decision of Commission of July 16, 1903.
    Affirmed by Department July 7, 1904.

RESIDENCE: Pontotoc COUNTY					CARD NO.			
POST OFFICE: McGee, I.T.					FIELD NO.			

NAME	RELATION- SHIP TO PERSON FIRST NAMED	AGE	SEX	BLOOD	TRIBAL ENROLLMENT		
					YEAR	COUNTY	PAGE
1 Lee, Samuel S.		32	M	I.W.	1893	Pay roll No. 2	141

TRIBAL ENROLLMENT OF PARENTS

	NAME OF FATHER	YEAR	COUNTY	NAME OF MOTHER	YEAR	COUNTY
1	Silas W. Lee	Dead	Non Citizen	Kate Lee	Dead	Non Citizen

(NOTES)

First married to Biddie Chisholm, Chickasaw by blood, un U.S. Law and again under Chickasaw law.
After her death he married a white woman
Two children by Biddie Lee on Chickasaw Card #???. Transferred from Chickasaw Card #D.27.
    See decision of Aug. 17, 1904.

SEP. 1, 1904

RESIDENCE: Pickens   COUNTY   CARD NO.

POST OFFICE: Whitebead, I.T.   FIELD NO.

NAME	RELATION-SHIP TO PERSON FIRST NAMED	AGE	SEX	BLOOD	TRIBAL ENROLLMENT		
					YEAR	COUNTY	PAGE
1 Paher, Susan	NAMED	48	F				

TRIBAL ENROLLMENT OF PARENTS						
NAME OF FATHER	YEAR	COUNTY	NAME OF MOTHER	YEAR	COUNTY
1 *(Illegible)* Stacey	dead	non citizen	Margaret Stacey		non citizen

(NOTES)

Certificate of marriage to white man ub 1873 filed Sept. 28, 1898.
Transferred from Chickasaw Card #D.31. See decision of Aug. 17, 1904.

Sept. 1, 1904.

RESIDENCE: Pickens   COUNTY   CARD NO.

POST OFFICE: Durwood, I.T.   FIELD NO.

NAME	RELATION-SHIP TO PERSON FIRST NAMED	AGE	SEX	BLOOD	TRIBAL ENROLLMENT		
					YEAR	COUNTY	PAGE
1 Hiser, Mincy	NAMED	41	F	I.W.	1897	Pickens	83

TRIBAL ENROLLMENT OF PARENTS						
NAME OF FATHER	YEAR	COUNTY	NAME OF MOTHER	YEAR	COUNTY
1 Milton Page		non citizen	Ann Page	dead	non citizen

(NOTES)

On Chickasaw roll doubtful list Pickens Co. Page 83, as Minnie Hiser
Married Jany. 29, 1874 to William *(Illegible)* Chickasaw citizen. After his death, was married on Jan. 15, 1879, to
N.K. Hizer, non citz. under Chickasaw law -
Transferred from Chickasaw card #D.43. See decision Aug. 17, 1904.

Sep. 1, 1904.

RESIDENCE: Pickens   COUNTY   CARD NO.

POST OFFICE: Ardmore, I.T.   FIELD NO.

NAME	RELATION-SHIP TO PERSON FIRST NAMED	AGE	SEX	BLOOD	TRIBAL ENROLLMENT		
					YEAR	COUNTY	PAGE
1 Granden, Martha A.	NAMED	48	F	I.W.	1893	Chick Pay Roll #2	101

TRIBAL ENROLLMENT OF PARENTS						
NAME OF FATHER	YEAR	COUNTY	NAME OF MOTHER	YEAR	COUNTY
1 A. Boutwell	Dead	non-citizen	Pamelia G. Boutwell		non-citizen

Chickasaw Enrollment Cards 1898-1914
Chickasaw by Blood   Volume V

(NOTES)

On Chickasaw pay roll #2 page 101 as Mat Howard

Married in 1874 to John Parker a Chickasaw Indian, Subsequently married three white men, L.S. Hurand, F.D. *(Illegible)* and J.? Granden.

Transferred from Chickasaw card #D.681. See decision of Aug. 17, 1904.

Sep. 1, 1904

RESIDENCE: Tishomingo COUNTY					CARD NO.			
POST OFFICE: Tishomingo, I.T.					FIELD NO.			
NAME	RELATION-SHIP TO PERSON FIRST	AGE	SEX	BLOOD	TRIBAL ENROLLMENT			
					YEAR	COUNTY		PAGE
1 Williams, John F.	NAMED	50	M	I.W.	1897	Pickens		79

TRIBAL ENROLLMENT OF PARENTS							
NAME OF FATHER	YEAR	COUNTY	NAME OF MOTHER	YEAR	COUNTY		
1 Wm D. Williams	dead	non Citizen	Eliza Williams	dead	non citizen		

(NOTES)

On Chickasaw roll as J.F. Williams

Married Chickasaw woman Jany. 1, 1874

Married white woman Dec. 23, 1888.

Affidavit of P.F. Kemp as to marriage ceremony filed Sept. 19, 1898.

Certified copy of marriage record filed Oct. 4, 1898.

Transferred from Chickasaw card #D.87

See decision of August 17, 1904.

Sept. 1, 1904.

RESIDENCE: Tishomingo COUNTY					CARD NO.			
POST OFFICE: Tishomingo I.T.					FIELD NO.			
NAME	RELATION-SHIP TO PERSON FIRST	AGE	SEX	BLOOD	TRIBAL ENROLLMENT			
					YEAR	COUNTY		PAGE
1 Poyner, Louisa J	NAMED	43	F	I.W.	1897	Tishomingo		83

TRIBAL ENROLLMENT OF PARENTS							
NAME OF FATHER	YEAR	COUNTY	NAME OF MOTHER	YEAR	COUNTY		
1 *(Illegible)* Corbett	dead	non citizen	Percilla Corbett	dead	non citizen		

(NOTES)

(All notations illegible)

Sept. 1, 1904.

| RESIDENCE: Pickens COUNTY | | | | | CARD NO. | | | |

| POST OFFICE: Duncan, I.T. | | | | | FIELD NO. | | | |

NAME	RELATION-SHIP TO PERSON FIRST NAMED	AGE	SEX	BLOOD	TRIBAL ENROLLMENT			
					YEAR	COUNTY		PAGE
1 Weaver, James Wilson	NAMED	39	M	I.W.	1897	Pickens		83

TRIBAL ENROLLMENT OF PARENTS							
NAME OF FATHER	YEAR	COUNTY	NAME OF MOTHER	YEAR	COUNTY		
1 Claybourne Weaver		non citz	Sarah Ann Weaver	dead	non citizen		

(NOTES)

(All notations illegible)

Sept. 1, 1904.

| RESIDENCE: Chickasaw Nation ~~COUNTY~~ | | | | | CARD NO. | | | |

| POST OFFICE: (Illegible), I.T. | | | | | FIELD NO. | | | |

NAME	RELATION-SHIP TO PERSON FIRST NAMED	AGE	SEX	BLOOD	TRIBAL ENROLLMENT			
					YEAR	COUNTY		PAGE
1 Mays, George W.	NAMED	41	M	I.W.	1893	Chic pay roll No. ?		151

TRIBAL ENROLLMENT OF PARENTS							
NAME OF FATHER	YEAR	COUNTY	NAME OF MOTHER	YEAR	COUNTY		
1 J.L. Mays	Dead	non citizen	Sarah Mays	dead	non citizen		

(NOTES)

(All notations illegible)

| RESIDENCE: Pontotoc COUNTY | | | | | CARD NO. | | | |

| POST OFFICE: Pauls Valley I.T. | | | | | FIELD NO. | | | |

NAME	RELATION-SHIP TO PERSON FIRST NAMED	AGE	SEX	BLOOD	TRIBAL ENROLLMENT			
					YEAR	COUNTY		PAGE
1 Bullock, Sarah Strickland	NAMED	43	F	I.W.	1897	Pontotoc		

TRIBAL ENROLLMENT OF PARENTS							
NAME OF FATHER	YEAR	COUNTY	NAME OF MOTHER	YEAR	COUNTY		
1 Reuben Belvin	D'd	non citz	Martha Belvin	D'd	non citz.		

(NOTES)

On Chickasaw roll doubtful list as Sarah Strickland
Husband of No. 1 on R.#8
No. 1 transferred from Chickasaw card D#9 *(remainder illegible)*

RESIDENCE: Chickasaw Nation ~~COUNTY~~					CARD NO.		
POST OFFICE: Wallville, I.T.					FIELD NO.		
NAME	RELATION-SHIP TO PERSON FIRST NAMED	AGE	SEX	BLOOD	TRIBAL ENROLLMENT YEAR	COUNTY	PAGE
1 Hogard, Minnie		24	F	I.W.	1897	Pickens	83

TRIBAL ENROLLMENT OF PARENTS

NAME OF FATHER	YEAR	COUNTY	NAME OF MOTHER	YEAR	COUNTY
1 Andrew Casey		non citizen	??olena Casey	D'd	non citz.

(NOTES)

No. 1 now the wife of John Hogard a non citz. white man Mar. 4, 1901.
No. 1 transferred from Chickasaw D#19. See decision of Sept 23, 1904.

RESIDENCE: Pickens COUNTY					CARD NO.		
POST OFFICE:					FIELD NO.		
NAME	RELATION-SHIP TO PERSON FIRST NAMED	AGE	SEX	BLOOD	TRIBAL ENROLLMENT YEAR	COUNTY	PAGE
1 Heald, Charles Hobart		59	M	I.W.	1893	Chick Pay roll No. 2	100

TRIBAL ENROLLMENT OF PARENTS

NAME OF FATHER	YEAR	COUNTY	NAME OF MOTHER	YEAR	COUNTY
1 W. Heald	D'd	non citz	Lucy Heald	D'd	non citz

(NOTES)

No. 1 married to Chickasaw citizen in *(illegible)* - In 1893 married white woman
No. 1 is father of Wm and Benj. on Chickasaw card #556
(Notation illegible)

RESIDENCE: Tishomingo COUNTY					CARD NO.		
POST OFFICE: Emet, I.T.					FIELD NO.		
NAME	RELATION-SHIP TO PERSON FIRST NAMED	AGE	SEX	BLOOD	TRIBAL ENROLLMENT YEAR	COUNTY	PAGE
1 Collins, Thomas W.		63	M	I.W.	1893	Chick Pay roll No. 2	112

TRIBAL ENROLLMENT OF PARENTS

NAME OF FATHER	YEAR	COUNTY	NAME OF MOTHER	YEAR	COUNTY
1 George Collins	D'd	non citiz	Mildred A. Collins	D'd	non citz.

(NOTES)

No. 1 married to Eby Wadkins a Chickasaw woman in 1861
(Other notations illegible)

Chickasaw Enrollment Cards 1898-1914
Chickasaw by Blood   Volume V

RESIDENCE: Chickasaw Nation COUNTY						CARD NO.		
POST OFFICE: Marlow, I.T.						FIELD NO.		

NAME	RELATION-SHIP TO PERSON FIRST NAMED	AGE	SEX	BLOOD	TRIBAL ENROLLMENT		
					YEAR	COUNTY	PAGE
1 Tomlinson, Mary Y	FIRST NAMED	67	F	I.W.	1893	Pickens	PR#2 110

TRIBAL ENROLLMENT OF PARENTS

	NAME OF FATHER	YEAR	COUNTY	NAME OF MOTHER	YEAR	COUNTY
1	*(Illegible)* Gilliam	D'd	non citz	Caroline Gilliam	D'd	non citz

(NOTES)

No. I married to George C. Moore a Chickasaw in 1852.
lived with him until his death in 1863
Married J.W. Tomlinson a white man in 1881
No. I transferred from Chickasaw card #0.191
See decision of Sept. ??, 1904.

RESIDENCE: Chickasaw Nation ~~COUNTY~~						CARD NO.		
POST OFFICE: Sulphur, I.T.						FIELD NO.		

NAME	RELATION-SHIP TO PERSON FIRST NAMED	AGE	SEX	BLOOD	TRIBAL ENROLLMENT		
					YEAR	COUNTY	PAGE
1 Campbell, Sarah	FIRST NAMED	32	F	I.W.	1896	Doubtful *(illegible)* Pickens County	83

TRIBAL ENROLLMENT OF PARENTS

	NAME OF FATHER	YEAR	COUNTY	NAME OF MOTHER	YEAR	COUNTY
1	*(Illegible)* Manning		Non citz	Martha Manning		non citz.

(NOTES)

(All notations illegible)

RESIDENCE: Chickasaw Nation ~~COUNTY~~						CARD NO.		
POST OFFICE: Davis, I.T.						FIELD NO.		

NAME	RELATION-SHIP TO PERSON FIRST NAMED	AGE	SEX	BLOOD	TRIBAL ENROLLMENT		
					YEAR	COUNTY	PAGE
1 Short, Robert P.	FIRST NAMED	23	M	I.W.	1893	Tishomingo	PR#2 131

TRIBAL ENROLLMENT OF PARENTS

	NAME OF FATHER	YEAR	COUNTY	NAME OF MOTHER	YEAR	COUNTY
1	Daniel Short		non citz	Harriet Short	D'd	non citz.

Chickasaw Enrollment Cards 1898-1914
Chickasaw by Blood   Volume V

(NOTES)

No. 1 formerly husband of Hattie *(illegible)* on Chickasaw Card #1368   *(No. 1 Dawes' Roll No. 500)*
No. 1 married to Hattie N. Lillard nee Johnson a Chickasaw Indian Dec. 12, 1886,
Dovorced from her Nov. 15, 1896
Married to Nellie Bailey an *(illegible)* Citizen Dec. 15, 1897
No. 1 transferred from Chickasaw card D#225
See decision of Sept. 19, 1904.

RESIDENCE: Chickasaw Nation   **COUNTY**   **CARD NO.**
POST OFFICE: Durwood, I.T.   **FIELD NO.**

NAME	RELATION-SHIP TO PERSON FIRST NAMED	AGE	SEX	BLOOD	TRIBAL ENROLLMENT		
					YEAR	COUNTY	PAGE
1 McLish, Esther	FIRST NAMED	48	F	I.W.	1893	Chick Pay roll #1	137 #47
2 " Holmes	Son	9	M	1/4			

TRIBAL ENROLLMENT OF PARENTS

	NAME OF FATHER	YEAR	COUNTY	NAME OF MOTHER	YEAR	COUNTY
1	*(Name Illegible)*	D'd	non citz	Annie *(Illegible)*		Choctaw and Cherokee
2	Holmes McLish	"	Pickens	Esther McLish		Claims Cherokee

(NOTES)

No. 1 claims to be an intermarried Chickasaw   *(No. 1 Dawes' Roll No. 501)*
First married to   Benj. Frazier   in 1869 lived with him until his death
then   "   " Houston Brown   " 1872 "   "   "   "   "   "
then   "   " Jim Wolf   " 1880 "   "   "   "   "   "
then   "   " Holmes McLish   " 1893 "   "   "   "   "   "
          Claims all four husbands were Chickasaws
No. 1 transferred from Chickasaw card D#381. See decision of Sept. 8, 1904
No. 2 was born Sept 22, 1894   *(No. 2 Dawes' Roll No. 4950)*
Holmes McLish, father of No. 2, on 1893 Chick Pay Roll *(remainder illegible)*

                                                                     Sept. 23, 1904.

RESIDENCE: Chickasaw Nation   ~~COUNTY~~   **CARD NO.**
POST OFFICE: Ardmore, I.T.   **FIELD NO.**

NAME	RELATION-SHIP TO PERSON FIRST NAMED	AGE	SEX	BLOOD	TRIBAL ENROLLMENT		
					YEAR	COUNTY	PAGE
1 Fitch, D.H.	NAMED	56	M	I.W.	1896	Pickens47	

184

Chickasaw Enrollment Cards 1898-1914
Chickasaw by Blood   Volume V

TRIBAL ENROLLMENT OF PARENTS

	NAME OF FATHER	YEAR	COUNTY	NAME OF MOTHER	YEAR	COUNTY
1						

(NOTES)

No. 1 married in 1882 to Emily Colbert, a Chickasaw from whom he was   *(No. 1 Dawes' Roll No. 502)*
divorced in 1891. Emily Colbert former wife of No. 1 is Emma McGlasson on Chickasaw card #577
No. 1 transferred from Chickasaw card #D335. See decision of Sept. 8, 1904.

Sept. 23, 1904.

RESIDENCE: Choctaw Nation   *COUNTY*   *CARD NO.*
POST OFFICE: Krebbs, I.T.   *FIELD NO.*

	NAME	RELATION-SHIP TO PERSON FIRST NAMED	AGE	SEX	BLOOD	TRIBAL ENROLLMENT		
						YEAR	COUNTY	PAGE
1	Coleman, Maggie	FIRST NAMED	29	F	I.W.	1897	Chick residing in Choc Nation	82

TRIBAL ENROLLMENT OF PARENTS

	NAME OF FATHER	YEAR	COUNTY	NAME OF MOTHER	YEAR	COUNTY
1	*(Illegible)* Fink	D'd	non citz	Elizabeth Fink	D'd	non citz.

(NOTES)

No. 1 widow of Louis H. Priddy, Chickasaw roll 1st Dist. Choc Nation page 67   *(No. 1 Dawes' Roll No. 503)*
No. 1 married *(Illegible)* W. Coleman an U.S. Citizen Feby 20, '99
No. 1 on 1897 Roll as Mary Priddy.
No. 1 on Oct. 15, 1902, Name was Maggie A. Russell
No. 1 transferred from Chickasaw card #D.231. See decision of Sept. *(illegible)*

Sept. 23, 1904.

RESIDENCE: Pickens   *COUNTY*   *CARD NO.*
POST OFFICE: Woodford, I.T.   *FIELD NO.*

	NAME	RELATION-SHIP TO PERSON FIRST NAMED	AGE	SEX	BLOOD	TRIBAL ENROLLMENT		
						YEAR	COUNTY	PAGE
1	Williford, Joe	NAMED	38	M	I.W.	1897	Pickens	77
2	" Nannie		38	F	I.W.	1893	"	PR#2 158

TRIBAL ENROLLMENT OF PARENTS

	NAME OF FATHER	YEAR	COUNTY	NAME OF MOTHER	YEAR	COUNTY
1	John Williford		non citz	Mary Williford	D'd	non citz
2	Bill Lynn	D'd	"	Sally Lynn		"

185

Chickasaw Enrollment Cards 1898-1914
Chickasaw by Blood   Volume V

(NOTES)

No. 1 on Chickasaw roll as Joe Wilford   *(No. 1 Dawes' Roll No. 504)*
No. 2 Nannie Williford was married first to M. Lane under U.S. law and afterward   *(No. 2 Dawes' Roll No. 505)*
under Chickasaw law. Chickasaw Commissionclaims that she "Married out" If this is true, Joe also
"married out" when he married Nannie
Nos. 1 and 2 transferred from Chickasaw card D#41.
    See decision of Sept. 18, 1904.

                                                                              Sept. 23, 1904.

RESIDENCE: Choctaw Nation	COUNTY				CARD NO.			
POST OFFICE: Kiowa, I.T.					FIELD NO.			
NAME	RELATION-SHIP TO PERSON FIRST NAMED	AGE	SEX	BLOOD	TRIBAL ENROLLMENT			
					YEAR	COUNTY	PAGE	
1 Colbert, Ova	NAMED	19	F	I.W.				
TRIBAL ENROLLMENT OF PARENTS								
NAME OF FATHER	YEAR	COUNTY		NAME OF MOTHER	YEAR	COUNTY		
1 Ed Robinson		non citz		Frances Robinson		non citz		

(NOTES)

No. 1 is wife of Oscar Colbert on Chickasaw card #212. She was married to Oscar   *(No. 1 Dawes' Roll No. 506)*
Colbert *(Illegible)* 1902 United States license both parties having always been residents of the Choctaw Nation.
No. 1 transferred from Chickasaw card #D#353
See decision of Sept. 23, 1904.

                                                                              Sept. 23, 1904.

RESIDENCE:	COUNTY				CARD NO.			
POST OFFICE: Ardmore, Ind. Ter.					FIELD NO.			
NAME	RELATION-SHIP TO PERSON FIRST NAMED	AGE	SEX	BLOOD	TRIBAL ENROLLMENT			
					YEAR	COUNTY	PAGE	
1 Jennings, Mary E.	NAMED	39	F	I.W.	1893	Pickens	P.R.#1 No. 137	
TRIBAL ENROLLMENT OF PARENTS								
NAME OF FATHER	YEAR	COUNTY		NAME OF MOTHER	YEAR	COUNTY		
1 John Wagnon	dead	non citizen		Paulina Wagnon		non citizen		

(NOTES)

Also on page 83 as Mary Jennings, Pickens Co. 1897 roll
No. 1 transferred from Chickasaw card #D227.
See decision of *(illegible)*

                                                                              Oct. 31, 1904.

Chickasaw Enrollment Cards 1898-1914
Chickasaw by Blood   Volume V

RESIDENCE: Pickens COUNTY   CARD NO.

POST OFFICE: Bradley   FIELD NO.

NAME	RELATION-SHIP TO PERSON FIRST NAMED	AGE	SEX	BLOOD	TRIBAL ENROLLMENT		
					YEAR	COUNTY	PAGE
1 Thacker, Zachary T.	FIRST NAMED	52	M	IW	1893	Pickens	PR#2 210

TRIBAL ENROLLMENT OF PARENTS

NAME OF FATHER	YEAR	COUNTY	NAME OF MOTHER	YEAR	COUNTY
1 Samuel J. Thacker	dead	non citizen	Mary Ann Thacker	dead	non citizen

(NOTES)

No. 1 transferred from Chickasaw card #0199.
See decision of *(illegible)*

RESIDENCE: COUNTY   CARD NO.

POST OFFICE: McMillan, I.T.   FIELD NO.

NAME	RELATION-SHIP TO PERSON FIRST NAMED	AGE	SEX	BLOOD	TRIBAL ENROLLMENT		
					YEAR	COUNTY	PAGE
1 Bean, Mark	NAMED	49	M	IW	1897	Pickens	83

TRIBAL ENROLLMENT OF PARENTS

NAME OF FATHER	YEAR	COUNTY	NAME OF MOTHER	YEAR	COUNTY
1 Isaac Bean		non citizen	Nancy Bead	dead	non citizen

(NOTES)

No. 1 transferred from Chickasaw card *(illegible)*
See decision *(illegible)*

RESIDENCE: Pickens COUNTY   CARD NO.

POST OFFICE: Provence, Ind. Ter.   FIELD NO.

NAME	RELATION-SHIP TO PERSON FIRST NAMED	AGE	SEX	BLOOD	TRIBAL ENROLLMENT		
					YEAR	COUNTY	PAGE
1 Owens, Samuel	NAMED	49	N	IW	1897	Doubtful Cit	83

TRIBAL ENROLLMENT OF PARENTS

NAME OF FATHER	YEAR	COUNTY	NAME OF MOTHER	YEAR	COUNTY
1 Joel Owens	dead	non citizen	Angeline Owens	dead	non citizen

(NOTES)

No. 1 divorced wife Rachael Yates is on Chickasaw card #1368 and on final roll #3870
(Other notations illegible)

Oct. 31, 1904.

187

RESIDENCE: Chickasaw Nation **COUNTY** **CARD NO.**
POST OFFICE: Walden, I.T. **FIELD NO.**

NAME	RELATION-SHIP TO PERSON FIRST NAMED	AGE	SEX	BLOOD	TRIBAL ENROLLMENT		
					YEAR	COUNTY	PAGE
1 Carter, Florence	NAMED	28	M	1/4	1897	Pickens	86

TRIBAL ENROLLMENT OF PARENTS

NAME OF FATHER	YEAR	COUNTY	NAME OF MOTHER	YEAR	COUNTY
1 Eli Carter	dead	non citizen	Mary Carter		

(NOTES)

(All notations illegible)   *(No. I Dawes' Roll No. 4914)*

RESIDENCE: **COUNTY** **CARD NO.**
POST OFFICE: Hastings, I.T. **FIELD NO.**

NAME	RELATION-SHIP TO PERSON FIRST NAMED	AGE	SEX	BLOOD	TRIBAL ENROLLMENT		
					YEAR	COUNTY	PAGE
1 Morris, John W.	NAMED	49	M	IW			

TRIBAL ENROLLMENT OF PARENTS

NAME OF FATHER	YEAR	COUNTY	NAME OF MOTHER	YEAR	COUNTY
1 W.H. Morris	dead	non citizen	*(Name illegible)*		

(NOTES)

(All notations illegible)   No. 20, 1904

RESIDENCE: **COUNTY** **CARD NO.**
POST OFFICE: Platter, I.T. **FIELD NO.**

NAME	RELATION-SHIP TO PERSON FIRST NAMED	AGE	SEX	BLOOD	TRIBAL ENROLLMENT		
					YEAR	COUNTY	PAGE
1 Summers, Bettie	NAMED	69	F	IW	1897	Panola	83

TRIBAL ENROLLMENT OF PARENTS

NAME OF FATHER	YEAR	COUNTY	NAME OF MOTHER	YEAR	COUNTY
1 *(Name Illegible)*			*(Name Illegible)*		

(NOTES)

No. 1 formerly wife of Stephen Colbert, a recognized Chickasaw by blood, he died about 1884
(Other notations illegible)

Nov. 20, 1904.

Chickasaw Enrollment Cards 1898-1914
Chickasaw by Blood   Volume V

RESIDENCE:	COUNTY					CARD NO.		
POST OFFICE:						FIELD NO.		

NAME	RELATION-SHIP TO PERSON FIRST NAMED	AGE	SEX	BLOOD	TRIBAL ENROLLMENT		
					YEAR	COUNTY	PAGE
1 Tucker, George R.		46	M	I.W.	1897	Pickens	78

TRIBAL ENROLLMENT OF PARENTS

NAME OF FATHER	YEAR	COUNTY	NAME OF MOTHER	YEAR	COUNTY
1 Wm Tucker	dead	non citizen	Katie Tucker	dead	

(NOTES)

Chickasaw wife died and he married a white woman in 1898.
No. 1 formerly husband of Eliza Tucker *(remainder illegible)*
On Chickasaw intermarried roll Pidkens Co. page 78 as George Tucker.
No. 1 Originally listed for enrollment on Choctaw card #D.54, Sept. 28, 1898. Transferred to Chickasaw card #D.356, May 24, 1902, and transferred to this card Nov. 26, 1904.
   See decision of Nov. 10, 1904.

RESIDENCE: Choctaw Nation	COUNTY					CARD NO.		
POST OFFICE:						FIELD NO.		

NAME	RELATION-SHIP TO PERSON FIRST NAMED	AGE	SEX	BLOOD	TRIBAL ENROLLMENT		
					YEAR	COUNTY	PAGE
1 Jennings, Lizzie						Ieshatubby	
2 " Robert							
3 " Mary							

TRIBAL ENROLLMENT OF PARENTS

	NAME OF FATHER	YEAR	COUNTY	NAME OF MOTHER	YEAR	COUNTY
1						
2						
3						

(NOTES)

Husband, Richard Jennings and two children *(remainder illegible)*   *(No. 1 Dawes' Roll No. 4927)*
No. 1 on 1885 Choctaw Census Roll *(remainder illegible)*   *(No. 2 Dawes' Roll No. 4928)*
Nos. 1 and 2 originally listed for enrollment Sept. 14, 1899 *(remainder illegible)*   *(No. 3 Dawes' Roll No. 4929)*
Nos. 1,2,3 transferred to this card *(remainder illegible)*

Chickasaw Enrollment Cards 1898-1914
Chickasaw by Blood   Volume V

RESIDENCE:	COUNTY				CARD NO.			
POST OFFICE:	Miami, Texas				FIELD NO.			

NAME	RELATION-SHIP TO PERSON FIRST NAMED	AGE	SEX	BLOOD	TRIBAL ENROLLMENT		
					YEAR	COUNTY	PAGE
1 Carr, James J.	NAMED	36	M				

TRIBAL ENROLLMENT OF PARENTS							
NAME OF FATHER	YEAR	COUNTY	NAME OF MOTHER	YEAR	COUNTY
1 E.F. Carr	Dead	non citizen	Nancy Carr	dead	

(NOTES)

Jennie Carr, former wife of No. I died in 1892
Claims through his former wife Jennie Factor who was the mother of Henry *(or Hensy)*
     on Chickasaw card #853 and #2520 on final roll *(remainder illegible)*
Afterwards he married Maude Carr
No. I originally listed for enrollment Sept. 20/98, on Chickasaw card #??
Transferred to this card Dec. 15, 1904.

RESIDENCE:	COUNTY				CARD NO.			
POST OFFICE:	Tahlequah				FIELD NO.			

NAME	RELATION-SHIP TO PERSON FIRST NAMED	AGE	SEX	BLOOD	TRIBAL ENROLLMENT		
					YEAR	COUNTY	PAGE
1 Paul, John C	NAMED						

TRIBAL ENROLLMENT OF PARENTS							
NAME OF FATHER	YEAR	COUNTY	NAME OF MOTHER	YEAR	COUNTY
1					

(NOTES)

First married to Kittie Paul, formerly Durant, a recognized citizen by blood of the Chickasaw Nation. After eight years they separated and he has successively married Harriet Jennings and Amanda Gordon, both non citizens. No. I originally listed for enrollment Sept. 27/98 on Chickasaw card #D-57. Transferred to this card Dec. ??

RESIDENCE:	COUNTY				CARD NO.			
POST OFFICE:	Tishomingo				FIELD NO.			

NAME	RELATION-SHIP TO PERSON FIRST NAMED	AGE	SEX	BLOOD	TRIBAL ENROLLMENT		
					YEAR	COUNTY	PAGE
1 ?rwin, Jennie	NAMED	54	F	I.W.	1893	Pay Roll #1	108

TRIBAL ENROLLMENT OF PARENTS						
	NAME OF FATHER	YEAR	COUNTY	NAME OF MOTHER	YEAR	COUNTY
1	Daniel Watson	dead	non citz			

(NOTES)

No. 1 formerly the wife of *(remainder illegible)* recognized and enrolled citizen by blood of the Chickasaw Nation; who is identified upon the 1878 Chickasaw Annuity Roll, Tishomingo Co. #103. He died about 1881. Afterwards No. 1 married John S. Irwin, a white man
No. 1 originally listed for enrollment Feby. 7, 1900, *(illegible)*
Transferred to this card Dec. 15, ????
On May 21, 1901, application was made by the town officer of Eufaula Canadian Town for enrollment of No. 1 as a Creek by blood. She was subsequently *(illegible)* by the Commission and said enrollment approved by Secretary on March 28, 1902. On May 12, 1902, she elected to be enrolled as a Chickasaw by intermarriage and on Oct. 31, 1902, the Commission *(illegible)* remanded by Depart,emt and on June 30, 1904, said *(illegible)* was by direction of the Secretary (I.T.D. 5304-1904) *(illegible)*

RESIDENCE: Pickens ***COUNTY***				***CARD NO.***				
POST OFFICE: Healdton, IT				***FIELD NO.***				
	NAME	RELATION-SHIP TO PERSON FIRST NAMED	AGE	SEX	BLOOD	TRIBAL ENROLLMENT		
						YEAR	COUNTY	PAGE
1	Trentham, Joseph							

TRIBAL ENROLLMENT OF PARENTS						
	NAME OF FATHER	YEAR	COUNTY	NAME OF MOTHER	YEAR	COUNTY
1						

(NOTES)

No. 1 denied by *(illegible)*
No. 1 admitted by U.S. Court, Southern District *(remainder illegible)*
No. 1 admitted as an intermarried Chickasaw by Choctaw and Chickasaw Citizenship *(illegible)*
(Other notations illegible)

RESIDENCE: ***COUNTY***				***CARD NO.***				
POST OFFICE: Kittie, I.T.				***FIELD NO.***				
	NAME	RELATION-SHIP TO PERSON FIRST NAMED	AGE	SEX	BLOOD	TRIBAL ENROLLMENT		
						YEAR	COUNTY	PAGE
1	Allen, Winfield Scott		53	K	1/2	1897	Pontotoc	

TRIBAL ENROLLMENT OF PARENTS						
	NAME OF FATHER	YEAR	COUNTY	NAME OF MOTHER	YEAR	COUNTY
1						

(NOTES)

(All notations illegible) *(No. 1 Dawes' Roll No. 4942)*

RESIDENCE: Pickens COUNTY					CARD NO.		
POST OFFICE: *(Illegible)* I.T.					FIELD NO.		
NAME		RELATION-SHIP TO PERSON FIRST NAMED	AGE	SEX	BLOOD	TRIBAL ENROLLMENT		
						YEAR	COUNTY	PAGE
1	Morris, Olive J		42	F	I.W.	1893	Chic Payroll	#2 180

TRIBAL ENROLLMENT OF PARENTS

	NAME OF FATHER	YEAR	COUNTY	NAME OF MOTHER	YEAR	COUNTY
1	Sammie C. Buckley	dead	Non Citizen	Mary Buckley	dead	non citizen

(NOTES)

Jan 3, 1875, No. 1 was married to James Jones a recognized citizen by blood of the Chickasaw Nation.
James Jones died in 1877
No. 1 successively married William Staten, Andrew Pickett and S.F. Morris, all non citizens, *(remainder illegible)*
(Remaining notations illegible).

RESIDENCE: Pontotoc COUNTY					CARD NO.		
POST OFFICE: Purcell, Ind. Ter.					FIELD NO.		
NAME		RELATION-SHIP TO PERSON FIRST NAMED	AGE	SEX	BLOOD	TRIBAL ENROLLMENT		
						YEAR	COUNTY	PAGE
1	Taylor, William V.		47	M	I.W.	1893	Pickens	P.R.#2 ??

TRIBAL ENROLLMENT OF PARENTS

	NAME OF FATHER	YEAR	COUNTY	NAME OF MOTHER	YEAR	COUNTY
1	*(Illegible)* Taylor	dead	non citizen	Katie Taylor	dead	non citizen

(NOTES)

No. 1 formerly the husband of Lucy McLaughlin *(Illegible)* a recognized citizen by blood of the Chickasaw Nation.
In 1888 No. 1 married Nettie Wtkins, a non citizen white woman.
No. 1 identified on 1893 Chick Pay Roll #2 page 210 as *(Illegible)* Taylor.
No. 1 originally listed for enrollment on Chickasaw card D-221
Nos. 26, 98 transferred to this card Feb 5, 1905 see decision of *(illegible)*

RESIDENCE: COUNTY					CARD NO.		
POST OFFICE: Purcell, I.T.					FIELD NO.		
NAME		RELATION-SHIP TO PERSON FIRST NAMED	AGE	SEX	BLOOD	TRIBAL ENROLLMENT		
						YEAR	COUNTY	PAGE
1	Howard, Frank		54	M	I.W.			

TRIBAL ENROLLMENT OF PARENTS						
NAME OF FATHER	YEAR	COUNTY	NAME OF MOTHER	YEAR	COUNTY	
1 *(Illegible)* Howard	dead	non-citizen	Mary Howard	dead	non citizen	

(NOTES)

(Illegible) No. 1 was married to Kitty Howard a recognized and enrolled citizen by blood of the Chickasaw Nation, Chick Card #452, final roll #1328.

In April, 1901, they separated and were divorced.

No. 1 originall listed for enrollment on Chickasaw Card D-241 and transferred to this card *(Illegible)*, 1905, see decision of Jan. 20, 1905.

RESIDENCE: COUNTY   CARD NO.

POST OFFICE: *(Illegible)*, I.T.   FIELD NO.

NAME	RELATION-SHIP TO PERSON FIRST NAMED	AGE	SEX	BLOOD	TRIBAL ENROLLMENT		
					YEAR	COUNTY	PAGE
1 Bean, Thomas	FIRST NAMED	45	M	I.W.	1893	Pontotoc	P.R.#2 45

TRIBAL ENROLLMENT OF PARENTS						
NAME OF FATHER	YEAR	COUNTY	NAME OF MOTHER	YEAR	COUNTY	
1 F.T. Bean	dead	non citizen	Nancy Bean	dead	non citizen	

(NOTES)

No. 1 formerly the husband of Harriet Sealy, a recognized and enrolled citizen by blood of the Chickasaw Nation, on Chickasaw Card #296, final roll #444 as Malinda Sealy.

In 1902, No. 1 married Mollie B. Jones, a non citizen white woman

No. 1 also on 1896 Chick census roll, page 97

No. 1 originally listed for enrollment on Chickasaw Card D336

Nov. 1, 1900, transferred to this card Feb. 5, 1905, see decision of *(illegible)*

RESIDENCE: Pontotoc   COUNTY   CARD NO.

POST OFFICE: Ada, Indian Territory   FIELD NO.

NAME	RELATION-SHIP TO PERSON FIRST NAMED	AGE	SEX	BLOOD	TRIBAL ENROLLMENT		
					YEAR	COUNTY	PAGE
1 Perry, Joe	NAMED	11	M	1/4			
2 " Dillard	Bro	9	M	1/4			

TRIBAL ENROLLMENT OF PARENTS						
NAME OF FATHER	YEAR	COUNTY	NAME OF MOTHER	YEAR	COUNTY	
1 Charlie Perry	Dead	Pontotoc	Eliza Perry		Chick Roll	
2 " "	"	"	" "		" "	

Chickasaw Enrollment Cards 1898-1914
Chickasaw by Blood   Volume V

(No. 1 Dawes' Roll No. 5013)   *(No. 2 Dawes' Roll No. 5014)*

March 17, 1905

CANCELLED Stamped across card

RESIDENCE: Pickens COUNTY					CARD NO.		
POST OFFICE: Marietta, Ind. Ter.					FIELD NO.		
NAME	RELATIONSHIP TO PERSON FIRST NAMED	AGE	SEX	BLOOD	TRIBAL ENROLLMENT		
					YEAR	COUNTY	PAGE
1 Blake, John Y		24	M	I.W.			

TRIBAL ENROLLMENT OF PARENTS							
NAME OF FATHER	YEAR	COUNTY	NAME OF MOTHER		YEAR	COUNTY	
1 L.L. Blake		non Citizen	*(Name Illegible)*			non Citizen	

(NOTES)

No. 1 was originally listed for enrollment as a citizen of the Choctaw Nation on Choctaw Card #509 in pursuance of a judgment of the U.S. Court for the Southern District of The Indian Territory, Chitizenship Case No. ??

No. 1 was denied as a Choctaw by decree of Choctaw and Chickasaw Citizenship Court of June 30, 1903 (Tishomingo Case No. 98)

No. 1 was married to Callie Blake on Chickasaw Card No. 590 Sept. 11, 1901.

Name of No. 1 placed on this card April 4, 1905 in accordance with a decision of the Commission of that date holding application was made for enrollment of No. 1 as an intermarried Citizen of the Choctaw Nation within the time prescribed by the Act of Congress approved July 1, 1902.

RESIDENCE: Chickasaw Nation COUNTY					CARD NO.		
POST OFFICE: PO Box *(illegible)*					FIELD NO.		
NAME	RELATIONSHIP TO PERSON FIRST NAMED	AGE	SEX	BLOOD	TRIBAL ENROLLMENT		
					YEAR	COUNTY	PAGE
1 McCoy, Clay		54	M	I.W.			

TRIBAL ENROLLMENT OF PARENTS							
NAME OF FATHER	YEAR	COUNTY	NAME OF MOTHER		YEAR	COUNTY	
1 Henry McCoy	dead	non Citizen	*(Name Illegible)*			non Citizen	

(NOTES)

No. 1 of the husband of Sallie Goldsby McCoy, on Chickasaw Card #1404; final roll of citizens by blood of the Chickasaw Nation

No. 1 admitted by Dawes Commission in *(illegible)*

No. 1 admitted by U.S. Court Southern District *(remainder illegible)*

April 17, 1905.

Chickasaw Enrollment Cards 1898-1914
Chickasaw by Blood   Volume V

RESIDENCE:	COUNTY					CARD NO.		

POST OFFICE: Sterrett, Ind. Ter.   FIELD NO.

NAME	RELATION-SHIP TO PERSON FIRST NAMED	AGE	SEX	BLOOD	TRIBAL ENROLLMENT		
					YEAR	COUNTY	PAGE
1 Hamblin, James Benjamin	NAMED	23	M	White			
2 " Frank	Bro						
3 " Ben	Bro						
4 " Gertrude	Sister						
5 " Maude	Sister						
6 " P (illegible)							

TRIBAL ENROLLMENT OF PARENTS

	NAME OF FATHER	YEAR	COUNTY	NAME OF MOTHER	YEAR	COUNTY
1	Henry C. Hamblin	I.W.	Chickasaw Card 1151	Jessie I. Hamblin	IW.	
2	" " "	"	" " " "	" " "	"	
3	" " "	"	" " " "	" " "	"	
4	" " "	"	" " " "	" " "	"	
5	" " "	"	" " " "	" " "	"	
6	" " "	"	" " " "	" " "	"	

(NOTES)

Nos. 1 to 6 inclusive placed on this card in accordance with an order of the Commissioner to the Five Civilized Tribes of July 24, 1905, holding that application was made for their enrollment within the time prescribed by the Act of Congress approved July 1, 1902.

Nos. 1 to 6 inclusive are children of Nos. 1 and 2 on Chickasaw Card ??

July 24, 1905.

RESIDENCE:	COUNTY					CARD NO.		

POST OFFICE: Emet, I.T.   FIELD NO.

NAME	RELATION-SHIP TO PERSON FIRST NAMED	AGE	SEX	BLOOD	TRIBAL ENROLLMENT		
					YEAR	COUNTY	PAGE
1 Hayes, Charley	NAMED	M	I.W.	1893			
2 " Daniel	Son	M		1893			
3 " Minnie	Dau	F					
4 " Maggie	Dau	F					
5 " (Illegible)	Son	M					

TRIBAL ENROLLMENT OF PARENTS

	NAME OF FATHER	YEAR	COUNTY	NAME OF MOTHER	YEAR	COUNTY
1					dead	non Citizen
2					"	

3					"	
4					"	
5					"	

(NOTES)

No. 1 was formerly husband of Mattie McKinney, daughter of William McKinney *(No. 2 Dawes' Roll No. 4988)*
Mattie McKinney died July *(remainder illegible)* *(No. 3 Dawes' Roll No. 4989)*
Nos. 1 to 5 inclusive transferred from *(remainder illegible)* *(No. 4 Dawes' Roll No. 4990)*
(No. 5 Dawes' Roll No. 4991)

Oct. 26, 1905.

RESIDENCE: Choctaw **COUNTY** **CARD NO.**
POST OFFICE: Antlers, Ind. Ter. **FIELD NO.**

	NAME	RELATIONSHIP TO PERSON FIRST NAMED	AGE	SEX	BLOOD	TRIBAL ENROLLMENT		
						YEAR	COUNTY	PAGE
1	Adams, John Quincy							

TRIBAL ENROLLMENT OF PARENTS

	NAME OF FATHER	YEAR	COUNTY	NAME OF MOTHER	YEAR	COUNTY
1	Heber ? Adams					

(NOTES)

RESIDENCE: Chickasaw Nation **COUNTY** **CARD NO.**
POST OFFICE: Ryan, I.T. **FIELD NO.**

	NAME	RELATIONSHIP TO PERSON FIRST NAMED	AGE	SEX	BLOOD	TRIBAL ENROLLMENT		
						YEAR	COUNTY	PAGE
1	Ryan, Stephen Walker		46	M	I.W.	1896	Pickens	

TRIBAL ENROLLMENT OF PARENTS

	NAME OF FATHER	YEAR	COUNTY	NAME OF MOTHER	YEAR	COUNTY
1	John Ryan	dead	non citizen	Elizabeth Ryan		non citizen

(NOTES)

No. 1 on Chickasaw Roll Pickens County Doubtful List Page ??
No. 1 first married to Carrie Cheadle, a Chickasaw woman Dec. 15, 1875, with whom he lived until her death in ???
Married Sallie Wylie a white woman Aug. 11, 1896
No. 1 transferred from Choctaw Card *(remainder illegible)*
No. 1 an application for identification as a Mississippi Choctaw MCR #54 now pending from Dept. in case of Alberta Gains *(remainder illegible)*

Nov. 2, 1905.

Chickasaw Enrollment Cards 1898-1914
Chickasaw by Blood   Volume V

RESIDENCE:	COUNTY					CARD NO.		
POST OFFICE: St. Paul Minnesota						FIELD NO.		

NAME	RELATION-SHIP TO PERSON FIRST NAMED	AGE	SEX	BLOOD	TRIBAL ENROLLMENT		
					YEAR	COUNTY	PAGE
1 Jones Mary E.	NAMED	34	F	I.W.			

TRIBAL ENROLLMENT OF PARENTS

NAME OF FATHER	YEAR	COUNTY	NAME OF MOTHER	YEAR	COUNTY
1 William Thompson	Dead		Casandrew Thompson	Dead	non citizen

(NOTES)

No. I placed hereon under order of the Commissioner to the Five Civilized Tribes *(remainder illegible)*

RESIDENCE:	COUNTY					CARD NO.		
POST OFFICE: Baker City						FIELD NO.		

NAME	RELATION-SHIP TO PERSON FIRST NAMED	AGE	SEX	BLOOD	TRIBAL ENROLLMENT		
					YEAR	COUNTY	PAGE
1 Compton, Sallie	NAMED	39	F	1/4	1897	Pontotoc	
2 Melton, Ed	Son	24	M	1/8	1897	"	
3 " Jesse	"	21	M	1/8	1897	"	
4 " Rosa	Dau	15	F	1/8	1897	"	
5 Compton, Pearl							

TRIBAL ENROLLMENT OF PARENTS

	NAME OF FATHER	YEAR	COUNTY	NAME OF MOTHER	YEAR	COUNTY
1	Drew Gentry	Dead	non citizen	Mary Gentry	Dead	Chick roll
2						
3						
4						
5						

(NOTES)

Nos. 1,2,3,4 & 5 transferred to this card from Chicasaw card No. D.238, March 30, 1906.

(No. 1 Dawes' Roll No. 4997)   *(No. 2 Dawes' Roll No. 4998)*   *(No. 3 Dawes' Roll No. 4999)*

   (No. 4 Dawes' Roll No. 5000)   *(No. 5 Dawes' Roll No. 5001)*

March 30, 1906

Chickasaw Enrollment Cards 1898-1914
Chickasaw by Blood   Volume V

RESIDENCE:	COUNTY					CARD No.		
POST OFFICE:						FIELD No.		

	NAME	RELATION-SHIP TO PERSON FIRST NAMED	AGE	SEX	BLOOD	TRIBAL ENROLLMENT		
						YEAR	COUNTY	PAGE
1	Robinson, O.P.	NAMED	63	M	I.W.	1896		

TRIBAL ENROLLMENT OF PARENTS

	NAME OF FATHER	YEAR	COUNTY	NAME OF MOTHER	YEAR	COUNTY
1	Joseph Robinson			Martha Robinson		

(NOTES)

(All notations illegible)

RESIDENCE:	Creek Nation	COUNTY				CARD No.		
POST OFFICE:	Muskogee, I.T.					FIELD No.		

	NAME	RELATION-SHIP TO PERSON FIRST NAMED	AGE	SEX	BLOOD	TRIBAL ENROLLMENT		
						YEAR	COUNTY	PAGE
1	Durant, Maggie	NAMED	28	F	I.W.			

TRIBAL ENROLLMENT OF PARENTS

	NAME OF FATHER	YEAR	COUNTY	NAME OF MOTHER	YEAR	COUNTY
1	McLemore	dead	Non Citz	Froney Bailey	dead	

(NOTES)

No. 1 placed hereon under order of the Commissioner to the Five Civilized Tribes of Jany. 11, 1897 – holding that application was made for enrollment with in the time provided by the Act of Congress approved April 26, 1906. No. 1 formerly the wife of Judias Durant No. 1 on Chickasaw Card No. 62, Roll No. 190.

1/11/07

RESIDENCE:	COUNTY					CARD No.		
POST OFFICE:	Wheeler, Ind. Ter.					FIELD No.		

	NAME	RELATION-SHIP TO PERSON FIRST NAMED	AGE	SEX	BLOOD	TRIBAL ENROLLMENT		
						YEAR	COUNTY	PAGE
1	Layman, John S.	NAMED	58	M	I.W.			

TRIBAL ENROLLMENT OF PARENTS

	NAME OF FATHER	YEAR	COUNTY	NAME OF MOTHER	YEAR	COUNTY
1	A.W. Layman					

(NOTES)

No. 1 transferred from Chickasaw Card #D-273 *(remainder illegible)*   *(No. 1 Dawes' Roll No. 642)*
Feb. 2, 1907.

Chickasaw Enrollment Cards 1898-1914
Chickasaw by Blood   Volume V

RESIDENCE: Chickasaw Nation   COUNTY   CARD NO.
POST OFFICE: Woodford, I.T.   FIELD NO.

	NAME	RELATION-SHIP TO PERSON FIRST NAMED	AGE	SEX	BLOOD	TRIBAL ENROLLMENT		
						YEAR	COUNTY	PAGE
1	McGee. Florence	NAMED	15	M	1/8			
2	" Mattie	Sis	14	F	1/8			
3	" John	Bro	11	M	1/8			
4	" Allison	"	10	"	1/8			
5	" Wade	"	8	"	1/8			
6	" Ruby	Sis		F	1/8			
7	" Oliver	Bro		M	1/8			
8	" Elsie	Sis		F	1/8			

TRIBAL ENROLLMENT OF PARENTS

	NAME OF FATHER	YEAR	COUNTY	NAME OF MOTHER	YEAR	COUNTY
1	Jesse McGee	1897	Pickens	Dora McGee		Chick Freedman
2	" "	"	"	" "		" "
3	" "	"	"	" "		" "
4	" "	"	"	" "		" "
5	" "	"	"	" "		" "
6	" "	"	"	" "		" "
7	" "	"	"	" "		" "
8	" "	"	"	" "		" "

(NOTES)

Nos. 1 to 8 inclusive transferred from Chickasaw card No. D-51 Feb. 18, 1897.   (No. 1 Dawes' Roll No. 5049)
   See decision of *(illegible)*   (No. 2 Dawes' Roll No. 5050)
Father of Nos. 1 to 8 inclusive on Chickasaw roll card #55? *(remainder illegible)* (No. 3 Dawes' Roll No. 5051)
(Other notations illegible)   (No. 4 Dawes' Roll No. 5052)   (No. 5 Dawes' Roll No. 5053)
      (No. 6 Dawes' Roll No. 5054)   (No. 7 Dawes' Roll No. 5055)   (No. 8 Dawes' Roll No. 5056)

RESIDENCE: Choctaw Nation   COUNTY   CARD NO.
POST OFFICE: Sterrett, I.T.   FIELD NO.

	NAME	RELATION-SHIP TO PERSON FIRST NAMED	AGE	SEX	BLOOD	TRIBAL ENROLLMENT		
						YEAR	COUNTY	PAGE
1	Black, Willie	NAMED	22	M				
2	" May	Sis		F				
3	" Effie	"	14	F				

TRIBAL ENROLLMENT OF PARENTS						
NAME OF FATHER	YEAR	COUNTY	NAME OF MOTHER	YEAR	COUNTY	
1 George ? Black			Martha F. Black			
2						
3						

(NOTES)

(All notations illegible) (No. 1 Dawes' Roll No. 5057) (No. 2 Dawes' Roll No. 5058) (No. 3 Dawes' Roll No. 5059)

RESIDENCE: Chickasaw Nation   *COUNTY*   **CARD NO.**
POST OFFICE: Center, I.T.   *FIELD NO.*

NAME	RELATION-SHIP TO PERSON FIRST NAMED	AGE	SEX	BLOOD	TRIBAL ENROLLMENT		
					YEAR	COUNTY	PAGE
1 Rolston, Sarah E.	NAMED	47	F	I.W.			

TRIBAL ENROLLMENT OF PARENTS						
NAME OF FATHER	YEAR	COUNTY	NAME OF MOTHER	YEAR	COUNTY	
1						

(NOTES)

No. 1 Enrolled by Department *(remainder illegible)*   *(No. 1 Dawes' Roll No. 646)*
" " transferred from Chickasaw card No. *(remainder illegible)*

RESIDENCE: Choctaw Nation   *COUNTY*   **CARD NO.**
POST OFFICE: Sterrett, I.T.   *FIELD NO.*

NAME	RELATION-SHIP TO PERSON FIRST NAMED	AGE	SEX	BLOOD	TRIBAL ENROLLMENT		
					YEAR	COUNTY	PAGE
1 Black, Martha	NAMED	63	F	I.W.			

TRIBAL ENROLLMENT OF PARENTS						
NAME OF FATHER	YEAR	COUNTY	NAME OF MOTHER	YEAR	COUNTY	
1						

(NOTES)

(No. 1 Dawes' Roll No. 644)

Index

www.ingramcontent.com/pod-product-compliance
Lightning Source LLC
Chambersburg PA
CBHW030241030426
42336CB00009B/202